New Cures, Old Medicines

Women and the Commercialization of Traditional Medicine in Bolivia

D1715257

LYNN SIKKINK
Western State College

CASE STUDIES IN CULTURAL ANTHROPOLOGY:
JANICE E. STOCKARD AND GEORGE SPINDLER,
SERIES EDITORS

WADSWORTH
CENGAGE Learning™

Australia • Brazil • Japan • Korea • Mexico • Singapore • Spain • United Kingdom • United States

WADSWORTH
CENGAGE Learning

New Cures, Old Medicines:
Women and the
Commercialization of
Traditional Medicine in
Bolivia
Lynn Sikkink

Assistant Editor: Erin Abney

Editorial Assistant: Arwen Petty

Media Editor: Andrew Keay

Marketing Manager: Kim Russell

Marketing Assistant: Dimitri Hagnere

Marketing Communications Manager: Tami Strang

Consulting Editors: Janice E. Stockard & George Spindler

Content Project Management: Pre-PressPMG

Creative Director: Rob Hugel

Print Buyer: Paula Wang

Permissions Editor: Mardell Glinski Schultz

Production Service: Pre-PressPMG

Cover Designer: Rob Hugel

Cover Image: Lynn Sikkink

Compositor: Pre-PressPMG

For product information and technology assistance, contact us at **Cengage Learning Academic Resource Center, 1-800-423-0563**

For permission to use material from this text or product, submit all requests online at
www.cengage.com/permissions
Further permissions questions can be e-mailed to
permissionrequest@cengage.com

Library of Congress Control Number: 2009920556

ISBN-13: 978-0-495-83711-4

ISBN-10: 0-495-83711-3

Wadsworth/Cengage Learning
10 Davis Drive
Belmont, CA 94002-3098
USA

Cengage Learning products are represented in Canada by Nelson Education, Ltd.

For your course and learning solutions, visit
academic.cengage.com.

Purchase any of our products at your local college store or at our preferred online store **www.ichapters.com**

Printed in Canada
1 2 3 4 5 6 7 12 11 10 09

This book is dedicated to my parents,
Don and Arlene Sikkink

Contents

Foreword

ABOUT THE SERIES

These case studies in cultural anthropology are designed for students in beginning and intermediate courses in the social sciences, to bring them insights into the richness and complexity of human life as it is lived in different ways, in different places. The authors are men and women who have lived in the societies they write about and who are professionally trained as observers and interpreters of human behavior. Also, the authors are teachers; in their writing, the needs of the student reader remain foremost. It is our belief that when an understanding of ways of life very different from one's own is gained, abstractions and generalizations about the human condition become meaningful.

The scope and character of the series have changed constantly since we published the first case studies in 1960, in keeping with our intention to represent anthropology as it is. We are concerned with the ways in which human groups and communities are coping with the massive changes wrought in their physical and sociopolitical environments in recent decades. We are also concerned with the ways in which established cultures have solved life's problems. And we want to include representation of the various modes of communication and emphasis that are being formed and re-formed as anthropology itself changes.

We think of this series as an instructional series, intended for use in the classroom. We, the editors, have always used case studies in our teaching, whether for beginning students or advanced graduate students. We start with case studies, whether from our own series or from elsewhere, and weave our way into theory, and then turn again to cases. For us, they are the grounding of our discipline.

ABOUT THE AUTHOR

Lynn Sikkink grew up in the Midwest, part of an academic family who loved to travel. By the time she was ten years old, she said she wanted to be an archaeologist. With her parents and three siblings, she spent a year in Spain as a twelve-year-old and a year in a Danish High School; these experiences helped to set her on the course of anthropology. It was in college that she began to pursue this field of study formally, getting a B.A. in anthropology from the University of Colorado, Boulder, and inspired by wonderful teachers such as Paul Shankman. Before graduating with an undergraduate degree, Sikkink also spent a year as an exchange student in Cuzco, Peru, which provided the foundation for further studies in the Andes. After working as a "shovel bum" for a couple of years in the Rocky Mountain west, during which time she worked on the Dolores Archaeological Project in Colorado and the Shute Creek Project in Wyoming, she returned to school and to her Midwest roots. At the University of Minnesota, she received her M.A. in 1988, based on an ethnoarchaeological project set in Peru and directed by Christine Hastorf.

After almost two years of fieldwork in Bolivia, Sikkink wrote her dissertation on Andean women and rural exchange networks, and was awarded a Ph.D. from the Department of Anthropology in 1994, under the direction of both Stephen Gudeman and Christine Hastorf. She has continued to conduct fieldwork in Bolivia while teaching. Over the past twelve years, she has held positions at Lawrence University, San Jose State University, and Western State College, where she currently teaches.

Sikkink is married and has an eleven-year-old daughter who says she wants to be an oceanographer. Sikkink also continues to enjoy the outdoor life—hiking, canoeing, skiing, and camping, especially in the company of friends.

ABOUT THIS CASE STUDY

In this newest addition to the Case Study in Cultural Anthropology series, anthropologist Lynn Sikkink invites us along on her journey into the diverse marketplace settings of Bolivia to explore the practice and meaning of traditional medicine. Through her focus on the collection, processing, distribution, and sale of herbs and medicines at a variety of marketplace venues—from rural to urban, highlands to lowlands, market stall to shop—Sikkink introduces students to the field and practice of both medical and economic anthropology. Her approach also provides students with an introduction to the rich perspectives offered by cultural anthropology in general.

Sikkink conducted her research across almost two decades of fieldtrips to five different market venues in Bolivia; thus her research is by design multisited. Rather than presenting an account of the practice and meaning of medicine in just one rural Bolivian village, she is able to highlight the changing content, meaning, and dynamics of the traditional medical *system* by following people as they buy and sell medicines and avail themselves of medical services at various sites across the Bolivian landscape. This wide angle of vision provides students with a privileged insight into the linkages between and across these diverse marketplaces. In addition, Sikkink's approach makes it possible for students to understand how change in traditional medical systems comes about, as well-traveled vendors introduce new herbs, medical products, and ideas at one venue, and those goods and services are then further circulated, filtering up, down, and across market hierarchies with the continuing movement of both buyers and sellers.

The Bolivian rural household is the subject of much discussion as Sikkink explores the roles of both men and women in them. She underscores in particular women's responsibilities as managers of household plant and medicinal resources. Women's historical and continuing roles in the cultivation, collection, processing, and exchange of plant resources, Sikkink argues, provide them with the skills—the essential cultural "toolkit"—that enable them to become the dominant purveyors of these goods in the rural marketplace. Sikkink considers the degree to which this extension of a household role into a market venue ends up empowering local women. She focuses on other gender issues in this study as well.

In her analysis of the Bolivian system of traditional medicine, Sikkink introduces students to the local lexicon of "hot" and "cold" herbs and medical products, to a variety of diagnosed ailments (such as the power and meaning of curses and "fright"), and to local medical vendors and practitioners, including a curandero and a naturista. In addition, she familiarizes students with a variety of specific local herbs and treatments—love charms, medicinal teas, and dragon's blood, for example. She chooses coca leaf as a special window to show how local medical products and practices are changed as "outside" markets and cultural values penetrate the Bolivian medical system. The *hybrid* nature of the Bolivian and other traditional medical systems is a major focus of Sikkink's study; she provides students with examples of how the processes of commercialization and globalization change the content, practice, and meaning of the local medical system at different market levels. In fact, Sikkink devotes a full chapter to the critical contemporary issue of traditional medicine and the intellectual property rights of indigenous peoples in a world where biotechnology firms and international markets are reshaping the demand and supply of plant resources.

In her case study, Sikkink treats readers to colorful and vibrant descriptions of Bolivian markets. Her account of vendors and the content of their market stalls and inventory of their herbs and medical products are visually enhanced by rich ethnographic photographs, documenting the diverse array of wares available in various market settings. We invite you to join Lynn Sikkink in her exploration of Bolivian marketplaces as sites for understanding the changing meaning and practice of traditional medicine.

Janice E. Stockard and George Spindler
Series Editors

Preface

I first went to the Andes as an exchange student in college. I lived for a year in Cuzco, Peru, and celebrated my twenty-first birthday on a hiking trip to Machu Picchu. During that year, I lived with a Peruvian family, attended the university, and took classes in archaeology, cultural anthropology, and Quechua language, concentrating on all things Andean. Although I had wanted to major in Spanish before I lived in Peru, and my language skills certainly improved from being immersed in the language, including taking college courses in Spanish, it was in Peru that a love for the field of anthropology was sealed. When I returned to the University of Colorado, Boulder, I switched my major to anthropology, and was further inspired by the excellent courses and professors there. I went to field school on the Dolores Archaeological Project and decided to specialize in archaeology.

While at the University of Minnesota for gradate studies, I began some training in ethnobotany—the study of cultural uses of plants. This interdisciplinary field was partly responsible for drawing me in the direction of cultural anthropology and ethnographic studies, as I became fascinated with how people in different places express themselves, culturally, in so many different ways. Looking at plant use opens up a window into that cultural variation.

During my graduate studies, I continued to be interested in archaeology, but my research focus turned to contemporary Andean people. I conducted master's fieldwork in Peru, in conjunction with the Upper Mantaro Archaeological Project, and advised by Dr. Christine Hastorf. This research was ethnoarchaeological—looking at modern households as a way to get a handle on how the remains of cultural activities find their way into what becomes the archaeological record. To explore this issue from an ethnobotanical angle, I took soil samples from modern households to look at the seeds and other vegetation in various locales. I know many of the householders in my study got a good laugh from my actions (as did I), but I was impressed with their willingness to go along with the strange requests of gringo research. It was during the time I spent in Peruvian households watching crop-processing steps, sharing meals with people, playing

Working in the field in Peru, the author learns about agricultural work by helping with the winnowing of *tarwi*, an Andean legume.

with kids, and talking, that I realized I loved the contemporary part of anthropology best. I was especially drawn to the hard-working, frank and outgoing Andean women, who were as curious about me as I was about them.

I chose the neighboring country of Bolivia for my doctoral dissertation fieldwork, and have been returning to Bolivia ever since. This book draws on the fieldwork I have conducted throughout my stays there, beginning in 1989 with a preliminary research trip and including trips I took in 2006 and 2007 as this book was in its final stages. My fieldwork took me between city and countryside, into many different marketplaces, and into contact with a variety of people and their lives and stories. Traditional medicines as a topic presented itself to me in fieldwork trips after my dissertation, when I became more interested in these remedies as a specialized resource that women, especially, use as a way not only to heal members of their households, but also to economically support the same members through marketing. Although this book focuses on traditional medicines, it is my hope that readers will gain a better understanding of Andean culture in general by looking at all the ways in which traditional medicines figure into the history and culture of the Andes.

As I wrote this book manuscript, I had my San Jose State University students in mind. This group of mature undergraduate students came to class with questions, comments, and critiques, and through them shaped my own understanding of medical anthropology. I hope that my book is a salient contribution to discussions of medical anthropology, health, gender, and anthropology in other classrooms and places.

ACKNOWLEDGMENTS

I am extremely thankful to all my friends and colleagues in Bolivia for their support, guidance, and help. The Pillco Zolá family has been an anchor for me over the years as I have come and gone from Bolivia and San Pedro de Condo: Justo, Irene, Fidel, Olivia, Ramiro, and Emiliana deserve my first and deepest set of thanks. I offer special thanks also to Efrain Bueno, Iziquia, Don Carlos, and the many Condeño families and individuals who made me feel welcome and helped me out in so many ways, including with my research. In Cochabamba, my heartfelt thanks go to Carlos Prado and his wife Urbana, for their support and hospitality. I also want to thank the many vendors, doctors, healers, and others in Bolivia who generously gave of their time during my research into traditional medicines. Many friends from the United States have also spent time with me in Bolivia during various research trips: Lori Anderson, Alison Greene, Mary Liekefet, Alison Hurwitz, Melissa Michelson, Linda and Philip Miller, Timmy O'Neill, Rosalía Preiss, Liz Robinson, Gia Super, Sarah Linn, Kyoko Toriyama— with them, I was able to explore many different facets of Bolivia.

As a graduate student at the University of Minnesota, I was fortunate to have two exceptional advisors who helped me through the initial dissertation project, and who have been willing and available ever since to discuss my ideas as they continued to develop into this book. One of these advisors, Stephen Gudeman, read a version of the book manuscript and made insightful comments, which led to a new draft. Another advisor, Christine Hastorf, has continued to be an inspiration to me in the area of Andean studies as well as a friend; her support through the years has been important to the development of this material.

I have received funding from a range of sources for which I am sincerely grateful: I had a Fulbright Award in 1991 and 2000. I received several California State University grants while I was at San Jose State University, where I was also granted a sabbatical leave and awarded a Global Studies Fellowship. Lawrence University also funded two fieldwork trips to Bolivia in 1995 and 1996. While at the University of Minnesota, I received a MacArthur Pre-dissertation award, as well as funding from the McMillan Travel Fund, the William W. Stout Fellowship, a Doctoral Dissertation Fellowship, and grants from the anthropology department.

Assorted colleagues have contributed in myriad ways to the writing of this book. Alison Greene read an early draft and provided helpful comments, along with engaging me in great anthropological conversation beginning in our days as undergraduates together. Other colleagues contributed by providing various forms of intellectual and moral support: Clare Boulanger, Pamela Calla, Ricardo Calla, Chris Chiappari, Jan English-Lueck, Tom Layton, Ramiro Molina Rivero, Carol Mukhopadhyay, Peter Peregrine, George Saunders, Elvia Serrano, Kathryn Sikkink, Virginia Vitzthum, and Jim Weil. I would like to thank all of my many colleagues in the anthropology department at San Jose State University for providing a stimulating environment, and for the inspiration provided by their diverse research areas and anthropological approaches.

My new academic home at Western State College in Gunnison, Colorado, has provided wonderful opportunities for me. Thanks to all the faculty, staff, and administrators there for making me welcome, and for bringing me into the fold so quickly. Though it was inadvertent, had it not been for the offer of this new job, I would not have sent the manuscript out, finally. As it was, I sent it out the summer before starting at Western State College, and it was a lucky stroke as I have benefited ever since from the editorial assistance, positive feedback, and encouragement of the Wadsworth staff. Special thanks to Janice Stockard for her major role in editing, to Beth Kluckhohn and Arwen Petty for editorial assistance, and to Lin Gaylord for overseeing the entire process.

My own nuclear and extended family have been the most important source of strength and love during the time I've traveled back and forth to Bolivia, migrated between California and Colorado, changed jobs, and had new life adventures. Thanks to my parents, Arlene and Don Sikkink, to whom I dedicate this book, and who have been cheerleaders for my adventures and frequent contributors to them ever since my first trip to Peru. Also thanks to my siblings Jeff, Kathryn, and Julie, for everything. My in-laws, Linda and Philip Miller, created a home for my new family in our yearly migrations. Thanks also to the Distefanos, for everything.

My husband, Bryan Miller, has been unwavering in his support, love, and encouragement. Our daughter Lozen was born during my first job at Lawrence University. She turned three in Bolivia when we lived in Cochabamba on my Fulbright Award. She was in kindergarten the year I wrote the first draft of this manuscript during my sabbatical leave. Her enthusiasm for life and tenacity in approaching new things have guided my outlook, and made my life richer at every stage.

1

Andean Traditional Medicines in Rural Settings and Community Exchange Networks

Introduction

Setting and Environment

A Brief Introduction to Andean Medicine

Bolivian Language and Ethnicity

Fieldwork and Research Methodology

Summary

INTRODUCTION

In a high Andean settlement in Bolivia, an Aymara peasant woman prepares a collection of highland and lowland plants, bundling them in preparation for burning them as an offering to the gods. The highland plants in her bundle grow locally; the lowland plants she has acquired by trade. Another woman, living in the lowland "warm valleys" (*yungas*), makes tea from an herb that grows a day's journey away and several thousand feet up, but which she has bought in the marketplace.

In contemporary Bolivia, the use of traditional medicines is dependent on the exchange of plants and herbs through networks of women who traverse the highlands and lowlands. What was once traded directly in the Andes, through llama caravan trading trips and through a system of exchange partnerships, is now most often purchased in the marketplace. Even so, individual market vendors continue to assemble their herbal inventories through barter, swap, purchase, and

1

their own collecting activities. As a class of goods, Bolivian traditional medicines are in flux due to commercialization and borrowing from places within Latin America and beyond. The traditional system is kept alive, however, through the very practices of the purveyors of these goods—from small-scale rural vendors to owners of shops in the city that cater to natural healing.

In the process of collecting, assembling, trading, and using these remedies, the category of traditional medicines is continually altered through individual use and public buying and selling practices, yet "traditional" remedies retain their popularity. The very label "traditional medicine," as used by Bolivian healers and their patients, refers to what is essentially a hybrid system that is constantly changing as the "old" mixes with the "new," as ideas and products from the outside world find a place within a distinctively Bolivian system of traditional medicine. The use of traditional medicines is widespread across Bolivia in both rural and urban areas. The collection and exchange of the herbal ingredients and the production and consumption of the traditional medicines are activities that integrally connect the people of the city and the people of the countryside.

In this book's exploration of the changing world of traditional medicine in Bolivia, the primary focus will be the producers and vendors of this medicine, who for the most part are female. Indeed, women are responsible for most of the traditional medicine in circulation. Their activities and networks dominate every stage in the production and marketing of traditional medicines, forming the very backbone of the industry today—just as their predecessors did historically. In this book we ask, Why women? In pursuit of the answer to this question, we will focus our lens on the distribution of traditional medicines through marketplace venues, investigating the link between women's roles in urban commercial set-tings and their role as "exchangers" of goods in rural peasant households.

Several issues will guide our inquiry. We will explore the cultural and economic practices surrounding the sale and use of traditional medicines, and examine the work practices of the vendors of herbal ingredients and medicines. We will also focus on the content of traditional remedies and the emergence of new medicines. This issue, in turn, leads us to examine the trajectory of the plants themselves: What happens to them along the way as they move and are exchanged from suppliers to sellers to customers? Also, with foreign pharmaceutical companies undertaking increasing and intensifying "bioprospecting" activities in their search for new drugs, what are the intellectual property rights (and other international issues) that emerge for the people who have long used these plant resources for indigenous medicines and cures? What are the ecological issues that arise with increasing international demand for these primarily wild plant resources?

In our exploration, we draw on perspectives from two related fields, economic anthropology and medical anthropology. Taken together, these perspectives provide us with a privileged platform from which to view the production and marketing of traditional medicines from a ground-up perspective. We will track what happens to traditional medicines as they find their way into the marketplace system of Bolivia, ending up in tiny herbal remedy stands or in large natural medicine stores and clinics—and increasingly being converted into pharmaceutical-like products that are sold by emerging cottage industries. As part of our effort to understand the marketing of traditional medicines, we will also examine the role of Bolivian consumers, whose demand shapes both the kinds of traditional medicines offered for sale and the forms in which those medicines appear. As we will see, the practice of traditional medicine is shaped by the actions of individual buyers as well as sellers across a wide range of local indigenous marketplace settings.

As one subfield in anthropology, economic anthropology provides us with a perspective on persons as actors and participants in cultural systems of production, consumption, and exchange in diverse societies around the world. Economic anthropologists are interested in learning how individual persons and their families and communities "make a living," how people's lives are shaped and constrained by their own cultural and economic systems, and how these local systems link and interact with broader economic forces in the world. Economic anthropology provides us with rich perspectives on the ways in which diverse peoples engage in and react to the opportunities and challenges presented by a rapidly globalizing world. In Andean studies, economic anthropologists have conducted research on many aspects of Andean cultural life, focusing especially on agriculture, rural domestic economy, and exchange networks. (See, for example, Alberti and Mayer 1974, Harris 1995, Molina Rivera 1986.)[1] Many of these investigations are "community studies" that examine subjects such as labor practices, reciprocity, production and reproduction, landholding patterns, and irrigation systems in particular Andean locales. While some research has considered the topic of trade in the Andes (especially interzonal barter and reciprocity), none has focused explicitly on herbal remedies and medicines as economic products, as we will do here in this book.

As Bolivian traditional medicines enter the marketplace, they take their place alongside Western pharmaceuticals, other Latin American traditional medicines, and even Chinese medicine, and are used in conjunction with these agents. Globalization trends are certainly affecting people's access to traditional medicine, but this does not mean that the "traditional" medical system is being replaced by "outside" ones. Instead, a much more complex cross-cultural encounter is taking place, in which the local system is interacting with other medical systems and incorporating some of their features, albeit not all of them. In a way not predicted in general discussions of globalization, traditional medicines in Bolivia have enjoyed a resurgence of use. In 2007, the Bolivian government created a Vice Ministry of Traditional Medicines in recognition of the economic and cultural importance of traditional medicines. The demand for traditional medicine persists in part for economic reasons: These cures are generally more affordable than imported or manufactured pharmaceuticals. In addition, the Andean people's ongoing commitment to traditional and indigenous products continues to drive the demand for these medicines.

Certainly, the globalization of traditional medical systems is not just a recent phenomenon. Across histories and cultures, indigenous medical systems

---

1. For further examples of Andean ethnography, see Babb 1986, Brush 1977, Brush and Stabinsky 1996, Buechler 1997, Collins 1986, Deere 1990, Gudeman and Rivera 1990, Guillet 1992, Long and Roberts 1984, Mayer 2002, West 1981.

everywhere have come to incorporate elements of diverse and foreign origins. From this perspective, traditional medical systems have always been hybrid systems; this hybrid nature is not a distinctive feature of contemporary globalization. In Bolivian traditional medicine today, an inventory of the sources and origins of the different ingredients shows borrowings from diverse cultural settings around the world. Thus the study of contemporary traditional medicine in Bolivia requires an understanding of how products and ideas from Chile, Argentina, Peru, Brazil, Mexico, China, Europe, and the United States have, over time, been adapted and incorporated into Bolivian ideas about good health and healing. This situation is complex and defies simple assumptions about the inevitability and direction of globalization: A strong core of the plants and medical beliefs that make up Bolivian traditional medicine are of Andean origin, and the system itself, despite hybridization, is still uniquely Bolivian.

In the following chapters, we explore the expanding and changing use of these traditional medicines through an examination of the practices of various kinds of vendors in distinct marketplace venues whose business links urban and rural worlds. Our focus is on the vendors themselves, their wares, and their customers, as well as the dynamic interaction between countryside and city in Bolivia in the realm of traditional medicine. We will look at traditional medicine as "merchandise"—that is, as goods that circulate along established paths, sold by individuals who travel between city and country marketplaces, and sometimes across national borders. This perspective provides an excellent vantage point for understanding the nature of the rural–urban interface in the Bolivian medical world, as well as the internationalization of traditional medicines. It also highlights how Bolivian demographics and the process of commercialization have contributed to new notions of traditional health and healing as people come together to trade.

In this book, we will consider the marketplace from more than an economic perspective. Specifically, we will examine the marketplace to learn about medical ideas and practices, as the source of medical information (as well as products) for the general populace. As the sale of herbal remedies and healing services has become more widespread, traditional medicine has become a more viable option for a broader population, beyond the peasants of the countryside. Simultaneously, traditional medicine has emerged as an attractive business opportunity for a larger number of urban vendors and healers who can earn their living in the city or in other marketplace settings where traditional medicines are traded and sold. Although these traditional medicinal practices are adapted for use in urban areas, they cannot be dismissed as adulterated or distorted forms of the real thing. Rather, they are legitimized by their wide use and the number of people who believe in the efficacy of the urban hybrid system. The use of these medicines also provides an opportunity to learn how people fashion new forms of health systems in changing contexts, and it reveals the way in which a large percentage of the population now addresses its health issues.

In our focus on the commercialization of traditional medicines, we will explore trade activities in diverse Bolivian locales, but always with an eye toward how they are linked to rural economies. Selling traditional medicines is certainly a business opportunity and a strategy for maintaining a healthy rural household economy, but it also has implications for what people believe, how they take care of themselves and one another, and which health decisions they reach. Exploring this avenue takes us beyond a narrow economic approach to our subject.

The perspectives of medical anthropology will also serve to further illuminate our understanding of Bolivian traditional medicine. As another subfield of anthropology, medical anthropology highlights the issues of health, illness, and healing in different cultural and belief systems. Many medical anthropological studies have focused on Andean societies and cultures. Indeed, there is a wealth of research on Andean "medical pluralism" describing the situation in which diverse cultural ideas and practices are combined in one medical system. Some of the work on medical pluralism has focused on Bolivia; early studies examined in particular how beliefs about illness and healing in Bolivia could be considered evidence of a distinctive Andean cultural tradition (see especially Bastien and Donahue 1981). Later research focused on the theme of how biomedicine and Andean ethnomedicine are integrated in the practices of Bolivian healers and their patients.[2] Recent studies have turned to focus on the distinction between the "two systems" of biomedicine and ethnomedicine. In these studies, medical anthropologists have emphasized the blending of elements from multiple systems and sources. Different elements are brought together in specific contexts by healers and health-seekers, thereby ensuring that the practice and content of traditional medicine continues to shift over time and space. (See, for example, Koss-Chioino et al. 2003.)

The approach we take in this case study emphasizes how medicines and ideas about them flow through marketplaces as well as health systems. We focus on the commercial aspects of the promotion and use of traditional medicines, which are as important as the innate qualities of the medicines themselves. By focusing on "the business of health" in Bolivia, we will learn how the marketing of medicines—from their barter and sale in rural fairs to their promotion in natural medicine cottage industries—has not only been a means of exchanging and distributing medicines, but has also stimulated change in medical ideas and practices. In short, beyond its economic functions, the marketplace has served as site for the reworking of indigenous cultural practices.

We will, of course, also consider the marketplace as a site of economic interaction, and the economic activities of "rural people" and "urbanites," both groups whose members travel back and forth between city and country, resulting in the diffusion of new ideas and practices. Rural fairs (*ferias*), for example, are one economic site where we can observe the meeting and mixing of rural medical ideas and practices with urban ones; analogous urban marketplaces (*mercados*) provide another site from which to observe the rural–urban exchange. Not surprisingly, many of the same products and some of the same vendors can be found at each site. Earlier Andean ethnographic research (conducted in the 1970s and 1980s) focused to a large degree on the *isolation* of rural communities, whose

---

2. See Alba and Tarifa 1993, Arnold and Yapita 2002, Bastien 1992, Cáceres Ch. 1988, Crandon-Malamud 1991, Fernández Juárez 1999, Lira 1985.

patterns of kinship, rituals and religious beliefs, and farming and irrigation systems differentiated them from their urban counterparts. These more distinctively rural patterns and practices, it was assumed, constituted evidence of continuity with a pre-Hispanic past. (For examples, see Allen 1988, Bastien 1978, Harris 1982, Platt 1982, Rasnake 1988, West 1981.) More recent anthropological investigations of Andean communities have called into question both the degree of the rural communities' isolation and as their retention of pre-Hispanic cultural features. Although most Andean scholars have now moved away from "essentializing" Andean culture as homogeneous, there is still a tendency to seek out more isolated groups, which are considered to be more "authentically Andean" in some sense. One Andean ethnographer, Orin Starn (1991), has called for scholars to pay greater attention both to contemporary political change and to the cultural differences differentiating Andean societies from one another. Starn has labeled the traditional ethnographic tendency to focus on cultural similarities as the search for *lo andino* ("that which is Andean")—a depiction that fails to catch important cultural differences of Andean peoples and their unique communities.

Increasingly anthropologists have turned to urban Andean populations as the targets of their studies. In Bolivia, the ethnographic lens has focused especially on poorer migrant groups who have relocated to urban areas. These populations have been shown to maintain continuing ties to rural areas, and these recent studies have, therefore, helped to elucidate the dynamic flow of people and cultural practices within and between rural and urban areas in Bolivia. (See, for example, Albro 2000, Goldstein 2004, Himpele 2003, Luykx 2000, Paulson and Calla 2000.)

What is still largely mostly missing from the anthropological record is research into the dynamic patterns of migration and movement of Andean people who live in more than one community and regularly travel between rural and urban spheres. Admittedly, studies of this kind are more difficult to conduct, as they require greater mobility on the part of the anthropologist and a broad understanding of both rural and urban cultural life. This book is intended to help bridge the divided focus that has characterized most of the ethnographic work conducted in the Andes. Its topic—the commercialization and marketing of traditional medicines in Bolivia and changes occurring in traditional ideas about health and illness—provides us with an unusual vantage point from which to observe these important cultural dynamics.

SETTING AND ENVIRONMENT

Bolivia is both a highland Andean and lowland Amazonian country. It has major landholdings in both regions, and includes territory at the mid-elevations, on the mountain slopes, and in the valleys connecting the highlands with the lowlands. Current residents of Bolivia (as well as their ancestors) have always traveled between these zones, motivated to do so by the variety of resources to be acquired at the different elevations and in different ecosystems. Exchange, therefore, is now and has long been a salient feature of life for Bolivians.

Our focus in this book is the highland peoples, but the traditional medicines they use come from all regions, and today even from areas outside Bolivia. Two major ethnic groups, the Aymara and the Quechua, populate the highlands today. The areas examined in this book were historically Aymara areas. Over time, however, intermixing of Aymara with Quechua peoples and languages has occurred that makes it difficult to draw a clear line between these two ethnic populations.

Despite the difficulties of life on the cold and dry high plateau (*altiplano*), most of Bolivia's population resides here; approximately 75 percent of the people live in the altiplano on 30 percent of Bolivia's territory, rather than in the larger area of lush valleys and lowlands (Queiser Morales 1992:6). The northern altiplano sustains higher numbers of inhabitants, especially around Lake Titicaca. The central and southern altiplano also supports a surprisingly high number of people, given the harsh living conditions, which include cold temperatures, periodic droughts, and the risk that frost poses for agriculture. The geology of the southern altiplano is rich in resources. Indeed, since Spanish colonial times, the operation of mines has influenced and supplemented the local economy, even while it has claimed lives and otherwise sapped the vitality of the people of this region.

In modern times, economic opportunities in the lowlands—including government projects that have opened more arable land—have not resulted in a major demographic shift of altiplano inhabitants to the lowlands. Put simply, the continuing occupation of the altiplano cannot be attributed to economic reasons alone. Highlanders talk of the "weakness" they experience in the lowlands because of the hot temperatures, the insects and snakes, and the illnesses (such as malaria) that are common at those lower elevations. In leaving the altiplano, they must also accustom themselves to a different diet and to growing different crops; these are ventures that many people are reluctant to try. Partly because the altiplano is dry and cold, campesinos consider it to be a much healthier environment. Although some migration to Bolivia's lowlands has occurred, it has been slow and often of temporary duration only, similar to the "unseasonal migrations" described by Jane Collins for Peruvian campesinos (1988).

Four of the five settings described in this book—Condo, Huari, Challapata, and Oruro—are located on the southern altiplano, in the highlands. (The fifth, Cochabamba, is located at a mid-elevation; its setting is described in Chapter 6.) The rural village of San Pedro de Condo, where I did my first stint of Bolivian fieldwork, serves as a good illustration of the environment and living conditions of southern highland Bolivia. Condo is situated on the dry and treeless altiplano of southern Bolivia, at 19° south of the equator and 67° longitude. (Refer to Map 1.1 on the next page for the location of Condo.) The altiplano is an intermontane plateau between the eastern and western cordilleras in Bolivia; it is a continuation of the highland plateau of the Andean region of Peru (called *puna*) in the north, and continues into the territory of Chile and Argentina in the south. Around Condo, the altiplano's average elevation is about 3,800 meters (12,500 feet), and the mountains surrounding the altiplano rise up as high as 5,200 meters (more than 17,000 feet). The climate of the altiplano changes as one moves from north to south, becoming even colder, drier, and more barren in its southern reaches. People here owe their existence mostly to animal herding

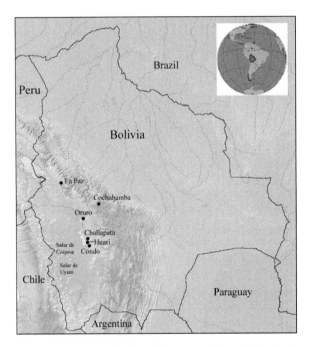

M A P 1.1 Map of Bolivia (Courtesy of Brett Soderberg)

(pastoralism) and to a high-altitude agriculture that is limited by the changing microenvironments within Condo's territory.

In pre-Hispanic times—more than five hundred years ago—the livelihood of local people was also based on a combination of crop farming and herding. One difference, however, is that the historical "agro-pastoral" livelihood focused on the herding of domesticated camelids, especially llamas and alpacas. Wild herds of vicuñas and guanacos also abounded and were probably hunted by local people. Other wild animals on this dry altiplano were typically small. Today the herds of vicuñas and guanacos are severely reduced and in danger of extinction. Sheep, cows, burros, and chickens—introduced by the Spaniards to South America— have become an indispensable feature of the contemporary Andean subsistence base, although the practice of sheepherding has exacerbated erosion in the area through overgrazing.

The wild vegetation on the altiplano consists primarily of plants and low-growing shrubs, not trees. The only stands of trees one might see are eucalyptus, which were successfully introduced as part of twentieth-century development programs to control erosion. In the hills above the altiplano proper, some native tree species remain, such as the *quinuar* tree (*Polylepis* spp.) with its characteristic papery red bark. In general, however, these native species have suffered from the long process of deforestation; across the generations they were used for fuel and construction material. Inhabitants of the Bolivian altiplano now rely on the *tola* bush (*Lepidophyllum* spp.) as fuel, along with dried animal dung from llama, sheep, and cows. Dung is an especially important fuel source at higher altitudes where vegetation is even scarcer.

Photo by Sarah Linn Gallardo

FIGURE 1.1   The hills and terraces surrounding Lake Poopó, between Huari and Condo.

The communities of Condo, Huari, Challapata, and Oruro are located along the southern end of a vast, drying lake basin. Bolivia's great lake system ends here in Lake Poopó (called *Aullagas* in pre-Hispanic times), which in contrast to Lake Titicaca's deep navigable waters is shallow (only one to several meters deep), saltier, and more sparsely inhabited along its shores.[3] Lake Poopó periodically dries up and will eventually become a vast salt flat like those located south of it, such as Uyuni and Coipasa; in the past, these salt beds were shallow, salty lakes like Poopó. One author calls Poopó the altiplano's "dead sea" (Queiser Morales 1992:8). Nevertheless Lake Poopó is filled with *pejerrey* ("king fish" or *Basilichthys bonariensis*), which were introduced from southern cone estuaries. *Pejerrey* are a source of food for the Uru groups who live along Lake Poopó and employ small boats outfitted with fishing nets. Condo is situated on Poopó's southernmost shore, where the landscape begins to give way to saltier, sandier soils; however, Condo's location—in a river valley against the hills—gives it the advantage of better soils to farm and a more reliable water supply than surrounding areas.

---

3. Lake Titicaca is extensively exploited by Aymara groups living on its shores, where they fish, farm, and herd (see Buechler and Buechler 1971, for example), and by Urus (a smaller ethnic group who speak their own language, identified as more ancient than Aymara and Quechua populations), who fish and hunt there. On Lake Poopó, it is the remnant Uru groups who exploit the lake by fishing and hunting, while their Aymara neighbors live away from the lake and do not exploit its resources. As Klein says about the Uru, "The Puquina speech of the Uru represented one of the three major altiplano languages in pre-Conquest Peru, along with Quechua and Aymara. By the time of the Spanish Conquest the Uru were a poor people living in small groupings among all the highland kingdoms ... [t]he cultural if not political and economic, deference paid by the Aymara to the Urus seems to imply that the Uru may have preceded the Aymara and have been remnants of an earlier and more advanced civilization. Some have even argued that they were the people of Tiahuanaco" (Klein 1982:18).

Condo is one of several communities that is close to Lake Poopó, yet not dependent on it. Located approximately midway between the mining centers of Oruro and Potosí, Condo is in the Department of Oruro, which encompasses not only Lake Poopó but also the smaller Lake Uru-Uru, plus a section of the Desaguadero River and the salt flat of Coipasa on its western edge. According to the geographer Carl Troll's classification, this area is between the altitudinal/longitudinal zones of dry *puna* and salty *puna* (1968). The annual cycle of seasons is marked by a rainy season (from November through April) and a dry season (from May through October). Temperatures are generally warmer in the rainy season, which is the Andean summer. Nevertheless, greater temperature fluctuations occur on a daily basis between night and day than tend to mark the winter/summer temperature changes (Troll 1968). When I lived in Condo, this meant shedding clothes when the sun was intense at midday, and always wearing a hat to protect my head from the sun at this high altitude; in the evenings on those same days, I would hurry to put on several extra layers of clothing and a wool hat. On winter nights in southern Oruro, the temperature can drop as low as −18 degrees Celsius (−4 degrees Fahrenheit); an average annual daytime temperature is 10 degrees Celsius (50 degrees Fahrenheit).

Part of the region to the south of Condo is inhospitable to agriculture. In those areas, the people depend mainly on animal herding and trading animal products such as wool, fat, woven items, and salt. Alongside pastoralism, they practice a limited form of agriculture based on quinoa (*Chenopodium quinoa*), a cereal crop that is suitable to cultivation in dry conditions. On the southern altiplano, quinoa is sown deep below the sand to take advantage of what little moisture there is, similar to the Hopi mode of corn planting. In Condo, however, there are better, wetter conditions, making it suitable for a more varied agriculture. This advantage arises in part because Condo is situated in a protected "corner" of the hills, alongside a river. Espinoza Soriano describes Condo's location like this:

> The village of Condocondo was founded in the cordillera of the Azanaques, in a bend in the Condo chain, on the banks of the river with this same name [Azanaques], but it enjoys a sheltered climate. The proximity to the mountains gives it a cheerful and agreeable aspect, which is uncommon in the villages of this region. Its soil is fertile and its hills contain silver[4] (1981:218).

Condo's comparatively good milieu for agriculture is nevertheless (and was historically) risky due to frosts and drought. At Condo's higher elevations, agriculture is impossible; there, inhabitants base their subsistence primarily on herding, supplementing their diet with agricultural products obtained through exchange with their relatives at lower elevations, through trading trips, and sometimes through direct access to lands around the village. The practice of "double domicile" also gives Condeños access to the resources of more than one zone (Molina Rivera 1987). In Condo, 28 out of the 35 households that I observed intensively had two residences— one in the village of Condo and one in an *estancia* (hamlet) located some distance away and usually at a higher elevation where herding prevailed.

---

4. This translation and those that follow are mine.

A BRIEF INTRODUCTION TO ANDEAN MEDICINE

The medical traditions of the Andes have a rich and deep history, embedded not only in the better-known Inca period, but also in a pre-Inca history that stretches back several thousand years. In this long history, the practice of medicine has centered on indigenous beliefs about well-being, ill health, and curing practices. In general, Andean people believe in establishing and maintaining a reciprocal relationship with their gods, who are beings that inhabit local mountains, water sources, and other facets of the natural world. According to indigenous belief, illness can result from improper relationships with these supernatural powers; health and good fortune can be assured through establishing a proper relationship with these supernatural powers. Although Andean people have long treated themselves with herbal and other natural remedies, they have also believed that offerings to the gods can maintain and reestablish the physical and spiritual equilibrium on which good health depends.

Even in some of the earliest Andean sites, archaeologists have discovered evidence of medicinal plants (Moseley 1992). Coca is one of the plants with a long history of medicinal use, and archaeological sites establish its early use far from its area of cultivation. Coca was clearly used not just for chewing and relief from physical exhaustion, but in spiritual and medicinal contexts as well. Evidence for coca use is present as early as 2000 B.C. on the coast of Peru (Plowman 1985). Although the presence of coca in the early archaeological record may or may not be related to medicinal traditions, it seems likely that the medicinal use of coca stretches back in time to its early appearance alongside other Andean plants such as quinoa, potatoes, and corn.

More direct evidence of specific Andean healing practices comes from the archaeological analysis of skeletal remains. Specifically, the archaeological record shows that ancient Andeans practiced brain surgery in the form of "trepanation." Holes were drilled into the skull, perhaps to relieve pressure on the brain caused by injury or illness. Many of the individuals undergoing trepanation not only survived surgery, but also apparently lived for many years, as evidenced by the healing that had ensued by the time of death. The practice of trepanation can be found as early as the Tiwanaku time period (A.D. 500–950). Its early origin demonstrates that, long before the Inca used it, trepanation was a familiar practice to their predecessors. Some of this evidence is found in the Kallawaya region of the Andes. Bastien (1978) believes that the Kallawaya healers have a very long tradition in the Lake Titicaca area, extending back well before they became "doctors to the Incas," as they are known even to this day. A shaman's tomb from the Kallawaya region that dates to A.D. 800 has yielded a snuff tablet, holly leaves, enema tubes, and various staffs with animal effigies, which were probably used in divination ceremonies (Wilson 1999:328).

On the southern altiplano around Condo, the earliest inhabitants are known as *chullpas*—a generic term for the "ancestors" who left behind burial tombs, although the term also refers to the tombs themselves. Old stone tools and ceramic sherds, found scattered around Condo's landscape, are often attributed to these people; locals claim they were made by *los chullpas*. The *chullpas* are thought to have had a "cult of the dead," although little is known of their medical practices. Today, artifacts of the Aymara era dominate the area around Condo: The basic

F I G U R E 1.2   The remains of pre-Inca burial chambers, or *chullpas*, in the foreground; the snow dusted peak of Thumpa appears on the horizon.

organization of local settlements, the local language, and many of the trade routes date back to the historical era of the Aymara Federation.

Prior to the arrival of the Inca, twelve Aymara federations existed, arranged in the north around Lake Titicaca and to the south, basically following the area encompassed by the altiplano and extending almost to the borders of what are now Chile and Argentina. Condo was part of the Killakas-Asanaqi Federation. These kingdoms drew upon both agriculture and herding as their resource base, but combined these productive activities with the direct control of lowland communities, from which they also obtained maize, coca, chili peppers, and fruit. Not only did Condeños engage in the transport and exchange of crops and animal products (especially wool, fat, and dried fish from their highland homes), but they also traded their local medicines. This trade marked the beginning of the direct medical interaction between the lowlands and highlands peoples. The legacy of this early trade is evident in modern marketplaces, where ingredients from many different ecological zones coexist in single medical inventories.

When the Inca appeared on the scene in the 1400s (approximately ninety years before the Spaniards arrived), they subjugated the Aymara kingdoms without closing down the established links between highlands and lowlands. Instead, the Inca exerted control over these supply lines through a system of taxation. In all of their endeavors, the Inca excelled in the empire-building strategy of taking over existing, sophisticated systems of trade and political organization—and controlling them and, through them, the local people.

In a similar way, the Incas drew on earlier, established medical traditions. They incorporated sophisticated healing techniques that they inherited from groups such as the Aymara, whose healers focused on removing illness from a sick person's body (Classen 1993:81). The most important of all their techniques was the use of herbal infusions. That the healers were referred to as *jampiyoq* ("medicine wielders") illustrates the degree to which herbal remedies were important in the Inca Empire (Classen 1993).

The Incas knew expertise when they encountered it, and the Kallawaya doctors on the eastern slopes of Lake Titicaca were certainly masters of plant lore and the use of herbal remedies, along with other cures. After the Inca conquered them, the Kallawayas were quickly employed by their vanquishers to serve as the official healers to the Inca elite, including the Inca ruler himself (Bastien 1978, 1992). In contemporary Bolivia, the Kallawayas retain their medical traditions and reputation as healers, traveling to take their expertise to people from other communities. They can be found peddling their medical wares and expertise in marketplace settings, as described in Chapter 6 of this book.

With the arrival of the Spaniards in the 1500s, older patterns of interaction between the highlands and lowlands populations began to change. Communities were cut off from each other as the Spanish succeeded in not simply taxing individual communities, but in rearranging human labor to control the extensive mining operations implemented in places such as Cerro Rico ("rich mountain") in Potosí.

The Spanish presence had drastic consequences for indigenous medical traditions. Especially damaging was the Spanish campaign launched against the perceived sorcery and witchcraft practiced throughout the Andes. Paralleling the Spanish Inquisition in the Old World (where anti-religious "heretics" were persecuted), the Spanish Inquisition in the New World sought to extirpate Andean "idolatry." The Spaniards' goal was to root out religious symbols and monuments of the Andean religion. In addition to undertaking the removal of sacred sites, the Spanish conquerors persecuted religious specialists such as local priests and the keepers of shrines. Indigenous healers (many of whom were women) were also targeted by the Inquisitors; especially vulnerable to attack were women who were found to be using "idolatrous" or "heretical" techniques (Griffiths 1996). For the Spanish conquerors, evidence that women were witches could be found in their use of coca leaf. Because it was used in indigenous divination rites and practices, coca was interpreted as evidence of communication with the devil. That coca leaf was used to divine medical problems and as medicine was overlooked. These Spanish trials became a convenient way to remove unconventional and "wayward" indigenous women from the population. Inquisition documents found in the Archivo Histórico Nacional in Madrid, Spain, reveal that women who had more than one husband, women who possessed healing powers, and women who did not conform to social expectations became the focus of witchcraft trials. Oftentimes these wayward women or witches were identified as such by the neighbors with whom they had disputes.

BOLIVIAN LANGUAGE AND ETHNICITY

Of course, I had studied Spanish before I embarked on my fieldwork. As further preparation for the field, I also received training in both Quechua and Aymara, the two indigenous languages of Bolivia. Although I cannot claim to have mastered either, this comprehensive language study did prepare me for the occasional monolingual speaker I sometimes encountered in my research. Usually the Quechua-only (or Aymara-only) speaker was an older woman.

Historically and ethnically, the area around Lake Poopó is Aymara. The great Aymara federations developed across the southern altiplano and continued to control the area to a certain extent even during Inca occupation. This historical legacy is reflected in the fact that the Aymara language[5] continued to be spoken throughout the duration of Inca rule. The Incas—whose original languages were *Puquina* and *Jaqi*—launched a "Quechuanization" program that was responsible for "converting" many Aymara speakers (Hardman 1985, Klein 1982:23). Later the Spaniards also continued to promote Quechua over other native languages.

This historical and linguistic picture is important because it illustrates that the inhabitants of the area around Condo—although dominated first by the Inca and later by the Spanish—continued to draw upon their original Aymara cultural heritage. This permeation of the Aymara culture was especially notable in the area of economic and political organization: The Aymara emphasized a subsistence livelihood supplemented by trade with various neighbors. The Aymara system of trade facilitated the collection and trade of traditional medicines on a broad scale. Although many other Andean communities have relied on trade in the past, the areas that were under heavy Inca rule came under the economic power and organization of Inca rulers; under the Inca administrative system, some goods moved "up" while other goods came back "down" the line. This exchange was a very different kind of trading system than the direct trading between communities that continued to flourish in the Condo area.

Reflecting the historical organizational dominance of the original Aymara groups, the Aymara language is still spoken today around the watershed system that includes Lake Titicaca, the Desaguadero River, and Lake Poopó. The Quechua language, however, continues to make inroads into some areas that were once dominated by Aymara groups. Quechua first entered southern Bolivia under Topa Inca's rule in 1470, but did not gain wide currency in Condo until approximately one hundred years ago, according to Condeños (Stark 1985:530). Although some older generations of people living in isolated pockets of Condo are still monolingual Aymara speakers, Quechua has become the more dominant of the two indigenous languages within the greater Condo region. Put simply, Quechua has become a kind of *lingua franca* in Bolivia, as it is in neighboring Peru. In part, Quechua gained dominance over other languages because it is the language of the market. It is also the language spoken in Cochabamba, which was colonized very early by the Inca and remains one of the richest agricultural

---

5. The Aymara and Quechua languages are similar because they have coexisted and influenced each other over at least 2,000 years of intertwined history (Hardman 1985). Through cultural contact, there have been "massive borrowings" in both directions between Quechua (a language family) and Aymara (from the Jaqi linguistic family). Many of the borrowings in the area of numbers and colors reflect market interactions, which indicates the importance of the marketplace as an economic and cultural crossroads (Hardman 1985).

regions in Bolivia. Cochabamba today attracts migrants from other parts of Bolivia, much as it has since Inca times.

As the official national language of Bolivia, Spanish is important in specific contexts. It is spoken in institutions established by the state, and it is the language of the Bolivian legal system. It is also the language of the Bolivian urban elite. Because men interact with state institutions more regularly—and travel to urban areas and other regions more frequently in search of wage labor—they are, therefore, more likely to receive schooling and experience in the Spanish language than are women. Not surprisingly, it is the men of Bolivia who speak Spanish most fluently.

In Condo, the population includes monolingual speakers (of Quechua, Aymara, or Spanish), bilingual speakers, and trilingual speakers. I surveyed the members of thirty-five households on the subject of language. In eighteen households, residents used all three languages; in thirteen households, mostly Quechua was spoken; and in five households, mostly Aymara was used. In fourteen households, members used both Quechua and Spanish. In three households, residents spoke both Quechua and Aymara. This area is clearly very complex linguistically, partly because it is situated on the margins of both Quechua and Aymara language zones (Albó 1991).

FIELDWORK AND RESEARCH METHODOLOGY

My first trip to Bolivia took place in 1985, when (along with my sister and brother-in-law) I visited the lakeside archaeological site of Tiwanaku, Lake Titicaca, and the views and museums of La Paz. At the time of our trip, the Bolivian government faced a looming economic and political crisis. Fearing massive public protests, the government sent military tanks into the streets, stationing them at the corners of the main plazas. Travel was restricted. We had to get special travel passes just to leave the city and go to Lake Titicaca. It was a difficult time to be in Bolivia, and certainly not a particularly opportune moment to be introduced to the charms of local life and the marketplace. Somehow, even at that tense moment, I became drawn to Bolivia—to its raw beauty, its cultural richness, and even its political dramas.[6]

In 1990, I began my first extended period of research in Bolivia, which I conducted over a twenty-month period in San Pedro de Condo. Ethnographic studies have historically focused on a particular community or group of people. Although such an intensive focus on one group or place has enabled anthropologists to produce rich ethnographic accounts, this methodological approach has not been without its limitations. Sometimes anthropologists have created a false sense of "boundedness," describing the people they study as ethnically and culturally separate and distinct from other neighboring groups. This fiction of cultural difference—Condeños as culturally distinct from Huareños, for example—is a characteristic of early ethnographic accounts in particular. In these accounts,

---

6. Over the years I have witnessed a series of political crises rock Bolivia, and then watched as periods of relative calm bring renewed hope for improved economic and social conditions in the country.

communities are described as closed and separate cultural units. Absent are perspectives on the connections between the community under study and other communities, the rest of the nation, and the world at large.

During my original fieldwork I did focus on one specific community, Condo. Over time, however, I was continually struck by the frequency with which people arrived in Condo (or left it), whether on short trips, for seasonal wage labor work, or for extended stays lasting years, during which time they maintained their ties to rural homes and kin. People, goods, services, and ideas all flowed both ways, in and out of the community—which was anything but isolated and unto itself. This dynamic nature of culture is important to study and understand, but it is sometimes difficult to grasp because of the confusion caused by all the movement. As I observed the exchange patterns and networks based in Condo, I began to get a real sense of the ways in which this was not a bounded, isolated, separate community. The emerging picture was one of a vital community that thrived on connections and was inextricably linked through the movement of people to other communities across a broad region.

Thus, rather than focusing my research lens on Condo as a community apart, I began to look at the way local persons interacted culturally in a wider setting, beyond Condo itself. I took inspiration from anthropologist Sherry Ortner's (1999) approach in her work on Sherpas in Nepal. Rather than examine "Sherpa culture" as the focus of her ethnography, Ortner investigated mountaineering and the way in which Sherpas have supported it and interacted within its framework. She found that the experience and activity of mountaineering had changed the Sherpas and their cultural practices. Elsewhere she calls this "practice anthropology," reflecting the fact that the anthropological lens is focused on what people do, their strategies for doing it, and the creative ways in which they accomplish what they set out to do. The focus is not on painting a fixed picture of a separate homogeneous culture and community (Ortner 1984).

Cultural interaction and dynamism is also what Stephen Gudeman and Alberto Rivera seek to capture in *Conversations in Colombia* (1990). In that book, they offer perspectives on Colombian culture by presenting conversations they conducted with informants in Colombia, their own conversations with each other, and their discussions together about economic theory.

The ethnographic research employed in this book examines the branching interconnections that link Condo with the communities beyond it. Our lens is focused on the networks of exchange and commerce built upon the circulation of traditional medicine. During the course of my ethnographic excursions in Bolivia, I worked to trace, follow, and physically walk these networks, from one community and marketplace to the next. Beginning with Condo, I became interested in the ways in which market vendors participated in the Huari and Challapata marketplaces. I began to visit and study these locales. I also frequently visited Oruro, which is Condo's closest big-city neighbor.

After completing my initial fieldwork in 1994, I continued to visit my rural field site in Condo as well as to spend time in Oruro and Cochabamba. In 2000, I was able to spend six months living in Cochabamba with my family, during which time I studied the impressive marketplace there, focusing especially on medicine

Photo by Bryan Miller

FIGURE 1.3 The author on the ridge above Condo, collecting notes on Condo's territory and geography.

vendors. I originally went to Cochabamba to interview Condeña vendors, but once there I became interested in the general ways in which traditional medicines are commercialized. The kernel of this present study took shape in 2000. In addition, in exploring traditional medicines and their networks of exchange, I have revisited the original research that I conducted in 1990–1991, as well as material collected during fieldwork trips in 1995, 1996, 1999, 2003, 2006, and 2007.

In compiling these data, I have drawn on a variety of ethnographic methods. I collected large amounts of data in an intensive survey of thirty-five Condo households that I conducted during my original fieldwork; from this material emerges some of the rural patterns of bartering and selling traditional medicines described in the following chapters. In addition, I conducted several marketplace surveys in Huari and Challapata, where I interviewed many vendors. I devoted long hours to observing marketplace transactions, drawing on one of the signature methods of anthropology, "participant observation;" to that end, I spent many hours sitting at vendors' stands, and in some instances attempting to sell the product myself.[7] My experience as a regular marketplace customer also helped me gain insight into the organization and patterns of interaction in the marketplace.

I continue to return to Bolivia and to Condo to conduct further research, most recently in August 2007. In Condo, I have a Condeño family and more than twenty godchildren. Through these multiple visits I have been able to collect

---

7. Participant observation is also at the heart of the general ethnographic research that I conducted Condo, where I collected data on agricultural practices, fiestas, kinship, marriage, healing, and local politics, among other topics.

longitudinal data about many marketplace and household events in Condo. The life histories of female vendors that I collected there form the core of the ethnographic research presented in this book.

In Cochabamba, I also collected life histories, conducted marketplace surveys, and spent many hours observing marketplace transactions. Because my research in Cochabamba has now spanned seven years, I have gained perspective on both the cultural continuities and the changes occurring in this setting.

SUMMARY

Andean traditional medicines originate in specific environmental and cultural settings, such as the one described in detail in this book—San Pedro de Condo. Although these medicines have a long history of use in rural household settings, they are also collected and assembled as items to be exchanged in urban marketplace settings, alongside other local commodities such as crops. In the past, the chief mechanism for the circulation of herbs and other items used in healing was direct exchange, sometimes across the great distance that separates highland products and customers from lowland ones. Today traditional medicines are mainly circulated through marketplace settings, such as those found in Condo and Cochabamba. These markets, which remain "traditional" in some of their characteristics, are just beginning to be targeted by a process of governmental regulation. In these marketplaces, more than the medicines themselves are sold or bartered; ideas about their use are also shared. Thus medicines and medical advice are exchanged in tandem by a variety of practitioners, many of whom now work in the market settings and new venues explored in Chapter 2.

2

Traditional Medicines in New Contexts: Old Cultural Practices in New Venues

INTRODUCTION

Bolivian traditional medicines have long been used in a variety of contexts beyond their native habitats. Plants and other medical products have journeyed, transported by Andean travelers, across the trade routes and pathways that integrated communities and allowed goods to flow in particular patterns. As these medical resources entered into circuits of commercial exchange, some of the rural Andean patterns of social organization continued to be used as part of the exchange process, as was the knowledge of the properties of the plants themselves. Because much of the healing takes place at the level of the rural household in the Andes, and because it is women who perform these healing duties as they manage and exchange medicines as one of their roles, gender is important to the system of traditional medicines and the means by which they are distributed.

The medicines themselves are classified into categories of "hot" and "cold," which allows them to be directly applied to their opposite "hot" and "cold" ailments. Although a much deeper understanding of medicinal plants, their uses, and healing in general is held by specialists (many of them males), the hot and cold system allows for the prescription of traditional medicines to move readily from household to marketplace. In the marketplace, both the vendors and the customers themselves are familiar with this division of hot and cold, and they often draw upon it as a way to classify medical items, foods, illnesses, bodies, and other conditions. The system of hot and cold condenses meaning and presents it in an accessible way. This ability to classify enables Andeans, many of whom are not official healers, to navigate the medical system and apply medical remedies. The hot and cold folk categories are widely understood, and a focus on a few Andean herbal remedies and their division into hot and cold categories reveals some of the basic features of this medical system, including its flexibility and capacity to adapt over time.

THE HOT AND COLD SYSTEM IN TRADITIONAL HEALING AND EXCHANGE

With a small hotplate purchased from my local hardware store, I boil another kettle of water for the lab module that my students are conducting as part of an ecological anthropology course. Today we are doing labwork in the Anthropology Laboratory at San Jose State University, a room that is more often occupied by the students in physical anthropology and archaeology, but which now contains a setup of boxes of manufactured teas and vials of dried plants, alongside the equipment for brewing: cups, strainers, and even sugar cubes for those who want to sweeten the assignment.

In paper cups positioned around the room, small portions of medicinal teas (prepared from an array of Andean herbs) are already steeping. I reflect briefly on the irony of exploring these Andean traditional medicines in the heart of Silicon Valley, where new technologies reign. Our study of ethnobotany[1] in my course introduces the many uses of plants in diverse cultural contexts; it is a good way to introduce the various and changing medicinal uses of plants. The students are glad for a break from our normal class routine and are enthusiastically discussing the appearance, smell, and taste of these samples, which I have asked them to describe as a first step in the exercise. Cola de caballo, pupusa, sasawi, wira wira, romero, manzanilla—all contribute an element to the overall pungent aroma, and for a moment transport me back to the medicine stalls in the marketplace in Bolivia.

As I breathe in these memories, several students are demonstrating impressive powers of description: "Bouquet of newly mown hay from Grandma's barn," says one, adopting the pose of a sniffing wine taster. An older student, trained in Ayurvedic medicine, has shown himself adept at describing these potions in terms of astringency, sweetness, and bitterness. It's the bitterness that now causes the

---

1. Ethnobotany is the study of the relationship between plants and people in a given culture (Ford 1994). Ethnobotanists study the various cultural uses of plants as food, tools, and medicines, and in construction. Given that drug discovery has been an important research goal in this field, ethnobotany sometimes refers solely to the study of medicinal plants in a given culture (Balick and Cox 1997).

screwed-up expressions and laughter in the classroom lab. Several of the brews are so bitter that a number of students refrain from tasting them at all. The facial expressions of the more intrepid tasters report the degree of bitterness, especially when they taste sasawi.

The sasawi we have in lab comes from Doña Emiliana's market stand in Cochabamba, which means it is originally from my rural field site of San Pedro de Condo. "This is the one," I say, taking a small sip of the concoction myself as a way to bring back the memory more fully. (Certain tastes and smells facilitate remembering!) I encourage those who are more inclined to the tasting and sensory dimensions of our lab work in this class.

As a way of introducing the lab exercise to my students, I tell them the story of my own first experiments in the world of Andean medicines. About one year into my fieldwork on the southern altiplano of Bolivia, I got sick. The señora with whom I lived brought me sasawi, and I valiantly drank it for a day. That is, it took me a full day to drink a cupful of the bitter infusion. (During the lab exercise with my students, I see my own reaction from that day mirrored in their faces.) That was the first time I was seriously ill in Bolivia, and eventually a trip to the city for tests revealed that I had two different varieties of parasites. As treatment, the doctor prescribed metronidazole (Flagyl—a cure that people often say is worse than the illness), and I did get better. Back in my rural home in San Pedro de Condo, however, I had tried the local remedy of sasawi first; I may have taken it a little too late in the illness to benefit me.[2] As I told my students, had I tried the remedy sooner or kept it up longer, it might have cured me. Surely the bitterness indicated some effective principle actively at work.

In the hot/cold system of plant classification, one of the characteristics of a "hot" (cálido) plant is its bitterness, and the señora who was doctoring me believed that I had a stomach problem brought on by the "cold." For my students, the taste and smell of sasawi provide a useful demonstration of the sensory experience of a plant's medicinal quality. As we were able to discern from its brewed characteristics, the extremely bitter taste was reflected in its classification as a "hot" or "cálido" plant (*qoñi* in Quechua) in the Andean typology of medicines. In fact, the plant is considered to be *muy cálida* or even *picante* (spicy) and, therefore, useful for serious types of stomach problems such as severe diarrhea and dysentery. Because Bolivians perceive health to be a state of balance between the states of hot and cold, it made sense that the señora would treat me with the hottest plant she had available.

---

2. Sasawi is *Leuceria pteropogon* (Girault 1987); the label also includes *Tecoma rosaefolia* (De Lucca and Zalles 1992). This plant of the treeless glacial valleys of the Andes has relatives throughout the Andes of Argentina, Chile, and Patagonia. In Bolivia, sasawi is a plant that comes from the mountains that rise high above the altiplano (found at around 4,000 meters) and is a staple of Condo's traditional medicine inventory. It is collected from the upper elevations of Condo's mountain valleys, and is used at home for a variety of ailments characterized by gastrointestinal complaints. Lira writes about "sassawi" that "all illnesses fear it, even on hearing its name. They call it Saint Peter, because they say that it has a bad temper" (1985:129). In other regions, sasawi has uses beyond its prescription for gastrointestinal problems. Girault describes its uses among the Kallawaya healers, who are renowned as contemporary healers, but whose medical history stretches back into pre-Hispanic times, earning them the nickname of "Doctors to the Inca." The Kallawaya use of sasawi includes treatments for dizziness, smallpox, and uterine inflammations, as well as for the stomach problems for which it is known in Condo (1987:482).

In Condo, the categories of hot and cold are referred to as *cálido* and *fresco*, which are perhaps more accurately translated as "warm" and "fresh" (or "cool"). The distinction between hot and cold is common throughout the Andes and in Latin America in general, and it is frequently used as a way to categorize food, drink, medicines, and body types.[3]

There is ongoing discussion about the origins of hot and cold in humoral theory, and about the ways in which these categories relate to other concepts and practices. (See, for example, Foster 1967, 1988, 1994, Gudeman 1976, Ingham 1970.) Hot and cold are not merely distinctions used in medicine, but terms also used to describe various cultural oppositions. For instance, Stephen Gudeman (1976) relates hot and cold classifications to gender, sexual passion, and food. It is believed, he writes, that these elements must be balanced in the conjugal pairing of husband and wife—or one spouse may overpower the other.

George Foster, one of the founders of medical anthropology and a renowned Latin Americanist, found the hot/cold system of classification to be persistent because of its flexibility and adaptability to indigenous practices. He cites the example of "fright" (*susto*), an indigenous concept that was easily incorporated into the hot/cold system (1967:192). Arthur Rubel also discusses the varied causes, symptoms, and treatments of susto (1998).

In Condo, all foods can be labeled as either "cálido" or "fresco," based on properties such as general appearance, color, effects, and "richness." To an outsider the classification may seem arbitrary; in my own experience, I could never guess very accurately to which category a food belonged. Even for an insider the designations may vary, as I discovered when I interviewed husbands and wives and recorded food lists: Spouses sometimes argued and disagreed on designations.

What is clear about these categories is that eating too much of one type of food will make one ill, so that hot and cold substances must be balanced within the body. The components included in this balance especially reflect a person's body type of either cálido or fresco. Medicinal herbs that are either hot or cold, therefore, serve the purpose of balancing the effects of a hot or cold illness, or the adverse effects that may be caused by too much of a given food. Drink is also used to counterbalance the effects of food, which is why it is saved until after the meal. Pork is described as *bien fresco* ("really fresh/cool"). As such, it is desirable to drink some alcohol or soda after consuming a meal that includes pork. The drink serves to *matar el chancho* ("kill the pig"), so that it won't *revivir* ("come back to life"). Drinking alcohol, beer, soda, broth, or water after a meal is a way to truly complete the meal; chewing coca[4] serves this same purpose.

The Andean system of hot and cold may be partially based in humoral theory, but nevertheless differs from it in important ways. Joseph Bastien, a pioneering

---

3. The categories of hot and cold were incorporated into local medical systems in Latin America from Spanish colonial practices, although their reception may be due to widespread use of oppositions in Andean practices before the Spanish arrival. Oppositions of hot and cold did not originate in Spain, but in the Hippocratic corpus of ancient Greece, in which diseases were "attributed either to these opposites directly, or to their effect on other substances or parts of the body" (Lloyd, 1964:94).

4. Burchard (1976) claims that coca helps metabolize food; in the fresco–cálido system, it also helps to balance the body.

Photo by Sarah Linn Gallardo

FIGURE 2.1 In Andean traditional medicine, all plants are classified as either "hot" or "cold." Here Bolivian herbs hang from a traditional medicine vendor's stand.

medical anthropologist working in Bolivia, has studied the famous Kallawaya healers. His research on Kallawaya concepts of illness and health demonstrates that these cultural understandings differ from Greek humoral theory. Andeans stress the circulation of body fluids to maintain health, whereas the Greeks stressed balance. Bastien writes, "Greeks were concerned with balancing the pendulum; Qollahuayas [Kallawayas] are concerned with keeping it swinging" (1985:608). The idea of a pendulum, of course, seems to incorporate the notion of balance: not too much of one or the other opposite.

Van den Berg's research focuses on the Andean notion of balance in the environment. He finds that as a cultural concept, "balance" does not suggest a static equilibrium or homeostasis. Instead, it is a notion that is fluid, established by the encounter of contrary yet complementary forces. The achieved "balance," Van den Berg claims, is fragile because there is always flux and change is in such a concept (1990:123). Hence, it might be more productive to think of plants as occupying a position on a spectrum between the extremes of hot and cold. One Bolivian healer explained to me that he thinks of hot and cold as having three levels: a level three "cold" plant would have almost the same medicinal effects as a level one "hot" plant in his calibrated analysis of hot and cold.

George Foster has demonstrated that considerable disagreement may occur among people in one locale with regard to the hot/cold classification system (1988, 1994). After interviewing thirty people about the proper classification for a standard list of medicinal remedies, he found that a small number of respondents had a high level of agreement, but the majority did not. Some people even classified the same remedies differently at different times. This variation led Foster to conclude that the hot/cold classification system is used to *validate* the use of empirical remedies, rather than serving as a fixed system for prescribing treatments. Although the system is still employed when advising people how to maintain their health, the strict use of "cold" medicines for "hot" ailments is not consistently followed. Instead, hot and cold categories have become part of a narrative about health in which individual cases are modeled around a shared experience.

My introduction to the hot/cold system of medicines and my short-lived attempt to use sasawi as a cure was one of my many experiences with herbal remedies (albeit perhaps not the most successful). I came to observe how a wide range of illnesses was treated with local herbs, and over time I came to appreciate the flexibility of treatments and remedies. According to my study, the first level of healing in rural areas is to attempt to treat the illness with local herbal remedies (such as sasawi), before seeking other treatments. When I stumbled off to the city to seek a cure from the biomedical clinic there, the line between the cures of the countryside and those of the city seemed most distinct: I believed that sasawi was a cure of the countryside and of rural people. In time, I found this assumption was not completely true. Bolivian "urbanites" have roots in rural areas and traditions; likewise, rural people have connections to urban areas through kinship and commerce. These relationships draw the two "spaces" (rural and urban) together into a complex whole; neither is a distinct, separate sphere.

Traditional medicine in Bolivia is based on an inventory of plants that are collected and exchanged across highland and lowland regions, and combined with an array of plants originally introduced from the Old World. "Traditional medicine" is, therefore, practiced somewhat differently from place to place across Bolivia. At the same time, traditional medicine shares many similarities from region to region because of common themes, practices, and ingredients.

As I sought to impress upon my students in my laboratory experiment in ethnobotany and Andean traditional medicine, it may be more useful to speak of traditional *medicines* in Bolivia, to avoid suggesting uniformity across all regions. Andean people have, indeed, widely disseminated particular ideas and plants, and established a repertoire of healing beliefs, practices, and medicines. Nevertheless, there remain many ways in which to combine these elements. As a consequence, there are many variations in the larger indigenous system. Similar to the variability that Foster demonstrated for the hot/cold system, the inventory of plants and practices in contemporary traditional medicine in Bolivia reveals variability from place to place, and even from one practitioner to another (Foster 1988). Indeed, specific elements of the regional medical repertoire (including plants) apparently form a kind of shared medical toolkit that is part of the larger cultural system. Different elements from the toolkit are used for different purposes, at different places and times.

In marketplace settings (where medicine has been commercialized), diversity within traditional medicine systems has been gradually increasing. This proliferation of approaches is partly due to the economic practices of contemporary vendors, who in striving to build their business increase the variety of goods they offer for sale. Greater variation is also influenced, of course, by ethnomedical cultural beliefs—including those of the vendors and their customers. These beliefs mutually shape and influence one another, creating demand for new and diverse medical products.

Traditional medicine is also a system that has clearly shown the ability to adapt to change throughout its history. Over time, medical practitioners incorporate new products and ideas as they find them useful. This adoption leads to a "process of medical acculturation," which began early in the colonial period in Bolivia, when food plants and medicines were exchanged between the Old and New Worlds (Kay 1996:26). One study conducted in Mexico found that of the almost 2,000 plant species used in herbal remedies, 35 percent were indigenous and 65 percent were non-native and introduced from the Old World (1996:35).

Given the blending of medicinal ingredients and ideas within Latin American traditions, the plant cures and healing techniques used by people in Bolivia to cure themselves and others offers a wonderful window into changing traditions and culture in the Andes. Using the sensory experience of herbs that day in the classroom lab, I hoped to give my students a small glimpse into this world of Andean healing, with its flexible categories and shared toolkits, rooted in rich but ever-changing cultural traditions.

TRADITIONAL MEDICINES, COMMERCE, AND CHANGE

Although at first glance the category "traditional medicine" seems to hearken back to some bedrock Andean health system (based in ancient tradition), the set of medicinal ingredients that constitute traditional medicine becomes a site for studying the blending and transformation of medical practices and beliefs. On the southern altiplano, where I lived for twenty months while conducting ethnographic research, people did not use the term "traditional medicine." They spoke of "herbs" and "medicines," and called herbal medicines "*remedios*" (remedies) in situations where they were sold or bartered. As most rural people rely almost solely on these herbal medicines, it is simply "medicine" that they use. This system is deeply embedded in oral tradition. Unfortunately, it is in danger of losing its complexity and finer distinctions, as fewer people keep track of the myriad cures that are (and were) available. Because so many people live in the countryside and/or lack resources to avail themselves of biomedical facilities, 70–80 percent of the population relies on some form of traditional medicine.

Following a "hierarchy of resort,"[5] people in both rural and urban areas of Bolivia first try to treat themselves, and it is the mother of the household who is most often charged with taking care of familial ailments, especially her children's illnesses. She is the first-order healer in this indigenous medical system (McElroy and Townsend 1996, Romanucci-Ross 1989). In these household cases, sick

---

5. A "hierarchy of resort" refers to the sequence of options people avail themselves of in the treatment of illness.

people are treated with the medicines commonly used for a variety of ailments, including the sasawi plant, which is made into an herbal tea. These herbal remedies are either collected by a household member or obtained through trade from someone in the community. In other cases, the woman of the household will consult women vendors of traditional medicines in the marketplace, as these women are known to have specialized knowledge in the use of medicinal plants.

Although not technically considered "healers," these vendors fill the primary role in a "hierarchy of resort" for many lower-order ailments, and especially for "women's complaints." When an illness persists or is considered more serious, however, a sick person in the countryside may choose either to enter the bio-medical system or to employ the services of a local *curandero* (healer). Called a *yatiri*[6] in Aymara communities such as San Pedro de Condo, this healer is trusted to treat physical and spiritual problems. Patients choosing the biomedical route proceed to a local clinic, where they receive treatment from a male auxiliary nurse or health provider. Members of the medical staff receive some degree of Red Cross training, but they do not have official medical degrees. The services they render depend on their personal abilities, and the treatments they offer may be appropriate or not; sometimes, those treatments are even harmful. Unless there is a larger clinic nearby (one staffed by doctors or nurses), most rural inhabitants have to choose between these semi-skilled representatives of the biomedical system and local traditional medicine healers. Thus the hierarchy of resort in medical treat-ment works in favor of indigenous ethnomedicine—at least until the point where patients experience serious or life-threatening illnesses.

For serious health problems, some people choose to travel to a hospital, although there is a widespread belief that hospitals are expensive and dan-gerous places, where "people go to die" (Fernández Juárez, 1999). Given these economic and social considerations, traditional medicine retains a prominent place in rural areas.

In urban areas, and especially those populated by high numbers of recent migrants from the countryside, some of these same patterns persist. The difference lies in the greater availability of biomedical care as a result of the greater number of clinics, some of which (albeit not enough) are geared to meet the needs of poor people (see, for example, Klinman 1999).[7] The "hierarchy of resort" in cities is, therefore, a bit more complex and perhaps offers "better" options, although the extent of this difference very much depends on people's basic living conditions. Migrants to the city may shun clinics, where they are treated by "strangers," meaning the medical staff (Wayland and Crowder 2002). In cities, patients find a more varied and yet uneven distribution of traditional medicines.

---

6. A *yatiri* (which means "he who knows") is a shaman-like individual who offers diagnosis and treatment. These respected healers may also be referred to as *jampiris* in Quechua-speaking communities.

7. As an example of the composition of some newer sections of urban areas, in the peri-urban community of 2,500 in Klinman's study, 21 percent of the households were relocalized miners, 28 percent of the households included migrants from the countryside, and 36 percent of the households were lower-middle-class households from the nearby city of Cochabamba (Klinman 1999).

The creation of an inventory of Bolivian traditional medicines is not a modern phenomenon, but rather has a long history that is linked to commerce. For instance, in the early colonial period, the Huari fair—located just five kilometers from Condo—was a huge, international market. Beginning in the sixteenth century, Spaniards sold merchandise that originated in Seville at the Huari fair. Later, mule drivers from Argentina came to sell their mules and other livestock at Huari, in exchange for vicuña hides and medicinal herbs. Huari came to be known as an international market for traditional medicines, in which a particular array of "highland" and "jungle" medicines (some actually originating in places such as Spain, Chile, Peru, Argentina, and Bolivia) was brought together into a coherent, expanded medicinal inventory. This inventory was, in turn, distributed widely from this marketplace to other parts of Bolivia. We look more closely at the Huari fair in Chapter 5.

The Cochabamba market was another early site for the sale and consolidation of an inventory of Andean traditional medicines. The number of vendors there decreased during the late colonial period and early republican period, when officials attempted to squelch "backward" practices that ran contrary to modern Western medicine. Juan José Alba (1988) claims that between 1900 and 1930, sales in the *Jampi Qhatu* ("Medicine Market") of Cochabamba were "semi-clandestine" and that urban Bolivians referred to these indigenous goods as "garbage medicine" or *botica de basura*. This marginalization further served to set traditional medicines apart as a group. Today the medicine vendors who sell in the Cochabamba marketplace have not only rebounded but also profited from their characterization as purveyors of an "ancient tradition." We look more closely at the sale of medicines in the Cochabamba marketplace in Chapter 6.

The use of herbal medicines is certainly founded on "tradition," although it is also based on local plants and practices originating from many different regions and zones. Over time, the local repertoires of medicinal plants have been collected and bundled into larger assemblages. These treatments have been reclassified as "traditional," despite ongoing change and infiltration by outside plants and practices. Indeed, through this process, the system of medicines glossed as traditional medicine has become pluralized into traditional medicines. One hallmark of these traditional medicines is their cross-pollination, hybridization, and adaptability.

An element of economic supply and demand is at play here, too. Stands selling traditional medicines look quite different in the tourist zones of La Paz (labeled colorfully "The Witches' Market") than they do in the interior of an Oruro marketplace, or as they appear in Cochabamba or at the annual Huari fair. In La Paz, vendors understand full well the appeal of their "mysterious" charms; they wrap them up for customers in pieces of colored wool, reciting incantations for good luck or fertility or happy travels—and charging at least double the amulet's price in Cochabamba. At herbal medicine stands in non-tourist areas, by contrast, the particular goods offered go hand in hand with other services: At the very least, the vendor of medicines in these places will know how to tell the customer how to use the product. The extent to which a particular vendor can act as an effective healer, however, varies greatly.

HEALING IN THE CITY: A TRADITIONAL
MEDICINE PRACTICE

The vendors' stands in the marketplace look quite different from the businesses of urban natural medicine healers. Urban curanderos have practices that parallel those of biomedical doctors in many ways, although in other ways they lay claim to "authentic tradition." Natural medicine healers and curanderos often establish offices or clinics of some kind. One urban curandero in Cochabamba, Carlos, provides an excellent example of how contemporary traditional medicine is practiced, as he delivers medical services and products that meet the needs of urban customers with both old and new complaints. It is also interesting to note that, while most traditional medicine vendors are women, most curanderos are men. (There are exceptions to this norm, of course.) A visit to the urban curandero's home and clinic always provided me with some surprising insights into contemporary traditional medicine, plus a look at the wide cross-section of the Bolivian populace seeking advice and cures—as well as some respite from the crowded city in the valley below.

The first time I visit Carlos, I am greeted by his mother-in-law, who is sitting outside the door of their house in the sun shucking fava beans. The house that Carlos shares with his wife, two children, and mother-in-law (plus a fluctuating number of visitors) is located high up in Barrio Frutillar in the city of Cochabamba, a fairly new urban community that hugs the hillside, beginning on a major city street below and ascending to bumpy dirt tracks along the highest level of "streets." Carlos's house, in which his business is also located, is located approximately midway up the urban development and surrounded by other houses that have the patios and low-slung look you might find in the countryside. This house's patio is full of scores of lush-looking plants, some of them medicinal. The overall effect is of a welcoming refuge from the dirt and bustle of the city.

Seated on a bench padded with an old weaving, I await my turn along with a Quechua-speaking woman who is there to consult with Carlos about her ailment. Carlos caters to a diverse group of patients, from peasants who are monolingual Quechua speakers suffering from *aire* ([harmful] "air") to upper-class women trying to combat problems with migraine headaches. To all his clients, Carlos offers both cures and comfort. In the entryway and open area surrounding the garden, plants have been hung to dry, and mortars, pestles, and a brazier are in view. The smell of copal—an incense used in offerings—is in the air.

When my turn comes to meet with the curandero, we have a conversation that is less an interview about traditional medicines and more a series of rapid observations that Carlos makes about medicine, politics, and ecology. On the first day that I visit him, we cover a variety of topics. We discuss the countrywide strike that is in progress. Then we talk about his own philosophy and experience as a healer. Next we turn to ecological degradation and problems associated with the commercialization of medicinal plants. We also manage to discuss the effects of an anti-parasite health campaign as one example of the misguided use of biomedical cures.

Over the next few months, we have several similar conversations in which Carlos is both the interviewer and the respondent. Instead of following a set interview format, I ask some open-ended interview questions; these mark parameters and are less precise queries. The direction our conversation takes delights me, in that the open-ended style elicits rich data and new ideas. It turns out that Carlos has worked with several international investigators and patients: In 2000, when I spoke with him, he was working with people from Italy, Sweden, Denmark, and Mexico. Carlos also has close associations with the university in Cochabamba as well as the museum in downtown Cochabamba. His dearest wish, he confides, is to meet some of the Native American healers in the United States. In particular, he would like to meet Navajo and Hopi healers. Carlos is broadly educated and well read, and knows many people. Beyond his healing practice, he participates in an astonishingly large array of activities. In our six-month stay in 2000, my husband, daughter, and I are easily absorbed into the swirl of activities that surround him and his extended family.

Carlos comes from the countryside and descends from parents and grandparents who were healers. Thus he came to healing through the route that rural

Photo by Lynn Sikkink

FIGURE 2.2 Carlos Prado, here at a workshop teaching traditional medicine preparation, is a *curandero* who has adapted his practices to an urban clientele.

healers have most often taken: He inherited the role through his ancestors. From them he also learned a great deal about plants, including how to harvest them, what particular plants are good for, and how to integrate the use of plants within the hot/cold system of healing. As Carlos grew up, he began to travel (Peru, Ecuador, Argentina, and Bolivia) and to seek out healers in these new places from whom he learned about new therapies, plants, and rituals. He incorporated these elements into his emerging practice as an itinerant healer. Spending approximately eight years in the Amazon, he learned a great deal about what he calls "the shamanic tradition" and the role of ritual in healing. Traveling and visiting sacred places was of paramount importance in his development. Learning about plants and how to collect them was a secondary consideration, because anyone could learn these things, as Carlos put it. In his mind, the most important aspect of his training was the framework he gained by fully understanding "Andean cosmology," gaining insight into the working of the natural world. His knowledge also came from books. Carlos read about other traditions and means of healing and became a self-taught ethnologist of ethnomedicine—that is, he now has an understanding of healing from a cross-cultural perspective, including a technical understanding of biomedicine.

Moving to the city of Cochabamba, Carlos opened a practice where people can consult with him for a small fee—and the plants or medicines he prescribes are dispensed from the consulting room/pharmacy of his house. This curandero's practices seem a blend of disparate traditions when seen from the vantage point of his personal and professional development, but he calls his practice "traditional medicine" and relies above all on the legacy of his Andean ancestors. Carlos believes very strongly in the efficacy of making offerings to Andean gods both as part of the healing process and for communal well-being, an approach that he models on the practices of both rural *yatiris* and Amazonian shaman. Perhaps a better way to look at his practice is as a personal adaptation of traditional medicine to patients who live in diverse settings but who desire Andean cures. Indeed, his patients often distrust the treatments they receive at the hands of the biomedical establishment.

One example of Carlos's healing techniques can be found in the visit of a friend who once consulted him for a problem involving blood in the urine. Although this friend had consulted doctors in the United States, he found Carlos more familiar with the likely causes of his ailment. "Hematuria," said Carlos, using the scientific name for the condition. The curandero did not physically examine his patient, but instead used conversation as the diagnostic tool. He explained that he became very familiar with this condition through the taxi and bus drivers in Cochabamba, who often develop it from driving all day over bumpy roads in vehicles that have little in the way of a suspension system.

Carlos's observation was especially meaningful to his new patient, who, as an athlete, believed that his problems arose from running down long descents in the mountains that irritated his system. "Too much vibration," agreed Carlos. For his treatment of this case of hematuria, Carlos began by having his patient smell a pleasant liquid through a long gourd, as a way to relax him. He next produced a dried cactus rattle, which he shook to induce further relaxation, and then put hot compresses over his patient's back and kidneys.

Finally, Carlos prescribed and provided a medicine made from an infusion of herbs, which his patient was directed to take before meals. He also recommended that he consume less coffee, fat, salt, sugar, pasta, soda pop, and spicy foods. I mention this treatment in some detail to give a picture of the elements involved in Carlos's practice. That he uses a kind of aromatherapy, along with soothing sounds, underlines his attempts (influenced by shamanism and also "alternative healing" practices) to involve his patients' senses in the healing process. His use of compresses and herbal preparations derives more from the Andean legacy of his practice, which emphasizes that hot and cold elements should be "balanced." In addition, his admonitions to eat a healthy diet parallel what Andean naturopaths tell their patients in all consultations.

Carlos describes himself as a practitioner of "traditional medicine" rather than "natural medicine," a perspective that places his work more in line with Andean practice. His practice, however, incorporates elements similar to the natural medicine prescriptions of the institute-trained natural medicine doctors. One of these similarities resides in the fact that diet is a very important part of the healing process, and a component that is monitored by the naturopath. In Chapter 8, we look more closely at naturopaths—*naturistas*—and the "natural medicine" on which their practice is based.

Carlos's practice provides an example of one curandero's tailored selection of medical practices, beliefs, and cures, mostly herbal. His unique vision, although derived from Andean traditional medicine, is his personal response—his version of the "story" of Andean ethnomedicine. In this way, the traditional medicine clinic that Carlos operates shares some similarities with vendors' stands in marketplace venues around the city.

In both sites, the medical and healing products and services that are sold are based on herbal remedies, selected from a rich and varied Andean tradition, and chosen and displayed differently from place to place, and from person to person. The patients or customers who wish to be healed with these herbal remedies and through the use of ritual means patronize these businesses, matching the vendors' or healers' models of health with their own. Many of the patrons may have had bad experiences with biomedical cures, or at least question biomedicine's efficacy, and are now looking for "alternatives." Some of the customers—especially those from rural backgrounds— have personal beliefs that are rooted in the Andean healing tradition, while others are urbanites who choose to be healed in the traditional fashion. In these traditional medicine businesses, relationships between customer and healer develop over time. These relationships are nurtured in the public arena, which serves to bring together communities of people, perhaps not in "self-help" groups but rather in social circles where people share similar values and exchange ideas.

SUMMARY

In understanding uses of traditional medicines in new venues, it is important to pay attention to old ideas and contexts for traditional medicine use. Traditional medicines emerge from older, rural systems of use. The Andean hot/cold system, for instance, underpins not only traditional medicines, but also other elements of bodily conditions and substances that affect the body. In the marketplace, this system becomes a way for vendors to interact with their customers in a meaningful manner, as most people understand at least simplified versions of the hot/cold lexicon.

As part of an historic and widespread taxonomic system in the Andes, the hot/cold dichotomy is an integral part of medical belief and practice in Bolivia—and a vehicle for the commercialization of traditional medicine. The ways in which people seek healing in rural communities, including the particular hierarchy of resort they follow, are not the same as the approaches undertaken by their urban counterparts. The general pattern for seeking cures, however, is similar in both places. In rural and urban areas alike, people find healers in different venues, but healing expertise is still recognized as ultimately stemming from the rural tradition.

Although women may know a great deal about healing and, in their roles as vendors, prescribe medicines, men more commonly hold formal roles as curanderos in the Bolivian system. In their capacity as curanderos, these male healers can probably be linked to their rural (male) counterparts, the *yatiris* (shaman/healers). This chapter described the practice of one curandero to highlight the contemporary urban role of this class of healers. Keeping rural systems and practices in mind while looking at the urban marketplace helps to illuminate the links between the practices in these two locales. In the next chapter, we take a more in-depth look at issues surrounding the marketplace as a unique sphere of medical practice and activity.

3

Women's Roles in Andean Marketplaces: Shopping in the Andes

INTRODUCTION

Throughout Bolivia, open-air marketplaces abound. Although in some locales municipal marketplaces were planned and built as a way to provide official spaces for vendors to operate businesses, most marketplaces have grown organically on the spot: Stalls are set up in streets where people live and have storefront businesses, vendors occupy the city center's sidewalks with displays of their ground-level goods, small kiosks are wedged into corners along a busy street, and everywhere itinerant peddlers criss-cross urban spaces to bring their wares directly to customers. In rural areas, marketplaces have weekly, yearly, or fiesta-based schedules that concentrate marketing activities on specific days, creating an ebb and flow in cycles of buying and selling.

The marketplace is a microcosm of the social and economic relations of Bolivian people. It is also a place of desire: Vendors seek out business opportunities, customers look for good deals; along the way there is the hope of a mutually beneficial interaction. Sometimes a business breakthrough occurs, such that vendors are able to eventually move into more permanent and respectable storefronts. Many vendors, however, may sell little on any particular day given the intense competition from their fellow sellers, and barely manage to eke out a living in the marketplace.

This chapter probes the cultural economics of the marketplace. It focuses first on the opportunity, risk, and lure of the marketplace, and then turns to examine women's contributions to exchange relations. We also take a look at the informal economic sector in Bolivia and consider its significance in people's livelihoods and subsistence strategies. Finally, we consider how understanding Andean relations of exchange is critical for understanding Bolivian marketplace transactions.

To begin to set the stage geographically, we visit two marketplace venues that we will continue to consider in subsequent chapters. One is the most rural venue, Condo; the other is the most urban, Cochabamba. (For their locations, see Map 1.1.) These sites are endpoints on the urban–rural trajectory of the trade in traditional medicines. We begin with the Cochabamba marketplace—the largest single marketplace in Bolivia, located in the center of the country and at the nexus of trade.

COCHABAMBA'S LA CANCHA: TARZAN IN THE MARKETPLACE

As I was about to purchase camera batteries from an open-air stall, the vendor reached out to grab my hands, squeezing them and the peso boliviano bills that I hold. Our transaction froze as I followed her glance to the strange figure striding down the narrow aisle. "Tarzan!" shouted a number of people who were also watching his advance. I took one step into the vendor's already crowded space to let the apparition pass by. The man was dressed in nothing more than a loincloth on this cool day, and his movements were erratic yet strangely agile. His hair was a disheveled mat, he was barefoot, and his body had been stained a dusty brown. I looked back to the worried señora as she released my hands, and she answered the question I hadn't yet asked. "He lives in the marketplace. We're afraid of him because he's crazy! He comes by and takes what he wants. When he's hungry he grabs fruit and bread, sometimes money—no one can stop him because he's strong and quick. Even the police don't know what to do."

Even though I was a veteran marketplace observer, this event was something new and intriguing to me. This kind of surprise is what brought me back again and again to the marketplace with its unfolding scenes and drama. It was also one of the reasons I shopped for everything I needed in the marketplace, even when friends warned me of the danger of robbery there. For years I have enjoyed wandering through marketplaces around rural and urban Bolivia, but the Cochabamba marketplace was the largest and most complex terrain, extending approximately fifteen square blocks. Finding one's way around "La Cancha" was like finding one's way around Bolivia. A little bit of everything and everyone was there, and if you stayed long enough you might even see "Tarzan" go by, dressed for the jungle but surviving by hunting and gathering in the Andean marketplace.

The marketplace in general is a site of both opportunity and danger. "Tarzan" could survive there, living off the bounty of its wares as he strode through the aisles, taking what he needed. From his perspective, it is undoubtedly a sadder picture, as he obviously had nowhere else to go and no family to take care of him. He was clearly mentally disturbed, yet had found a kind of "home" in this marketplace. For their part, the vendors perceived him as a dangerous menace—if not to their personal safety, then to their livelihoods. They felt helpless to stop "Tarzan," and the police were unable to control his rampages. The scene I witnessed took place in 2000. It was because of the threat posed by people like Tarzan, as well as more conventional thieves, that the vendors finally took matters into their own hands and hired their own private security guards to patrol the marketplace in 2001. Each vendor paid a small fee to finance the guards' monthly salaries.

Later that same year, police tried to eject the marketplace security guards from the Cochabamba marketplace, resulting in the death of one passer-by. The vendors continued to support the security guards, rallying in protest of the incident. By June 2002, security guards were everywhere in the market, dressed in black paramilitary gear and carrying billy sticks. The police felt threatened by this parallel law enforcement organization, but the market sellers were proud of the young people they were employing and the way the marketplace atmosphere improved. I do not know what happened to Tarzan, but in 2006 the vendors continued to employ the security guards to keep thieves out of the marketplace. Making the market a safer place had proven successful in luring back shoppers who had previously drifted away because of the dangerous atmosphere they perceived La Cancha to have. In interviews with marketplace vendors, one theme that emerges is the marketplace as a site of great opportunity, but also a place of theft, danger, lawsuits, and competition with one's neighbors. (See also Buechler and Buechler 1996, Seligmann 2001, Weismantel 2001.)

Despite the chaotic appearance of the marketplace, the vendors have always organized as syndicated groups—as unions of fruit or flower sellers, for instance. This organization allowed them to take security measures into their own hands, neutralize the danger of robbery and thieves, and once again attract shoppers to the marketplace. In an ironic twist, this move has also brought more vendors into the marketplace, as marketing has become perceived as a more attractive business opportunity again. Competition is another kind of danger that presents itself in the marketing of wares. The over-saturation of vendors in the market threatens permanent vendors' livelihoods. Traditional medicine vendors complain of the competition with which they must contend and the difficulty of making a living when so many new and itinerant vendors are cutting into their sales.

On big market days, vendors flood the aisles, nooks, and crannies of the marketplace, selling wherever and whatever they can. Among them are increasing numbers of medicine sellers who find these events a good opportunity to make a least a little cash. The success of these newcomers impinges on the success of the permanent vendors, who already have a hard time making a profit. In times of economic crisis (which are unfortunately frequent), more people turn to the option of selling in the marketplace, which makes the enterprise less profitable for

Photo by Lynn Sikkink

F I G U R E 3.1 Throughout Bolivia, women make a living by selling produce and other items. Here, women sell in a marketplace in La Paz.

everyone. In the city, where many vendors dedicate themselves full-time to marketing, this kind of competition is especially threatening. In rural market-places, where vendors sell goods as a way to supplement their agropastoral liveli-hood, the competition is less damaging. Nevertheless, it may result in a higher concentration of sellers as they struggle to earn the small income that allows them to buy the things they need to sustain their rural livelihood. In the case of both urban and rural marketplaces and their corresponding vendors, the marketplace is an encounter point for people, goods, ideas, and practices.

THE MARKETPLACE AS A CROSSROADS

The marketplace is a site of both economic and social interaction for Bolivian people, and is a crossroads where dramatically disparate groups meet. In the Co-chabamba marketplace, the vendors come from either urban or rural backgrounds; their customers, while overwhelmingly urban, also include rural folk along with intermediaries, who buy goods for later resale. In addition to the primary re-lationships established around the buying and selling of particular goods, other relationships are built around people who provide services to others in the mar-ketplace, including to the vendors themselves. For example, vendors of prepared foods supply meals to both buyers and sellers, the security force patrols the mar-ketplace in sites such as Cochabamba, and the thieves find a different opportunity (an "anti-service") as they prey on vendors and customers alike.

In rural areas, the marketplace is also a site of both opportunity and risk for rural dwellers (*campesinos*) from different communities as well as for participating urbanites. Like the urban marketplace, the rural one serves as a sort of crossroads at which the local and national economies meet. Anthropologist Linda Seligmann describes the marketplace as "the crucial intersection between rural and urban sociospatial environments" (1989:695). In the countryside, the rural marketplace is in many respects modeled on household relations of exchange, although overall the marketplace is typified by a distinct set of economic relations and sociality. Whether rural or urban, the marketplace is directly linked to the national market economy, because the relations in the marketplace are based on gain rather than simple reciprocity. Nevertheless, this distinction does not mean that the two domains are completely separate: The market is affected by household exchange practices (as when barter takes place in the marketplace), and rural people are affected in their home communities by market notions of exchange.

The inhabitants of my rural field site of San Pedro de Condo (Condeños) are a good example of people who make use of the marketplace as a way to supplement their household economy. As agriculturalists and pastoralists, Condeños have subsistence livelihoods; families produce much of what they consume. Even so, their need for a cash income is great. The marketplace, then, is the source of both money and the essential things they buy with it—for example, animals, fuel, cooking oil, coca, and vegetables. Condeños follow the prices and fluctuations of the marketplace closely, and they attempt to choose advantageous moments to buy and sell certain goods. They also understand the benefits of buying in bulk, and when possible try to buy in economical quantities.

In short, Condeños, like other campesinos in Bolivia, are not separate from the market economy but are active participants in it, helping to shape the structure of the greater market through their own participation in it. Although many Condeños buy and sell in the marketplace, they consider that too heavy reliance on bought goods signals *vicio* (vice); likewise, anyone who relies too heavily on bought goods instead of eating the crops they produce is *vicioso* (full of vice). A useful perspective on "vice" is offered by Stephen Gudeman, who conducted research in Panama. Based on his research, "vices are both categories of goods and necessities carried to extremes ... vice and luxury are opposed to necessity as production for exchange is to production for use" (1976:40). Following a similar kind of logic, some Condeños told me that their good health came from eating foods *not* acquired in the marketplace, but rather grown and produced at home— even though this meant consuming a smaller variety of fruits or vegetables. This rural attitude is at odds with that of residents of urban areas; in the latter areas, every family's needs must be met with goods acquired in the marketplace, and the line between necessities and luxuries differently drawn.

In contrast to the perspective of Andean vendors presented in studies of urban marketplaces (Babb 1989 Seligmann 1989), for rural inhabitants the marketplace is a special domain into which vendors and buyers move and then retreat. Of course, their "retreat" is only a partial one because they remain dependent on the market to some extent. In addition, the rural marketplace has special spatial and symbolic significance for Condeños. This relationship is expressed during *Espiritu*, a Saint's

Photo by Lynn Sikkink

FIGURE 3.2 The work of cooking: women in Condo, cooking for a fiesta. Food preparation begins days ahead of time, and women put in long hours.

Day ritual marking both Pentecostal week and the newly harvested crops, and an event that is celebrated in the rural marketplace. The ritual enacted at *Espíritu* entails offering alcohol libations to the fields, the animals that helped in the production (the burros), the cold winds that bring frost to make freeze-dried potatoes (*chuño*), and *jach'a jara* (big market), where they will sell some of their products.

Distinct social and economic relations of exchange characterize the different contexts of rural life, including the home, community, and marketplace. For instance, reciprocity operates within these contexts in a way that connects rural vending to the household economy. Rural vendors may gift food items to one another, and relatives and neighbors often engage in a cooperative form of selling. This sense of community is distinct from the relations of exchange that mark urban marketplaces. There very little reciprocity is found, except among people related as close kin.

Because women exemplify the marketing enterprise in both rural and urban settings, oftentimes bridging the spheres of the household and the informal sector, it is important that we look at the gendered nature of the Andean marketplace.

GENDER AND THE MARKETPLACE

In both rural households and in marketplaces, women are in charge of much of day-to-day health care in Bolivia, prescribing plants to both family members and customers. From their household roles and experience in healing and health

FIGURE 3.3   The work of production: women in Peru, sorting and bagging potatoes.

FIGURE 3.4   Making freeze-dried potatoes, or *chuño*.

management, women have become medicine vendors par excellence, selling their medicines alongside their other products in the marketplace. What is it about women that prepares them for their work as vendors of traditional medicines? In rural Bolivian households, women take responsibility for much of the exchange work because these roles are related to their productive work. In these areas, women are largely in charge of crop-processing work, cooking, and the storage and care of household resources. In San Pedro de Condo, the household's resources that women produce and manage include traditional medicines. As local people say, "Women know what can be sold." Also, women seem well suited to sell this merchandise to what is largely a female clientele. Through Bolivian women's household experience as first-level healers, they acquire the expertise needed to successfully prescribe and to sell *remedios caseros* (home remedies) in the marketplace.

Andean women's roles in exchange are complex. They participate in both marketing activities and in nonmonetary exchange, and they shift readily between the two kinds of exchange. It is likely that women's role as modern market vendors has roots in older, nonmonetary forms of exchange. Across the Andes, women are well represented in marketplaces—from the huge markets in the department capitals, where they sell in both small and large quantities, to the smaller regional and local marketplaces. Because rural women are full-time agriculturalists, as vendors they may sell primarily their own agricultural products. Alternatively, they may buy goods in the market and resell them for profit, which they realize either as cash or as leftover, unsold goods. Another marketing strategy is for women to become vendors in the urban marketplaces, where they may make a career out of selling.

Related to women's active roles in exchange are their responsibilities as farmers and guardians of the family's storage facilities. Women perform many of the productive and crop-processing tasks that bring the "finished product" into their storage areas. The woman of the household is customarily in charge of this stored food. She keeps track of it, using appropriate quantities to feed the family while reserving portions of it for seed and to sustain the family through the lean periods before the next harvest and in years of crop failure. Linked to women's roles in cooking, the management of stored food is also connected to the yearly cycle of agricultural activities in which women oversee production and yields. For instance, it is the woman of the household who is responsible for storing the seed that will be used the next year's planting. This responsibility may descend from the planting tasks that were assigned to women in pre-Hispanic times. As ethnohistorian Irene Silverblatt writes, "The Andean division of labor had women put seeds in the earth as men broke the soil with their foot plows" (1987:29). Silverblatt describes Andean women in these roles as the "geneticist/agronomists" of the community (1978:44). Over time, a family's seed potato stock would have needed to be replenished with outside supplies. Exchanges related to seed potatoes, therefore, would have been crucial to ensure continuing good harvests. It is probable that in pre-Hispanic times women—as the traditional guardians of production and planting—would have been integrally involved in these seed potato exchanges.

Photo by Lynn Sikkink

F I G U R E 3.5   The work of crop-processing: woman threshing quinoa with a beer bottle.

Today women predominate in rural and urban marketplace activities across the Andes, and in Bolivia they are a cultural symbol of the marketplace. Advertisements, tourist posters, and artwork alike depict women huddled amongst the wares over which they preside, providing a backdrop for nationalist sentiments. Marketwomen in the capital of La Paz, with their gorgeous *polleras* (full skirts), gold earrings, and Borsalino bowler hats, are the main symbols both of bustling commerce and of the *cholo* or *mestizo* (mixed ethnicity) identity that characterizes much of the urban population.

Female marketers in the countryside occupy a less romanticized position, but even there women are integrally linked to marketing endeavors because of their very gender (Sikkink 2001a, 2001b). For instance, when Condeños (male or female) dream about girl babies, it means good luck in the marketplace. Women's participation in the marketplace is intimately tied to their roles in the household and in their community. At home, they keep track of the storehouses, prepare food, and feed their families, and their roles in the marketplace in many ways are a continuation of these duties. In the marketplace, women are clearly the dominant forces. In her study of a Peruvian marketplace, Florence Babb calculated that 80 percent of the vendors in one Andean marketplace were women (1989). In Condo, women also account for a majority of the marketers, especially when it comes to selling crops they produce with their own and their family's labor. Using a slightly different strategy are those rural female marketers whose "business" (*negocio*) relies on a "buy to sell" paradigm and who purchase goods from others to resell in the market.

FIGURE 3.6 La Paz marketwoman surrounded by her wares.

As it is generally rural women who collect, process, and manage the household resources, they are the ones who are able to calculate how to use these resources to other ends, such as in marketing. Although men are active in the household economy, women differ in their authority to manage and convert resources through exchange—for instance, selling household items to pay for the expenses of educating children. In discussing Peruvian urban street vendors in Cuzco, Seligmann (1989) claims that the division of labor in which women handle, prepare, and serve food and control the outflow of cash serves as a preparation for their roles in the marketplace. This description also applies to the situation in Bolivia, where Condeña vendors are the dominant marketers because of their roles in the household. In addition to becoming prepared for vending through their roles in the household, female vendors do well in the marketplace selling items such as potatoes or medicinal plants because the customers to whom they sell are mostly female. At home in rural households, women barter and trade with one another to a large extent; this behavior is paralleled in the rural marketplaces, where it is primarily women who buy from and sell to one another. Indeed, urban vendors who are originally from rural areas often owe their success in the marketplace to the skills they developed during their rural years.

If it is women who hold sway in the public arena of the marketplace, does that mean they necessarily have power in other contexts, including their own households? There is certainly a popular conception of marketwomen as feisty, authoritative women, whose increased economic power corresponds to increased personal freedom. Hans and Judith-Marie Buechler's (1996) account of one Bolivian urban marketwoman, Sofía Velasquez, emphasizes her autonomy as she undertakes a series of business ventures related to marketing. Sofía moves between rural and urban spheres, struggles through a series of national economic crises, eventually adopts the expensive urban *chola* dress to increase her success, and generally controls and maintains her own economic independence.

In contrast to Sofía, many rural women who market their wares, including the vendors of traditional medicines, do not necessarily become empowered because of their outside economic roles. Some may use their economic role to leverage some new power within their households; nevertheless, because vending is perceived as an extension of their household activities, women do not readily escape or transform the unequal gender constraints of their households. Indeed, not all husbands *allow* their wives to sell in the marketplace, despite the welcome income it might provide. Many rural vendors are single mothers.

Studies of gender relations and status in the Andean countryside offer at times contrasting perspectives and interpretations. Taken as a whole, the differing pictures presented by these investigations demonstrate the difficulty (and perhaps impossibility) of attempting to generalize about gender relations and hierarchy in rural households across diverse Andean societies. What is clear is that Andean gender relations are organized in strikingly different ways within different regions, different communities, and individual households. Part of the confusion stems from the assumption that similar terms used to describe the relationships between and relative status of men and women in households in diverse locales have the same meaning. For the Cuzco area in Peru, Catherine Allen (1988) describes the underlying gender principle in rural households as *warmiqhari* ("woman-man"). For the Laymi people in Bolivia, Olivia Harris (2000) also characterizes the operating gender principle there as *chachawarmi* ("man-woman"). Indeed, "man-woman" is a gender principle that accurately describes men's and women's relatively egalitarian and complementary relationships in rural households in *many* Andean societies. Unfortunately, some scholars have wrongly assumed that "egalitarian" and "complementary" can be universally applied to gender organization in *all* Andean rural households.

In her Bolivian research, Harris did find that separate male and female household tasks gave each gender access and control over the resources most closely linked to the performance of their work. Indeed, in their conversations with Harris about gender relations, both Laymi men and women emphasized what can be called the "complementary unity" of males and females in the household, reinforcing an interpretation of separate-but-equal arrangements. However, in contradiction to romanticized accounts of "complementarity" that stress "harmony" and "balance" (Grillo Fernández 1994), Harris's research found that "when men act as a group ... the asymmetry of the gender relationship is revealed" (2000:179). In sum, in collective contexts Laymi men exercised considerable power over women and occupied a higher position in the rural gender hierarchy.

Gender equality can certainly be demonstrated for some Andean households, and perhaps is illustrated most strikingly in Sarah Hamilton's study, *The Two-Headed Household* (1998). Working in Chanchaló, Ecuador, Hamilton found that both

Photo by Lynn Sikkink

FIGURE 3.7 In many rural households, both women and men work together at many tasks.

women and men refer to the *dos cabezas* of the household, according to which a husband and a wife assert respect for each other and maintain that neither controls more valuable resources than the other. In contrast to the Laymi case described by Harris, Hamilton found that in the Chanchaló case, this gender principle translates into equality at both the household level and the collective or community level. Equal standing in the gender hierarchy in this case may, in fact, be a legacy of the years Chanchaló people spent as members of the local hacienda, where women's economic contributions became indispensable and were highly valued by all community members. Hamilton concludes that "the model of traditional Andean gender complementarity in household production and reproduction, convincingly presented in several ethnographies, does not fit Chanchaló. There are no 'separate-but-equal' spheres of activity for women or men, either in practice or in people's perception" (1998:166).

Thus gender inequality does not characterize all Andean male–female relations any more than does "complementarity" or "egalitarianism." Inequality thrives not only in urban Andean life, but also in the most isolated of rural communities. In the case of Condo, men hold almost all public offices, dominate municipal and communal meetings and assemblies, and interact more frequently with representatives of the government and non-governmental organizations (NGOs). Clearly Condeño men are better able to make their voices heard and their interests known than are their female counterparts. The Condo case shows that a smoothly working gender division of labor in the household cannot be assumed to demonstrate "complementarity," nor can it be claimed as evidence of gender equality. As contemporary Bolivian scholars participate in the developing discourse over assumed traditional Andean gender equality, it is easy to overlook the reality that in many rural contexts, men continue to speak for women and represent their interests in the public world (Luykx 2000, Paulson and Calla 2000).

The key to what may best be described as Andean women's *relative* equality with men may lie in their labor participation in the household, and especially in their ability to engage in entrepreneurial exchange activities. Women often emphasize this explanation in their personal accounts. For instance, the Buechlers' informant, Sofia Velasquez, reflects, "With respect to the power of women in Bolivia, I can say that their power is connected to their work" (1996:167). Women's participation in income-producing work has long been proposed as the primary factor in creating more egalitarian gender relations (Alberti 1988). Supporting this interpretation is the observable shift in household gender relations (in favor of women) that occurs when women enter the relatively public arena of the marketplace, and especially when they begin to sell goods more frequently and in larger volumes, thereby bringing in larger incomes.

In my own research on rural and urban marketplaces, I have observed that marketwomen are to some extent able to negotiate their own economic and gender status and opportunities; that is, their positions within the household and society change in response to their participation in economic activities. One way in which women develop their market careers is through the extension of their roles and experience from one realm (i.e., the household) to the other (i.e., the market), and back again. Although women sometimes operate in different circuits of exchange than do men, women also work *between* circuits of exchange—and in the Andes this reinforces their power. Whether we characterize marketwomen as "bridges" between spheres and circuits of economic activities, it is important to see them as active entrepreneurs. Perhaps they might best be conceived as economic "brokers" who negotiate between urban and rural spaces (Seligmann 1989, 1993). To the extent they are able, they use the economic skills and knowledge honed in domestic contexts to build their own businesses and positions of authority in the marketplace. Their success will, of course, depend on their personal situations and the national economic conditions under which they labor, but also relies to a large extent on their personal flexibility and creativity.

Female marketers do not simply sell goods, but also provide services along with their wares. One service is giving advice to buyers on how to prepare or use their products. Other services include cutting, husking, or shelling the crops they sell, converting raw meat and crops into prepared meals, and combining herbs into medicinal packets. Given this multitude of responsibilities, economic anthropologist Florence Babb (1989) describes women's role in the marketplace as not only a distributive one, but a productive one as well. Another economic anthropologist, Enrique Mayer, claims that "urban informal enterprises rely on the commercialization of women's labor through selling and processing food" (2002). This labor commercialization comes about because much of the work done in the marketplace resembles housework: Women may perform crop-processing steps prior to selling the finished products, they may sort crops into size grades, and they may care for and feed their own children from their stand in the market.

Thus the true picture is one in which women's household roles project onto the marketplace stage. Somewhat unfortunately, this image of a *natural* and seemingly easy transfer of women's roles from one context to another obscures the fact that women must learn many new skills to successfully market their goods. For instance, they must learn to handle money, do arithmetic, and lower or raise their prices when appropriate. They must learn to build ongoing relationships with some buyers, who will become their *caseras* ("habitual customers"); at the same time, they must learn to judge which customers to mistrust and avoid. Buechler and Buechler note that marketwomen's use of kinship ties and other relationships as a business resource is especially important in Bolivia, where very few sources of formalized credit are available (1996:72). Thus a variety of skills essential to success in the marketplace are built upon women's fulfillment of their responsibilities in rural households, including distributing food and seed from their stores, relying on exchange relationships with *compadres* ("co-parents") and neighbors, and dealing differentially with members of their community. Also important in some marketplace settings are language skills. In rural fairs, Quechua and/or Aymara are sufficient to conduct business; in contrast, in urban settings, it is increasingly important to be able to communicate in Spanish. The most successful Condeña vendors, for example, are women who speak at least some Spanish.

In situations where both men and women sell their goods in the rural marketplace, they tend to sell different goods, ones that link to their roles and economic activities in the household. Typically, women in Condo sell their crop products at either the Sunday Challapata market or the annual Huari fair, where their customers are other women who are in charge of cooking these items. Sometimes, when it is economically advantageous to do so, female vendors even travel to sites such as mining centers to sell their crops. Men, too, may sell their own crops, especially when there is no woman in the household to do so, or in cases where the wife is too shy, is too inexperienced, or feels handicapped by not speaking Spanish. Women are also the marketers (and usually the gatherers) of the medicinal herbs that they exchange. This is an important business for marketwomen, especially at the annual Huari fair. The majority of their customers are also other women.

Paralleling Condeña female vendors' roles as the sellers of traditional medicines are male vendors' roles as sellers of musical instruments, especially *zampoñas* (pan pipes). They make these instruments to sell to male customers, who will play them during fiestas. The manufacture of musical instruments, however, is on the decline. Young men are choosing not to learn this skill from the few older instrument makers. Increasingly the skill is limited to a handful of men from the Kallapa *ayllu* (community segment). Nonetheless, these parallel roles indicate some degree of "complementarity" in vending practices in Condo and are further reflective of the gendered division of labor in rural homes.

In the Challapata, Bolivia, market, men almost exclusively run the stands that offer radios, tape players, typewriters, and other technology-based products for sale. These male vendors undoubtedly enjoy some measure of success from their enterprise. By contrast, the exclusively male *cargadores* ("porters") are among the poorest participants in the marketplace, barely eking out a living from their efforts. Porters are infrequently Condeño men, who disdain the job and leave it to

Photo by Lynn Sikkink

FIGURE 3.8 Making the musical instrument known as *zampoñas* (pan pipes), this man prepares for the Huari fair. This activity parallels women's selling of traditional medicines at Huari.

"poorer" neighbors in the region. In the Challapata marketplace, female participation is greatest in the small stands of self-produced farm goods. The percentage of women who have market stands engaged in the business of resale is not high. However, other kinds of stands—for instance, those that sell condiments, ingredients for ritual offerings, and clothes (all technically processed or manufactured goods)—belong primarily to women vendors. Perhaps this gender-based division occurs because the buyers at these stands are predominantly women, or because the goods themselves are considered "female" and will be used by women in their households. Interestingly, Condeña vendors claim that "men do not like to sell," and that if they have to sit on a street in front of their wares, "they feel ashamed" because they are among women and engaged in a "womanly" task.

Just as it is women in rural households who tend to sell in the local markets, so it is also women who often control the money that enters the household. This responsibility is linked to their role as guardians of the household food stores. Women keep the money they bring home to use for household expenditures and their children's needs. A husband may question his wife about her expenditures and savings, and in some cases may be suspicious that she is not making a full report. In general, however, it is the woman who controls the household cash. When one husband complained to me that his wife was spending too much money, claiming that *he* never spent a centavo, she chided him. She countered, "Yes, you never buy anything for the house! ... from now on I'll feed you only cooked wheat, flavored with a little salt—no more bought food for you."

Even when the husband earns money through wage labor, he is expected to deposit the money with his wife. He recognizes that she will use the funds for the expenses of the household. Some men choose to spend a portion of their wages on alcohol for their friends—especially buying beer or other distilled drinks for their friends, which is a way of increasing their social standing. Anticipating this possibility, women will try to wrest the earnings from their husbands at opportune moments, and then physically hide money from them.

In sum, rural women's roles as marketers are functionally linked to their roles as managers of their households. Many women gain some expertise in vending through selling at rural fairs, building on the skills and experience acquired through their domestic economic responsibilities.

Next we look at the marketing opportunities for women that exist within the "informal economic sector" in Bolivia. It is there that women have the opportunity to hone their abilities as vendors of traditional medicines.

THE INFORMAL ECONOMIC SECTOR

The "informal economy" of the marketplace offers a flexible and valuable opportunity for workers who seek to gain a foothold in notoriously poor national economies, such as that found in Bolivia. For many people, the informal economy may provide their only opportunity to earn cash. As opposed to the formal economy, the informal economy provides a space in which people can create their own businesses and opportunities, circumventing some of the restraints present in the formal economy. Indeed, the informal economy is sometimes described as being "underground" because these business activities are conducted outside of the formal economy. Although people operating in the informal economy may have legal goals—to sell legal goods and services to make a living—they may employ illicit means to achieve them, including tax evasion. After the collapse of the Bolivian mining industry, the government instituted policies of "free market shock treatment" that drove many public workers into the informal economy (Stephenson 1999:188). Linda Farthing (1991), a journalist and astute observer of Bolivian politics, reports that following the implementation of these policies, approximately 60 percent of the urban population was forced to support itself in the informal sector of the economy.

In fact, the informal sector benefits not just individuals, but the entire economic system, as it is an important source for many goods and services and promotes cash flow. As a consequence, the government of Bolivia finds itself in an awkward position with respect to the informal sector: It cannot officially condone this market, it lacks the infrastructure to control it, and it recognizes that these economic activities are also important to the state. As Ghersi (1997) points out, "From an economic point of view, the most important characteristic of informal activities is that those directly involved in them as well as society in general benefit more if the law is violated than if it is followed." In *The Other Path* (1989), Peruvian economist Hernando de Soto describes the power of the informal economy. He shows how it serves not only the interests of individuals, but in bringing people together in community-like organizations also serves to protect people's interests as petty commodity producers and vendors. Notwithstanding the collective benefits the informal sector may provide to poor vendors, it is important to avoid romanticizing the situation by overly celebrating people's ability to stay afloat in difficult economic times (Gill 2000). The very existence of a burgeoning informal sector does, after all, signal the weakness of the state economy and highlight the failure of the neoliberal[1] program to provide economic opportunities for all Bolivians.

Itinerant merchants provide a good example of the informal economy in operation: They conduct business outside normal market structures and regulations to avoid paying taxes, profiting from their streamlined business practices. These individual businesses often operate on quite a small scale, and they are typically subsidized by the unpaid labor of household members—vendors do not calculate their own selling time as part of their profit margin. In his discussion of the link between the informal economy and the household base, Enrique Mayer, an economic anthropologist, suggests that the household is an essential factor that allows the informal economy to operate (2002:31). Both the household and the marketplace rely on the unpaid extraction of women's work in particular: Because women manage and oversee goods while simultaneously raising children and

Photo by Lynn Sikkink

FIGURE 3.9 The informal sector: sidewalk vendors in Bolivia.

---

1. The term *neoliberalism* is used widely in Bolivia to refer to unfettered capitalist and free-trade policies, which are often seen as adversely affecting the poor.

performing other household tasks, their economic contributions may be invisible and, therefore, may not be remunerated. It is clear that women have key roles to play alongside men in the informal economic sector. Ironically, that same sector may serve as both an avenue of empowerment for women (as well as for men) and a source of potential exploitation through unpaid labor.

The relatively unregulated nature of the marketplace[2] may provide economic opportunity and flexibility, but it may also disadvantage individual vendors and groups of vendors, who are always vulnerable to competition and crowding. In the Oruro marketplace, for instance, the permanent vendors of ritual ingredients have complained bitterly about part-time vendors selling in front of the marketplace and on sidewalks leading to the permanent stands. These occasional vendors would appear on the busiest shopping days; because they provided easy access to the same goods for shoppers, they managed to siphon off business from the permanent vendors. Although de Soto's (1989) depiction of the informal sector highlights its organization and economic opportunity, individual Bolivian vendors that I spoke with talked about unfair competition, diminished sales, and the increased difficulty of making a living in this arena.

SUMMARY

A general function of the Bolivian marketplace is to bring together rural and urban people, goods, ideas, and practices. For women, the marketplace serves as a bridge between rural household roles and business opportunities; it is a site where their expertise in exchange and healing can be developed into economic ventures. In fact, women's continuing ties to their original rural homes are often important in urban venues. Throughout the Andes, female vendors participate in the marketplace as active entrepreneurs, creating a female space in the public social and economic arena. In a poor country like Bolivia, women's participation in the informal economic sector is especially important in supplementing household income and supporting struggling families. In the following chapter, we begin our exploration of the rural origins of traditional medicines and women's roles as the vendors of them.

---

2. The degree of regulation varies depending on location and item being sold. Because many basic staples, such as meat, are almost solely distributed through the marketplace, the Buechlers call selling in the marketplace one of the "most regulated economic activities" (1996:223). Coca is another example of a highly regulated Bolivian commodity.

4

Marketing Medicines in Rural Bolivia: San Pedro de Condo

TRADITIONAL MEDICINES AS COMMUNAL RESOURCES: WHERE HERBAL REMEDIES COME FROM

In the enveloping darkness of the altiplano night and from the deep warmth of my bed, I tried to understand the statement, *"Ya es de día"* ("It's already day!"). It was my friend Izíquia, and as promised, she had arrived before dawn to rouse me out of bed for the plant-collecting trip. It was September, so the coldest part of winter had passed and Andean spring was under way. Even so, the air was typically cold, if not the bitter cold of June. Our other companion for the day was Emiliana, the daughter of the family with whom I lived; as I stumbled out of bed to find boots, hat, and mittens, I heard her moving around in the patio outside my door.

Izíquia was dressed in her pollera and sandals, to which she had added some wooly socks and a shawl. Despite her attire, as she stood waiting for us she exclaimed, *"Chiri!"* ("Cold!") several times. Nonetheless, she was in her usual cheerful mood, which seemed out of place at 3 A.M. I poured us some coffee from a little Thermos I had filled the night before. Although the coffee was no longer steaming hot, its warm, bitter sweetness was a welcome beginning given the trek ahead. Emiliana, who was visiting home from Oruro where she was studying at the university, was dressed much like me—in pants, sweater, and jacket. Despite their dissimilarities, she and Izíquia were childhood friends. Their lives had taken different paths: Emiliana's family had wanted her to have a profession, like her siblings, and Izíquia had become the head of her rural household at a young age. After Izíquia's one brother migrated to the city with his family, Izíquia managed all the agricultural duties as well as the sheep flock belonging to her family in Condo. Her father was long dead, and her mother had gone blind so that Izíquia had to tend to her, too.

While in her early twenties, Izíquia had worked in the mines. From that time, she had begun to collect and sell the herbs that constitute the traditional medicine inventory recognized by Condeños. When she could, she continued to sell her wares in the marketplaces in Huari and Challapata. In this way, like any responsible head of household, she managed a subsistence economy based in the rural household and obtained a small cash income earned through marketing. Following another fairly typical pattern, she contributed food to her brother's urban household, while he contributed occasional labor and some cash to her endeavors. In a sense, they considered the Condo home and farm to be a jointly run operation.

Despite her heavy responsibilities, Izíquia was fun loving and extremely extroverted: She actively sought me out and befriended me early in my stay. After some initial questioning on my part, Izíquia decided to "teach me" about collecting the traditional medicines that she relied on for her medicinal plant stand. The plants we were on our way to collect that day were found in the highest of valleys below Condo's 17,000-foot peaks, and Emiliana and I knew that Izíquia brought us along both for company and to help her with the chores.

The plants in these upper elevations of Condo are considered "communal resources," but this is an ambiguous label. Izíquia and Emiliana were from the Kallapa *ayllu* (community segment), a "lower" ayllu of the community of San Pedro de Condo. On our way to our high-mountain collecting site, we would be passing through lands belonging to an upper ayllu called Qollana, and the people from this ayllu were the ones who mainly used the high pastures. When I later consulted my map, which had been drawn by the Bolivian National Statistics Institute (INE), I discovered that the glacial valley and the lake at which we had collected plants appeared altogether outside the boundary drawn around Condo's territory; in fact, it seemed to be part of Huari's domain.[1]

Some of this uncertainty about the land's "ownership" is reflected in the stories told about the lake by inhabitants of Condo. Being directly below Azanaques—the highest peak in the region, which is considered a deity in the sacred landscape—the lake is considered "enchanted." Izíquia explained that it is also a

1. Political boundaries are always in dispute given the multiple ways that people reckon them. That the INE has placed the lake within Huari's territory (Condo's neighboring community) does not make it so, at least for Condeños.

"rich" lake, with gold and silver in its depths.[2] The Incas had built a canal from it to the altiplano below, she said, and the brewery in Huari was now using this water. Huari's use of water from this lake is considered to be "theft" by Condeños, and constitutes another point of contention in an ongoing territorial dispute between these neighbors. Nevertheless, this particular source of water is also the explanation that locals give for the delicious taste of the Huareño beer.

Because of the disputed nature of this valley, the plants collected there are "up for grabs" in a way, more than they are considered true communal resources. Inhabitants of Condo or Huari, regardless of their ayllu affiliation, may lay claim to them for different purposes. Izíquia was certainly aware of this dispute when we traveled there, as we had to cross other ayllus' grazing land en route to finally gaze down on the villages of Huari and Condo from our high elevation vantage point.

On our way up to this high valley, we passed through Condo's outlying hamlets (*estancias*) in the pre-dawn dark. Before we were halfway up the steep U-shaped valley that we were following to the lake named Qewiña Qota, the sun had risen and we began to shed some of our clothes. We skirted behind the ridge called Jisk'a Marka ("Little Village") and hiked past a U-shaped wall that kept

Photo by Lynn Sikkink

P H O T O 4.1   Pampa and hills. Many of Condo's herbal medicines must be sought in the plants that grow at high elevations.

---

2. A number of similar stories are told throughout the Andes about lakes with treasure in their depths. Mysterious water outlets also figure prominently in these tales. Some locals claim that an underground tunnel takes water from Lake Poopó to the Pacific (200 miles away). Partly based on this legend, two British researchers have recently proposed that Lake Poopó and Pampa Aullagas are features of "the lost city of Atlantis" (Allen and Snell, 1999).

animals in the higher reaches of the valley, as we continued climbing toward the ridge that the summit of Azanaques dominates. In local folktales, Azanaques is a deity, trickster figure, and dangerous force, about which numerous local stories are told. In one such tale, he beats his wife, Thunapa, causing her to flee to the edge of the Uyuni salt flat, which is just barely visible from Condo. (Thunapa is shown in Figure 1.2; for a full telling of the Azanaques/Thunapa story, see Sikkink and Choque 1999).

Along the way to Azanaques, I took a series of photos that I have since shown in many slide shows as the closest approximation to aerial views of my rural field site. (See Figure 4.2.) From our steep perch, it appeared that we were peering down vertically onto the high plain beneath us. From above, one gets a better feel for the broad expanse of this section of the southern altiplano, where Lake Poopó's shore cuts across the upper corner of Condo's territory. The only trees[3] in this vista appear as dark smudges around Condo's plaza, and the rest of landscape looks sandy or light green, depending on whether it is irrigated by one of the canals descending from the Azanaques River. As Izíquia, Emiliana, and I ascended, however, the variations in this landscape became less and less distinct.

Photo by Lynn Sikkink

FIGURE 4.2 Overview of Condo: highland valley, pampa, and Lake Poopó, with its salt-whitened shores, beyond.

---

3. The sole visible trees in these vistas are introduced eucalyptus trees, which are common throughout Bolivia. Native species such as Qewiña (as in the name of the lake we visited, where no trees remain today) and Qiswara (*Buddleja* spp.) can be found here and there, but the long history of deforestation and re-forestation of these native trees has prehistoric origins, as Gade demonstrates (1999:42–74). Nonetheless, deforestation accelerated during the colonial period and has become much more critical today, to the point that it now threatens to bring about the extinction of various native species.

After approximately four hours of hiking, we reached the lake-filled alpine valley. Izíquia quickly put us to work collecting the two plants she had come to find. *Papusa* (*Werneria* spp.) and *sasawi* (*Leuceria* or *Tecoma*) are native to the southern altiplano and grow in relative abundance in this location. Izíquia knew that at the Huari fair she could sell as many of these plants as we could collect. Izíquia was careful to collect only those portions of the plant growing above ground, but not the root—a method that allows the plant to regenerate more quickly. That day we collected several kilos of vegetation, although the plants would later lose both weight and value in the drying process. Nonetheless, Izíquia would be able to sell the bulk of these herbs at the upcoming Huari fair, while still keeping some for yearlong vending at the Challapata market, where she would also barter her plants for those from elsewhere as a way to diversify her inventory. She would also retain enough of the herbs for herself and her family's use at home. Sasawi, for instance, is used in a remedy for stomach ailments, and I was personally initiated to its application for this purpose when I was ill (as described in Chapter 2). When I walked the streets of the Huari fair a few weeks later, I caught the pungent aroma of the sasawi of our high-valley collecting adventure, which also reminded me of the less pleasant experience of my illness. The papusa produced a different memory—namely, one involving the steaming cups of tea I had frequently had for the dusk-time "meal" of tea and bread.

Herbs need not be used solely as medicines, as when papusa is used as a tea for evening meals with no reference made to its medicinal qualities. This tea is considered "warming" and a good drink for children who might have caught a chill, as well as for the family escaping the descending cold of the altiplano dusk. Herb teas—heavily sugared if possible—are often drunk as a hot beverage, either in the morning or in the evening. Used as both a tea and a medicine, papusa (*Werneria digital*) is of primary importance in the inventory of medicinal plants that come from the region around Condo. It is also one of the ingredients of the particular assemblage called the *mesa negra* ("black offering"). This usage creates a further demand for papusa, which may explain why it is widely sought after by Condeña herbal medicine collectors. Indeed, papusa is an economic staple of the traditional vendors from Condo, just as it is a staple in their kitchens. Its flower-scented flavor makes it a good everyday tea, but papusa also has the reputation of being a good medicine for coughs and stomach problems, especially for those involving inflammation. It is also prized as a remedy for the related problems of "colic" and indigestion, as well as being useful for the folk illness known as *empacho*, the condition of having a swollen belly in which undigested food is "stuck," causing various digestive problems (Kay 1996:53).

Both papusa and sasawi plants are characteristic of the inventories of Condeño traditional medicine vendors. Through their dealings, these herbs make their way from the high mountain valleys to the homes of urban dwellers as part of a rural–urban trajectory that ends in the transactions of vendors and customers in the marketplace.

SAN PEDRO DE CONDO: A VILLAGE
OF ENTREPRENEURS

With Lake Poopó and its salt-whitened shores visible from the village of San Pedro de Condo, the contrast between the barren pampas and the watery expanse on the skyline is striking. Rising up on the eastern side of the village are the hills and high peaks around which Condeños live in their dispersed pastoral settlements (*estancias*).[4]

As an early colonial "reduction" (*reducción*), Condo has been subjected to hundreds of years of state intervention; in addition, it has long played a key role in Bolivia's market economy. The nature of Condeños' involvement has certainly changed over time, with residents' participation ranging from purveyors of useful goods for mining centers to suppliers of goods and foodstuffs to other campesinos and to urbanites.

In Condo, vendors have carved out a unique niche, in that they have direct access to many herbs important to the traditional medicine pharmacopoeia. Although other regions have some of these same herbs available to them, Condeños have an advantage in that they draw on a diverse ecosystem (from lakeside *pampa* to the hills and valleys of the Azanaques range), marketing know-how (long involvement in markets, especially on the part of entrepreneurs from the Kallapa ayllu), and easy access to the Huari and Challapata markets.

Traditional medicines enter into the local exchange circuits differently from the way in which crops do. In fact, there is really no cash crop in Condo; goods such as potatoes, quinoa, animals, wheat, and fava beans form part of the household's subsistence base, but may be sold if the family needs money. For instance, *chuño* (freeze-dried potatoes) are metaphorically described as "money in the bank" because they may be stored for years as a hedge against bad harvests and lean years and can be sold in the marketplace when necessary. A family's economic buffer can be lost in one year if they sell their entire chuño supply. By contrast, if the family manages to accumulate a generous surplus in chuño, the decision to sell some is not so fraught with danger. When pondering the choice between feeding one's family and earning some cash, the immediate needs of the family prevail.

Unlike the food from the household's stores, traditional medicines are not part of the subsistence base. Herbs can be gathered in variable quantities, dried and stored, and then sold in the marketplace for cash, without having to calculate harvests in advance or risk not meeting the family's food needs. Of course, as illustrated in the collecting trip described earlier, this venture is not necessarily easy or without costs to collect and sell these home remedies. One needs to know where to get the plants and when they will be available. The plants must then be transported first to the house and eventually to a market setting, where the vendor may sit for long hours to make just a few sales.

Collecting trips also take time and labor away from people's subsistence activities, so this work must be balanced with the family's seasonal agropastoral

---

4. Condo's setting and history are described in more detail in Chapter 1.

responsibilities. Notwithstanding the time and effort expended in this kind of vending, the sale of traditional medicines represents an opportunity for enterprising rural dwellers. This activity was engaged in enthusiastically by a group of Condeña women I knew, who saw it as a way to bring cash into the household without depleting their food stores. Selling traditional medicines is an activity that can easily piggyback on the responsibilities of farming and running a household. And, as in the cases described later in this chapter, Condeña vendors sometimes make a full-time business out of the sale of medicinal plants in urban marketplaces, bringing rural medicines directly to urban customers.

SENSE OF PLACE: TRADITIONAL MEDICINES AND THE LOCAL GEOGRAPHY

The array of traditional medicines as found in a stand in the Cochabamba marketplace is representative of many different regions of Bolivia. Plants are always linked to particular places. Specific medicines come from specific contexts; to a person who knows its origins, each one is evocative of a unique landscape, much in the way that potatoes, quinoa, and maize are associated with particular zones.

In Condo, like most of the Andean countryside, the landscape is perceived and animated in specific ways. My perception of the southern Bolivian landscape, on first glimpse so desolate yet bright, changed during the time I spent there, as I heard the Condeños' stories that explained the unique arrangement of rocks, salt flats, reddened hills, and far off ridges that make up their home. Condeños describe the arrangement of landforms as the result of the past actions of gods in their guises of mountain deities: that rock catapulted from a sling during a fight, this hill as a hat knocked off during a fight, this salt and sand a trail of breast milk and barley flour from a departing god, this hill an abandoned child, those red rocks the blood of a wounded mountain/god. The stories vary from person to person, depending on the storyteller's age, gender, and community affiliation.

Just as the Andean geography is monumental, so are the beings that breathe life into mountains, plains, rivers, and rocky outcrops. A mountain is not just a place where a god walked, it is itself a god. Therefore, unlike other cultural landscapes that record in myths the passage of gods, ancestors, and trickster figures, and their effects on the landscape, Andean geography is a gargantuan arrangement of bodies, body parts, and the objects these beings used or left behind as they went on their ways in times past.[5] In Condo, a particular myth describes the bloody fight between a husband and wife mountain peak, details the wife's flight from her husband's side, and explains the current location of the female peak named Thunapa on the distant horizon of the altiplano (see Sikkink and Choque 1999 for more detail). In other regions, "myths may both shape and be shaped by landscapes" as well (Cosgrove 1993:281).

---

5. Lakoff and Johnson (1980) point out that in general metaphors are extended from the body to the land, but not in the reverse direction.

Andean communities themselves may be conceptualized as bodies. For example, as Bastien (1978) describes, a series of communities at different altitudes in the Kallawaya area are held together not only by ties of cooperation and reciprocity but because collectively they form a whole body. Strong objections were raised in this region during the time of agrarian reform because one segment of the community would be partitioned from the whole, which was perceived as an "amputation." Other authors have noted the links between Andean community segments, body imagery, and ritual (e.g., Gose 1994, Isbell 1985, Urton 1981).

As anthropologist Keith Basso (1996) has demonstrated beautifully for the Western Apache, not only do indigenous people have a particular "sense of place," but also there is an integration of time and space in the local landscape, brought to life through the stories that people tell about their geography's peculiarities. Telling stories about places "is a way of constructing history itself, of inventing it, of fashioning novel versions of 'what happened here'" (p. 6). Recognizing that senses of place are "the possessions of particular individuals" (p. xv), Basso goes on to explore how people exchange information about places so as to invoke specific emotional states, which are often associated with stories everyone knows about certain places, and that explain how these places earned their names. The Western Apache use place-based stories to instruct, to "shoot" listeners with moral arrows, and as a path toward gaining wisdom. The same stories are also used for comfort and/or as comic relief.

In other research on "place," Kathleen Stewart likewise links the Appalachian hills and hollers she has traversed with the stories and conversations that are woven around them by the people who inhabit that landscape. The particular sense of place among the people studied by Stewart in West Virginia "tracks along through an endless process of remembering, retelling, and imagining things" (1996:140). In anthropology, the study of "place," or landscape,[6] has received renewed attention through studies such as these. Anthropologists have always noted particular features about the places inhabited by the people they study, but as the late Clifford Geertz points out, if you look in the index of a standard ethnography, you will not find a separate heading for "place" (1996:259).

Recent anthropological studies of "place" reveal the very different and important ways in which diverse peoples discuss, interact with, and perceive the land upon which they live. As I found in my own fieldwork, land is never experienced merely as a passive environmental stratum. The landscape archaeologist, Barbara Bender, has discussed how different peoples create distinctive landscapes that are imbued with specific cultural meanings. According to Bender, landscapes are never inert; instead, each is created out of specific temporal and historical conditions and, therefore, reflects a different understanding of gender, age, and class, among other cultural distinctions (Bender 1993:1–3).

---

6. "Landscape" is the general conceptual category used in some of these recent studies (Bender 1993, Cosgrove 1993, Hirsch and O'Hanlon 1995, Humphrey 1995, J. Jackson 1994). The word *landscape* was introduced into English in the late sixteenth century from a technical term ("landschap") first used by Dutch painters (Hirsch and O'Hanlon 1995:2). As such, it connotes the perspective of objectification used in the practices of painting, map-making, song, and poetry (Humphrey 1995:135).

Using this insight, we can begin to comprehend how resources originating from unique locales, as part of distinctive landscapes of meaning, carry different cultural meanings. The vendors of traditional medicines carry these larger contexts into the marketplace, along with their products. Sasawi and pupusa come not just from Condo, but from the flanks of Azanaques, named after a mythical figure who plays a role in local legend. As ethnographers, we can contribute specific accounts of the ways in which people encounter places, perceive them, and invest them with significance. This information helps to underscore the link between cultural identities and land, which has become increasingly important in the light of ethnic-oriented land struggles (Feld and Basso 1996:4–8). As a result, we are in an advantageous position to ferret out some of the specific local meanings of small bags of medicinal herbs, transported into marketplace settings by peasant women.

In Condo, the local geography is particularly important to the social structure. The community segments called *ayllus* are land based and are located in specific relationship to one another within the wider Condo region and within the village of San Pedro de Condo. Features on the landscape are important to ayllu members not only as the basis of their livelihood and the source of the resources that they share as "commons," but also as animated parts of their world that have their own histories and have relationships with humans. The conception of the link between the body and the landscape varies from locale to locale, however, and is conditioned by gender and age. In Condo, the community is seen as a collection of separate parts bound into a whole through common concerns centered on communal land, such as the need to share and distribute fairly the water in their watershed. The community is held together, therefore, by the actions that community members take on behalf of the landscape, such as those demonstrated during a water exchange ritual that dramatizes and reorders communal rights and responsibilities (Sikkink 1997).

In years when rain comes late to Condo's landscape, a water exchange ritual called *yaku cambio* is enacted, which brings together the various segments of the community as part of the symbolic, cooperative "watershed." In seeking to bring rain, community members meet together to eat, drink, and exchange specific items from their particular ayllu, in a ceremony that brings together material goods from every corner of the territory. Participants bring small jugs of water that they have taken from their cherished water sources, and that they will mix and exchange with members from other ayllus. The exchange of water is the central focus of this ritual, which explains why this gathering is given the name of *yaku cambio* (literally, "water exchange"). Water from opposing ayllus (upper and lower) is mixed during the ritual, but people also exchange individual jugs of water, which they will take back to their particular local water sources. After the ritual, when participants pour the water they received from "outsiders" into their own springs or canals, the water source gets "angry" and "boils." This helps to cause a change in the weather system and, ideally, bring on rain (Sikkink 1997).

In this ritual, water is merely one of many items exchanged. Community members also bring specific goods to share that are emblematic of the places they inhabit. For example, members of the Kallapa ayllu bring *ch'uru*, tiny white shells

Photo by Lynn Sikkink

F I G U R E 4.3   During Carnival in Condo, community members meet on the land they share in common, sharing food and alcohol—and pouring libations to *Pacha Mama* ("Earth Mother").

from the shores of Lake Poopó that have a rice-like appearance. These shells are sometimes given to the people from the Sullkayana ayllu, along with flamingo eggs. The people from Kallapa then say, "Now you can cook rice with egg." People whose land is close to Lake Poopó offer pink flamingo feathers, which are also used in ritual offerings.

Herbal medicines are representative of various parts of the landscape that have different qualities, including different elevations and moisture, which materially highlights how various settlements are positioned on the landscape with their accompanying communal lands. Typically people bring and give plants that come from the territory of their ayllus, mostly wild herbs gathered by women. During yaku cambio, many participants give large bunches of plants, and those who receive them fill their bags with the sweet-smelling herbs. That these herbal remedies play an important part in the ritual emphasizes that plants are quite literally rooted in different parts of the landscape and stand for these various areas. People are connected to their landscape through these particular plants, and they exchange them during the ritual in an act of reciprocity, which not only brings people together in a common goal, but also reinforces their interdependence as a community of people who help to heal one another.

Not all the herbal remedies that a vendor takes to the city for sale evoke these sorts of local associations, but they nonetheless indicate the particular landscape from whence the plants came. Customers, in turn, register this sense of place when they buy herbs or purchase a particular remedy.

A TRAJECTORY FROM RURAL HOME TO
REGIONAL MARKETPLACE

Earlier chapters in this book introduced two of the marketplace settings in which Condeño vendors sell traditional medicines: the urban Cochabamba marketplace and the rural community of San Pedro de Condo. For people who live in Condo, these two sites serve as endpoints on a spectrum of marketplaces; they are characterized by different business and medical practices and beliefs, and the arrays of traditional medicines that represent these practices and beliefs. San Pedro de Condo is also the origin point and anchor for more distant marketplaces. From Condo come particular arrays of traditional medicines that are collected and taken to more distant locales, but that are nonetheless clearly tied to the people, places, and plants of the rural home community. A typical Condeño vendor of traditional medicines sells or barters at home in Condo, sells once a year at the Huari fair, sells almost weekly at the Challapata marketplace, and has ties to the urban Oruro market. (Refer to Map 1.1 for locations.) The Challapata and Huari marketplaces are described in Chapter 5.

The four marketplaces of Condo, Huari, Challapata, and Oruro are places where Condeño vendors (especially women) regularly sell, but they are differentiated in terms of the kinds of transactions that generally occur there (from reciprocity to barter to sales), the degree of participation by Condeño vendors, the particular arrays or inventories of medicines that vendors offer to customers, the way in which these arrays of medicines are assembled by the vendors, and the systems of healing in which these plants are embedded. Along with these general market characteristics, it is also important to consider the unique features of each marketplace and to acknowledge the activities of particular vendors as they go about their business in each locale. These variations highlight both the differences in the marketplaces and the interconnections among them. As the home of the vendors discussed in this chapter, Condo is generally the origin of many of their traditional medicines.

TRADITIONAL MEDICINE EXCHANGE AT HOME
IN SAN PEDRO DE CONDO

Rural communities such as Condo are the collecting sites for myriad herbal remedies, ranging from wild plants to common domesticates. From the diverse landscapes and elevations throughout Bolivia and beyond come the arrays of medicines that make up the pharmacopoeia referred to as "traditional medicine." For instance, in the Charazani region of Bolivia, where the Kallawaya people live, there is an astonishing array of medicines available, some of which are "brought to market" through the activities of itinerant healers (Bastien 1978, Girault 1987, Oblitas Poblete 1963). Nevertheless, the plant resources that make up the vendors' herbal inventories do not move in a simple "down-the-line" trajectory from rural areas to urban sites. Herbal remedies also move laterally among rural communities, and they are exchanged among individuals within communities as well. Traditional medicines may be given as gifts to close relations, neighbors, or friends. However, traditional medicines may also be sold from one community member to another, thereby circumventing the relations of reciprocity by which anthropologists usually characterize communal exchange.

A woman might, for instance, obtain a particular plant that she wishes to use in a treatment for one of her children, by buying it from a community member whom she knows has it in stock—because she also knows the herb is an object of that household's collecting activities. Many families will first attempt to supply their own needs by collecting these plants on their own, but it is impossible for every family to supply themselves with all the plants they wish to use in healing. Thus reciprocity, barter, and monetary exchange all serve as conduits for remedies: A mixture of exchange relations is involved in the movement of herbal remedies within the community itself, just as people employ a variety of healing strategies in the use of these home remedies.

As rural dwellers circulate plants beyond the community by using them as exchangeable resources, the plants become more firmly embedded in a system of monetary exchange. Consider the sasawi and the papusa that Izíquia, Emiliana, and I collected from the high mountain valley. After our trip, Izíquia took her plants home, dried them, and put aside a small amount for her household's members. The plants we gathered were then saved until the arrival of the Huari fair, six months later. Izíquia took the plants to this market, along with other items from her stock of plants, and sold approximately half of the volume of papusa and sasawi there. The rest of these herbs went back into her general inventory and became part of the remedies that she took to market at the weekly Challapata fair when she went to sell there. Unlike some Condeña medicine sellers, who sell in Challapata on most Sundays, Izíquia averages only one or two trips per month, although she still considers this marketplace to be an important part of her economic activities. At both the Huari and Challapata fairs, the plants are generally sold for cash by the vendors, although some might be used as part of reciprocal (nonmonetary) exchanges within the marketplace proper. Izíquia is amenable to both cash sales and barter, especially if she is offered something in barter that she needs at home, such as corn. Because barter continues to supply important goods in home communities and the marketplace, these varied kinds of exchanges continue to coexist.

Within the village of Condo, there is no regular marketplace. During fiestas, which bring a huge influx of people into the community, some vendors set up market stands, but they tend to sell items geared toward the fiesta, such as candles and confetti for use in the church. Some enterprising and intrepid vendors have beer booths in Condo's plaza.[7] Occasionally some of the fiesta's activity falls

---

7. Selling an item such as beer at a fiesta is not an activity for those with many pressing social obligations. A beer vendor who is unable to say no to her relatives or friends may end up "inviting" as many people as she has real paying customers. One woman complained to me after a fiesta about the difficulty of making money at this endeavor when she had to offer free beer to some people and pay for broken bottles. After her experience, this woman said she would never operate a beer booth again.

within the arena of traditional medicines—for instance, during carnival some of the Condeña vendors who typically sell in Challapata sell *mesas* (ritual assemblages) in Condo's plaza, for those conducting rituals at home. Generally, the same vendors who sell in Huari and Challapata operate these occasional stands during the fiestas in Condo, as they are the ones with both inventory and marketing know-how. A group of women who are known for their marketing activities are the same ones who sell regularly in Challapata, Huari, and Condo. Interestingly, though these women represent a cross-section of the villagers in Condo, a larger percentage of them come from the lower ayllu (community segment), named Kallapa, which Condeños say has always been known for its business orientation. It has reputedly produced a larger number of marketwomen, musical instrument makers, vehicle owners, and wage laborers than have the other ayllus.

Consider the further travels of the plants Izíquia collected. Izíquia sold some of the papusa and sasawi in larger quantities at the Huari fair. Here, middlemen (*intermediarios* or *resacatadores*, literally "rescuers") buy up large amounts of these local plants, which they then transport to the urban areas for resale. Thus some of Izíquia's plants may end up in La Paz, Sucre, or Cochabamba through the activities of these middlemen. Larger quantities of the same plants may also end up in these urban areas through the paths taken by individual vendors, who trade plants among themselves in an effort to assemble larger and more diversified inventories. For example, papusa that Izíquia collected might be sold to an intermediary and then resold by an individual vendor in Cochabamba. Alternatively, Izíquia might trade a small amount of papusa for some other plant; a Condeña vendor in the

Photo by Lynn Sikkink

FIGURE 4.4 Selling sweets and soda during the Fiesta of San Andrés in Condo.

same Cochabamba marketplace would then sell the papusa, albeit in a different section of the marketplace. Following a different route, some of the papusa might end up with individual rural customers who buy or trade the plant for their own use or for one of their family members; it would be used for cures in these rural households. Through these differing avenues, a variety of plants might continue to be sold or traded "down the line" through the marketplace, or they might circulate out immediately to individuals who use them as remedies.

The medicinal plants from communities like Condo are communal resources. Unless they originated in a privately owned field (such land accounts for less than 10 percent of Condo's land base, as most private fields are irrigated plots around the village of Condo), the plants come from communal herding areas or other spaces considered joint property of Condo's inhabitants.[8] When Izíquia collected plants at Qewiña Qota, she was exercising her rights as a community member to use these high mountain pastures. Other community members might potentially collect medicinal plants from these areas as well—an interesting proposition given that the plants are then sold in the marketplace, converting the communal resource into private income. Communal areas are not "protected" in any way, except by communal rights of access (someone outside the community would not be allowed to collect the plants gathered and used by Izíquia), and rural dwellers in both the Departments of Oruro and Cochabamba have complained bitterly that some of the plants that are part of the traditional medicine pharmacopoeia have become increasingly more difficult to acquire. As in the case of valerian (*Valeriana* spp.), a root that is a well-known natural sedative in the Andes and abroad, many of these plants are commercialized, indicating that the economic link between urban and rural areas can lead to overexploitation of key local resources, thereby engendering conflict and inequalities among community members.

The Qewiña tree (*Polylepsis* spp.), growing in the high valley of our collecting trip, is native to the Andes. It has suffered a long history of exploitation—mainly for fuel—resulting in its decimation. Although it still grows at some of Bolivia's highest elevations, and although twenty peaks in the Cordillera Occidental are still covered with *Polylepsis* forests (Gade 1999:48), it has become much scarcer, particularly at lower altitudes, due to human intervention and animal grazing. As a consequence, the medicinal resources of these forests have suffered. Between Cochabamba and Santa Cruz there is a region called Qewiñapampa ("Qewiña Plain") where many hectares of this tree once flourished (Carlos Prado, personal communication, April 9, 2000). A handful of families have commercialized this resource—turning the wood into charcoal used as fuel in *chicherías* (corn-beer bars) and in braziers for ritual offerings. Everyone suffers from the environmental consequences of such deforestation and the subsequent erosion, even though only a few individuals initially profited from the exploitation of the forest resources. In this scenario, medicinal resources decline alongside the destruction of an ecosystem, as when qewiña forests are destroyed; however, they are also decimated

---

8. Condeños do collect plants from the margins of their own fields and make use of "weeds" that grow among their crops. They also cultivate some herbs like chamomile for medicinal purposes.

through the direct process of exploitation—qewiña is also used medicinally in ritual preparations.

Not all medicinal plants are commercialized. For instance, some of the papusa and sasawi collected remains within Condo, as is true of all the resources that come from the environs of Condo. In this way the use of medicines at home parallels the subsistence economy in which people rely on local resources and market only a part of what they produce. Unlike local crops, however, some Bolivian plants (e.g., cat's claw) are collected, packaged, and sold internationally. Local Condeño plants are also part of the local system of healing. In the case of papusa and sasawi, it is not necessary to use these herbs in conjunction with the advice of a specialist. Instead, people simply make them into teas and self-administer the cure, in the same spirit as home remedies for the common cold are formulated everywhere in the world.

In a "hierarchy of resort" (Chapter 2), local plants are more readily used than are nonlocal plants. For instance, for minor illnesses people are more likely to self-administer a plant such as sasawi before they consult a local healer. Thus it is not just the services of people that figure into a hierarchy of resort, but the particular plants that people employ as well. Self-help is a less costly and more comfortable option than consulting an outsider or buying a treatment, whether it is herbal or pharmaceutical. In Condo, the first choice in a hierarchy of resort favors the use of at-home advice and local traditional medicines, collected by family members or acquired through trade without money changing hands. Those Condeños who move into urban areas (and who frequently move back and forth between urban and rural spheres) continue to use this logic in their healing: They treat themselves at home, often with herbs from Condo, and do not rely on the clinics that are available to them in the city.[9] Hence there is a similarity in the hierarchy of resort used in rural and urban areas, especially among people who shuttle back and forth between the two.

SUMMARY

Vendors of traditional medicines come from all parts of Bolivia. Nevertheless, in places such as San Pedro de Condo, where there exists a tradition of collecting and exchanging these resources, more women are likely to parlay the activity into an urban vending opportunity. Because locales are unique, particular products are linked to the landscape, the stories that define it, and the ceremonies that local inhabitants enact on behalf of their local geography. Examining Condo as a unique site with a particular "sense of place" provides a launching point for looking at the next set of marketplaces in which Condeña vendors are likely to participate—Huari, Challapata, and Oruro—as described in the following chapter.

---

9. In general, many people with rural roots feel uncomfortable with the care provided by urban clinics. They do not necessarily trust the personnel or the treatments that are offered (Crandon-Malamud 1991). Consequently, these clinics are underutilized, in part because of disparate views of "community" and an absence of trust on the part of rural folk (Wayland and Crowder 2002).

Selling Medicines at Condo's Regional Marketplaces: Huari, Challapata, and Oruro

THE HUARI FAIR: FROM COLONIAL FAIR TO REGIONAL MARKET

Condeños have long participated in the market at Huari, which is conveniently located just five kilometers away from the village of Condo. People in the region around Huari, including Condeños, remember when the Huari *feria* (fair) was a huge, international market. A local historian in Huari told me that the roots of the Huari fair stretch back to early colonial times (the sixteenth century), when the Spaniards sold the merchandise they had brought from Seville, such as clothes, scissors, razors, and cashmere. In later colonial times, mule drivers arrived from Argentina to sell their mules and other livestock on the Bolivian altiplano at Huari because these animals (so necessary for work in the mines and for transportation in general) were lacking in Bolivia. The Argentine mule drivers, in turn, traded for vicuña hides,[1] medicinal herbs, and other merchandise at the Huari fair and took

---

1. These wild camelids, once plentiful in this region of Bolivia, have become almost extinct because they must be shot in order to obtain their super fine fleece. The name Huari (Wari) actually means "vicuña" in Aymara.

these goods back to Argentina. In this way Huari became an "international market," and it persisted because it was centrally located between the Viceroyalty seat in Río de la Plata (Buenos Aires), the coast of Chile and Peru, and later because of the long-standing tradition of having the fair there.

Another important aspect of the Huari fair is its proximity to the shrine of Quillacas, on whose hill an apparition of Jesus materialized. With its saint's image installed to commemorate the miracle, the church became as important a destination to many Argentine pilgrims as it was to Bolivians. Throngs of people congregated at Quillacas on visits to the area, such as during the Huari fair. In modern days, the pilgrimage to this shrine continues to be important, although

Photo by Lynn Sikkink

FIGURE 5.1 Medicine vendors at the Huari fair sell local remedies to individuals and wholesalers alike.

Photo by Lynn Sikkink

F I G U R E 5.2 A vendor sells a wide array of medicinal wares (from plants to minerals and starfish) at the Huari fair.

fewer Argentines make the trip than in the past, and more modern Bolivian carnival elements (dancing troupes, drinking, and processions) dominate the proceedings.

In the Huari fair's heyday, merchants brought specialized goods from very long distances away. Peruvian sellers peddled dyes and condiments (including chili peppers and cinnamon); merchants from Chile brought dried fruit, incense, "medicines" (including starfish, sulfur, and ostrich eggs), guano (dung/fertilizer), and ostrich plumes; and from Argentina came cows, mules, burros, and horses, which the drivers herded overland on a one- to two-month trip[2] before the train line was installed. Huari, always a tiny community (then much smaller than Condo), hosted this event by providing the space; local farmers also planted barley on their wide pampa fields, which they later sold to the livestock owners as animal feed. Although this practice continued for many years, today the marketplace is dominated by Bolivian merchants, who nonetheless still rely on goods brought from Argentina, Chile, and Peru, and are sometimes described as "contra-bandistas" because they are purveyors of illegally imported goods, such as electronics whose border taxes weren't paid.

During the early history of the Huari fair, barter was the dominant form of transaction and represented a general *canje de comercios* (merchandise barter)

---

2. This trip brought them through Condo on the old Potosí road. The rural folk there traded their wheat and barley for fruit, which the travelers brought with them from the warm valleys.

between north and south. Some medicinal herbs came from the lowland regions of Bolivia, and also from Chile (especially *q'uwa*, an aromatic plant used like incense in many offerings). Other medicines traded in large quantities comprised local herbs, which are still collected and traded by Condeños today. Currently, much of the barter transaction has given way to vending. Although most Condeños sell their medicines at Huari, some still accept goods in exchange instead of money, especially in small-scale transactions. The Huari fair is important to vendors of herbal remedies all over Bolivia because it is the main site for the buying and selling of these special wares; as such, the Huari fair sets the prices of the goods for other marketplaces and even for itinerant vendors (Alba 1989).

The duration of the Huari fair used to be a full week (Sunday to Sunday beginning after Easter), and the town was always jam-packed with people. Elderly Huareños described to me how in their youth it was difficult to even push one's way through the crowds. The numbers of visitors and vendors have steadily declined through the years, because the fair has been superseded by the growth of many large weekly markets, including the Challapata market. Whereas several decades ago campesinos bought or traded for all their necessities at the annual Huari fair, as improved roads and transportation connected many regions of Bolivia, it became easier both for campesinos to travel to distant locales and for merchants to bring goods to regional markets. The Challapata market, for example, is an outgrowth of such a trend.

The Huari fair persists out of tradition, and because it offers special goods at low prices. Nevertheless, instead of being a unique forum for the exchange of herbal medicines, it has become part of an annual cycle of regional marketplaces to which full-time vendors travel to sell their goods. The fair in Huari now begins on a Friday and for the most part ends on Monday, although some vendors stay through Tuesday. The timing of the Huari fair remains important to Condeños because it allows local schoolchildren's parents to make some extra money and in turn buy school supplies. No matter what the national schedule is for the opening of school, classes never truly begin in Condo until after the Huari fair.

From all accounts, the Huari fair has drastically shrunk over the years. Despite the dire predictions of some participants—"perhaps next year it will be gone"—the Huari fair continues to provide marketing opportunities and tradition to those who come to sell and buy, even though it is now only one marketplace out of many.

Despite Huari's reduced stature and its annual occurrence, it is the most important vending venue for the largest number of Condeña vendors. Between 75 and 100 Condeña families sold traditional medicines at Huari in the 1990s. Out of the 35 Condeño households I surveyed intensively in 1991 about marketing activities, 15 participated in the Huari fair. Of these 15 families, 8 sold traditional medicines, while the other 7 sold meat, crops, prepared food, livestock, and vegetables. For the twenty Condeña women who sold regularly in Challapata, selling their herbal remedies at Huari was a continuation of their marketing practices during the rest of the year. In contrast, for the majority of the traditional medicine vendors from Condo, the Huari fair was the only locale in which they sold traditional medicines. The Huari fair serves as a kind of wholesale market for the large quantities of herbs such as pupusa and sasawi that vendors offer there.

Photo by Lynn Sikkink

FIGURE 5.3 Many women like the one on the right of this photo gather herbs all year long for sale at the Huari fair. Here she is at her high-altitude home with her son, mother, daughter, and daughter's blue-eyed doll.

Traditional medicine vending, which yields small amounts of money at other fairs, offers better prospects for profit at Huari. At the latter market, the vendors reported that they earned an average of more than 50 bolivianos (ranging from 20 to 100 bolivianos) for the two to four days they spent there, which equated to approximately 15 dollars in 1990. This potential profit is one of the reasons that so many Condeños sell traditional medicines there. Unlike in most rural markets, local crop products are not the main wares on display at the Huari fair. Although plenty of food is sold, some of it in the form of crops sold by the campesino-producers, in general Huari is dominated by goods such as traditional medicines and imported goods—everything from spices and ostrich feathers to radios and enamelware. In contrast to the Challapata fair, food vending is of secondary importance.

It is unclear how long Condeños have sold traditional medicines at the Huari fair, but it is certain that the annual gathering is a marketplace that has long been important to Condeños. Some vendors told me they learned about collecting medicinal plants from their mothers, who had also traded them as herbal medicines at the Huari fair. Others became involved in the venture because they saw it as a way to make some extra money. One Condeño told me that in the early 1900s there were only a few of these vendors, but that in recent years their numbers have burgeoned. With the modern-day acceptance of traditional cures, even among many *mestizos* and city dwellers, there has been an increased demand for these medicinal herbs and ingredients for offerings. Many urban vendors' wares, even at the bustling Cochabamba Jampi Qhatu ("medicine market"), come originally from the Huari fair, where they were peddled by small-scale local vendors. At the Huari fair, the majority of these small-scale vendors are actually residents of Condo. One Huareño estimated that 80 percent of the herbal medicine vendors were Condeñas; my own counts of the 1990 and 1991 fairs suggest that the percentage is closer to 60 percent. In 1986–1987, Alba counted 234 of his 300 vendors as being Condeños.[3] A local historian from Huari told me that the Condeñas have always dominated in this arena: "It has always been like that."

In studying the Huari fair, Alba (1989) came up with figures detailing the origins of different categories of vendors: locals versus nonlocals, and small-scale vendors versus wholesalers. He calculated that of the 300 vendors who sold traditional medicines, 50 percent exclusively sold those products and 43 percent both bought and sold medicines (the remaining 7 percent had some sort of mixed stands). Included in his numbers were both small- and large-scale vendors. The large-scale vendors are generally from La Paz, Oruro, or Cochabamba. These merchants buy products for later resale, although some also sell at Huari, often to small-scale vendors who want to broaden their inventories. Alba counted approximately 84 vendors whom he called wholesalers, and some of the largest of these stands were run by "mestizo-criollo Cochabambinos." At the 1990 and 1991 Huari fairs, I observed that the small-scale vendors are generally local women who collect relatively large quantities of local herbs (papusa, sasawi, and lamphaya in particular) that they generally sell to intermediaries, but who also buy or barter for nonlocal medicines that they offer at their stands to other campesinos who either buy in small quantities or barter for the medicines they need.

The stands that sold what Alba calls "magico-ceremonial" items, such as *misterios* (tiles for mesas), *alfeñique* (candy offerings), incense, copal, and *siwarios* (colored balls and powders used to cure illnesses like *susto* (fright), were mainly run by mestizo merchants from the cities, who sold their wares in large quantities. The very important herb called q'uwa, an incense-like plant, is sold at a special *tambo* (enclave or patio) where the q'uwa merchants share a space. The majority of q'uwa vendors come from the region along the Chilean border (Arica Department), and they concentrate on the exclusive sale of this one item. Because much q'uwa actually comes from the Chilean side of the border, q'uwa merchants must lease the land on which they collect the herb and then pay a tax to the Chilean border officials to transport it to the Huari fair—a very different situation from that faced by the Condeña vendors who sell local, communal resources. With the transportation costs of q'uwa included, this herb is relatively expensive, about 15 U.S. dollars per quintal (100 pounds[4]).

What accounts for Condeños' high numbers as vendors of traditional medicines? First, their preponderance is influenced by geographical/environmental

---

3. I believe this number is too high, because Alba does not indicate any other local origin of the vendors. When I made my observations and counts in 1990–1991, I recorded local vendors from Condo, Lagunillas, K'ulta, Qaqachaka, Cruz de Macha, and Huari; other vendors, mostly large scale, came from Cochabamba, Oruro, La Paz, Aiquile (department of Cochabamba), and Inquisivi (department of La Paz). It seems probable that Alba lumped all of the local vendors (who do live in contiguous territories) together as "Condeños," thereby giving him a higher number.

4. Compare this to the price of fava beans, an expensive food staple in Bolivia. In 1990, their price shot up to 48 bolivianos per quintal, or about 12 U.S. dollars.

factors. Condeños live in a tiered microenvironment, sheltered by hills on either side of the Azanaques River, where many of the important medicinal herbs of the altiplano grow. Of course, this explanation could also be given for a few other altiplano communities. Condo's location in the past as a crossroads between Potosí, the Pacific coast, and Peru, and its role as the hub of a pre-Inca Aymara Federation (Killakas-Asanaqi, as described in Chapter 1) also contribute to its leading role as a village of merchants.[5]

While the Huareños dedicated themselves to hosting the fair and growing fodder for the livestock as a kind of business venture, the Condeños found their niche as medicine sellers and so began a tradition of selling/trading. This activity may have originated among a few individual entrepreneurs who saw it as a chance to have a small, extra-agricultural commerce. Of course, this explanation still begs the question of why the women of the Kallapa ayllu are the leaders in this endeavor. Kallapa is known for its businesspeople, and women are the family members who generally participate in such marketing activities. The explanation that Condeños give for the dominance of this region in the traditional medicines trade is that the farmers from the Kallapa ayllu, while benefiting from larger agricultural plots, also suffered more crop damage over the years because their plots are on the pampa and, therefore, are more susceptible to frost. In certain years, their potato harvests in particular are destroyed. In searching for other activities to supplement their livelihoods, the women turned to selling traditional medicines and the men to making and selling musical instruments.

This explanation, which links environmental considerations to economic practices, is also supported by modern data. In 1989, when a drought occurred, Justino explained to me that many more people worked as traditional medicine vendors, and many had moved temporarily to the cities to pursue this activity there. In this way, the selling of traditional medicines, which was once a more localized activity (conducted in Condo and Huari), was "taken on the road" by the same vendors who originally sold their products closer to home, and then adopted by others. Research into peasant migration patterns shows that workers search for wage labor (or any alternative to agriculture) in bad years, but that their movement is not necessarily a permanent migration, as these workers often return to their villages to start over the next season. Guillermo Delgado (1985), a Bolivian anthropologist, has demonstrated that many miners in Oruro have returned to work as agriculturalists, and that at the mining centers women in particular maintain or "reactivate" agricultural practices as strategies for survival.

To sum up the foregoing information in terms of where the goods end up and their associated systems of healing, the Huari fair serves as a site for the provisioning of basically three kinds of customers, who in turn represent various medical beliefs and practices. First, individual customers buy remedies from the medicine vendors at the Huari fair. I once watched a vendor prepare an assemblage of 13 herbs for a

---

5. Several Condeños told me stories about their parents or grandparents who were traveling merchants, moving between the Pacific coast and the lowlands of Sucre. This trajectory is part of the old llama caravan trading routes. Today, some campesinos in this region still specialize in these long-distance trips (e.g., the Pampa Aullagueños), although they no longer travel to the Pacific coast.

customer. As the customer outlined her *problema de la matriz* ("uterus problem"), the Condeña vendor selected small bits of the 13 herbs. While she rolled them in a piece of newspaper for sale, the vendor explained to her customer how to take them in tea four times a day. Some of the herbs that the vendor included were not grown locally, which leads us to the second type of transaction.

Many medicine vendors provision their own stands by increasing and diversifying their own inventories at the Huari fair. For instance, Gabriela, a young Condeña who sold at Huari as a way to earn some extra money, collected only about four plants for sale there. Some of these she sold off in larger volumes; others she used in trade for other plants from the lowlands of Bolivia, or from Peru

Photo by Lynn Sikkink

FIGURE 5.4 The Huari fair: herbs drying in bulk before transport to other markets.

or Argentina, which would provide her with a richer inventory for the next marketing endeavor. In acquiring and selling exotic items like incense from Peru and resins from Argentina, vendors become purveyors of more "pan-Andean" (as opposed to local) healing knowledge and the herbs to accompany it. They pass this knowledge on with their wares when they sell them in the marketplace, and also share the information with their family and friends at home.

A third type of transaction involves the sale of herbs in bulk to intermediaries. Middlemen who buy up the plants in bulk, by buying from a number of different vendors, then dry the herbs for storage and transport. Patios and streets are lined with these herbs spread out on tarps, which give off the tangy aromas of papusa, sasawi, and chachacoma, among others (see Figure 5.4 on the previous page). Passersby joke that the air itself is medicinal. Unlike the remedies that circulate among rural community members, the plants that the intermediaries acquire enter into an urban pattern of exchange and healing. These plants are taken to the city, where they are resold to medicine vendors who then circulate them to their urban customers. In the city, these herbs are sometimes used alongside or in conjunction with pharmaceutical products or biomedical advice—in short, they become part of a healing system that is often referred to as "medical pluralism" (Crandon-Malamud 1991, Koss-Chioino et al. 2003).

Given the variety of ways herbal remedies from Huari will be employed, it is clear that they constitute a material aspect of the plural medical system. In addition, these communal medical resources become part of individuals' and vendors' medical inventories as they pass through the hands of intermediaries, and they may end up in urban homes or as ingredients in prepared remedies, which may then travel beyond the borders of Bolivia.

THE CHALLAPATA FAIR:
THE "NEW" REGIONAL MARKETPLACE

Challapata is called the "biggest indigenous [as opposed to mestizo or tourist] market in the Andes" (Molina Barrios, personal communication). Not far from Huari, Challapata claims the same advantageous location—it is located at a crossroads between Chile and Bolivia (and hence is an entry point for many goods), along the northern extension of an ancient Argentine trade route; it is also centrally located between the great salt flats of the southern Bolivian altiplano and the warm valleys, between which llama caravan trips were regularly run in the past. Moreover, Challapata is located along the road that connects Potosí and Oruro, and along the train line that during the early 1900s connected mining centers to urban areas.[6]

---

6. The rail lines throughout Bolivia are falling into disrepair and disuse, as a consequence of the mining crash and more recent privatization initiatives. Even the train that ran between La Paz, Oruro, and Cochabamba into the early 1990s is now defunct. After the railways were privatized, this line, which connected the Bolivian capital with the country's third largest city (Cochabamba), was abandoned. Despite recent attempts to revive it, the rail line has not been reopened. The loss of this transportation route is "a serious blow to the national infrastructure" (Finnegan 2003:46).

After agrarian reform, when rural markets were opened to the direct sale of produce to urban customers (Buechler and Buechler 1996:16), regional markets like Challapata flourished. Although its dusty streets and forlorn ambience on the weekdays provide no hint of its importance, on Sundays it springs to life, drawing buyers and sellers from rural and urban areas alike. The market participants (especially buyers) are mostly campesinos from the region, including people from the communities of Condo, Huari, Llapallapani, K'ulta, Cacachaca, Pampa Aullagas, Salinas de Garci Mendoza, and Uyuni, among others. Even Oruro urbanites come to shop in Challapata because meat and other food items are substantially cheaper there than in the city of Oruro, making it worth the six-hour (round trip) buying excursion to Challapata. Some of the buyers are intermediaries who buy food items to sell in large quantities in La Paz, Cochabamba, or Oruro. The vendors in Challapata, by comparison, are a mix of campesinos who sell their own wares, campesinos who have stands that amount to "businesses," and those people whom buyers call *comerciantes* ("merchants"—who are mestizos and/or urbanites) and who either sell in larger quantities or sell manufactured goods.

In contrast to the Huari fair, the Challapata market has grown in both size and variety over the years. According to local accounts, the market began sometime in the 1940s or 1950s as a small Sunday market, held in one of the plazas in the *pueblo viejo*, or old sector of the village. Before that time, Condeños relied exclusively on long-distance trading trips and local barter arrangements to meet their subsistence needs, and they bought (or bartered for) goods at the annual Huari fair. As a result of the ongoing participation of Condeños and other neighboring rural dwellers,

Photo by Lynn Sikkink

F I G U R E 5.5 Selling traditional medicines on Challapata's main plaza.

the Challapata market grew steadily. When one plaza could not contain the crowd, vendors set up stands along the adjoining streets. Stands, offering a wide variety of goods, gradually radiated out to the second large plaza of the old village—the church plaza. All along the route between these two main plazas, an increasing number of vendors began to sell their wares, especially during certain busy times of the year (e.g., All Saints' Day, Christmas, and Challapata's July 16 celebration of Vírgen del Carmen). In recent years, the weekly vendors have begun to arrive earlier to sell, with many of them coming on Friday evening. As a consequence, Saturday is now a market day as well, although Sunday remains the biggest day for sales. The number of people going to market on any given weekend fluctuates, because at certain times of the year there is a greater need to buy certain items, and hence for campesinos to sell their wares so that they can in turn buy.

The Sunday before All Saints' Day (November 1) is the biggest day of the year at the Challapata fair. Vendors from afar arrive to sell the special goods associated with this holiday, and wholesalers sometimes sell these items to the small vendors who in turn resell them. Likewise, campesinos bring larger volumes of goods to market to sell, hoping to use the money they earn that day to buy the items they need for All Saints' Day.[7] Vendors and buyers pack the market area, spilling out into the streets beyond the market's usual area, and business is brisk. During this celebration, vendors sell all of the items needed for constructing *tumbas* (commemorative altars): sugarcane, candies ("food for the souls"—the deceased), coca, cigarettes, alcohol, breads, prayer books, and other ingredients to make the special breads that adorn the altars.

In contrast to the brisk business conducted prior to November 1, the Sunday after All Saints' Day is probably the quietest and slowest of any market day in Challapata. Only about one tenth of the number of vendors and buyers come to the market compared to the week before, and business is so slow that many vendors simply stay home. Business picks up again in the weeks leading up to Christmas, and throughout the rest of the year generally follows a pattern of ebb and flow related to local fiestas and events, and national holidays.

Over the years, as the Challapata market has grown, Condeño participation has grown apace. The old walk to the market, which takes four to five hours from the village of Condo, has been replaced by a ride in a bus or truck, which takes less than an hour, including the stop in Huari. Every Sunday nearly 200 people leave Condo's plaza bound for Challapata, and about a quarter of these go to sell. The eastern side of Condo's territory is even more accessible to Challapata, and the people who reside there either travel in hired trucks or hitch a ride on the Potosí road to reach the market. On an average Sunday, perhaps 300–400 Condeños are present in the Challapata market. Many Condeños have come to depend on this market, where they can easily (and cheaply) buy their oil, sugar, spices, candles, vegetables, kerosene, and a wide selection of other goods. Likewise, Challapata has

---

7. In the cycle of selling to immediately buy (commodity → money → commodity), these transactions resemble barter much more than they do standard monetary transactions. Many such transactions are conducted in the Challapata marketplace (Sikkink 1994).

become an important source of income for many people—from those who sell occasionally to those who participate on a weekly basis.

The 20 traditional medicine vendors who sell in Challapata are mostly from the Kallapa ayllu (the "lower" ayllu). These women have fairly large inventories. At the market they are encircled by dozens of tiny bags, many of them hand-woven, in which they display their herbs. On average, five women sell items such as sugar tiles, candies, charms, and the wine and other items used in offerings. According to the vendor who was the first from Condo to sell these ritual goods, these vendors are distinct from the herbal remedy vendors. The five sugar-tile vendors come from the Sullkayana ayllu (the "upper" ayllu). Both groups of vendors (i.e., from the lower and upper ayllus) sometimes travel to sell their wares—for instance, to the mines between Oruro and Challapata (such as Pazña), where there is a demand for their goods. They also appear at the Huari fair, where their stands are some of the most diverse of the group from Condo.

While the opportunity to sell and buy at Challapata lures many people into the marketplace, as do the possibilities of seeing friends, buying something special, and watching the happenings of the bustling marketplace, the bustling market-place presents risks as well. Foremost is the risk of being robbed. Thieves, many of them from Oruro, especially prey on the campesina women who carry large sums of money because they are selling and/or buying. These thieves will also steal

FIGURE 5.6 A Condeña vendor of traditional medicines at work in Challapata with her daughter.

Photo by Lynn Sikkink

goods that the women are selling or have bought. Another risk for these campesinas arises from the selling process itself—for instance, selling at a "reduced" price that does not benefit the vendor, or being intentionally cheated by fast-talking buyers.

Accompanying these economic risks is Condeños' belief that some Challapateños are *lik'ichiris* (Aymara: "grease-suckers").[8] According to Condeño accounts, lik'ichiris are people who put their unsuspecting victims temporarily to sleep and then, with a needle, suck the life-giving fat from the victim's side. The victims are unaware that they have been preyed upon, until they are later stricken. Lik'ichiris' attacks are fatal if not immediately detected and cured by a healer. This fear of losing fat—seemingly a fear for one's health—is related to the risks of the marketplace, where one may be robbed or cheated, resulting in the loss of one's earnings, or "extra" (analogous to a body's fat).[9] An interesting body metaphor stands for the risks of the marketplace, therefore, in that the loss of the household's buffer is linked to the risks a body undergoes in the marketplace—the siphoning off of fat may even lead to death. A traditional medicine remedy for this condition is the ingestion of sheep's fat, particularly that associated with its internal organs, which is believed to replace the human fat that was lost.

The Sucre valley, to which some Condeños still make trading trips, is believed to harbor lik'ichiris among its residents, another association between the dangers to the body's health and the risks in conducting economic transactions, especially in strange locales. In Mary Weismantel's analysis (2001), the *pishtaco* (lik'ichiri) is neither a metaphor for economic exploitation nor a sign of a community's recent intrusion by outsiders, but rather an indication of the precarious nature of relationships between neighbors and the potential for conflict.

Thus both risk and allure characterize Condeños' participation in this marketplace, reflecting both its distance from the home community and the number of outsiders who populate it. The theme of danger presenting itself alongside opportunity is repeated in participants' dealings across marketplaces in Bolivia (as illustrated in Chapter 3), especially in those markets where the transactions are rarely based in reciprocity and close relationships between participants. Chapter 6 explores other dimensions of this issue for the Cochabamba marketplace.

Due to Challapata's size and the fact that many urbanites converge to buy at this weekly market, it is mainly characterized by monetary transactions. Shoppers peruse the wares on any given Sunday, asking prices and moving along until they find what they are looking for at a good price. A collective process aligns individual stands' prices with the prices asked by other vendors, which are rarely "set" in a formal sense. Within these parameters, buyers may seek to bargain. The Challapata market is, therefore, a good example of how the general forces of

---

8. Known as *qarisiris* or *pishtacos* (Quechua), these figures are widely described by Andean peoples, from Ecuador, Peru, and Bolivia (Weismantel 2001). The marketplace is but one of the many places where they might entrap unsuspecting victims.

9. Gringos are also sometimes believed to be lik'ichiris, a perspective that seems linked to their presence as foreigners and outside exploiters. Sometimes lik'ichiris are garbed in priests' robes. In the Challapata case, the belief that lik'ichiris reside in the village is also associated with the risks and fears inherent in a potentially exploitative marketplace.

supply and demand operate on a small scale, and also exemplifies a market at the crossroads of rural and urban economic spaces and practices.

Interestingly, the Challapata market does not operate as much by economic rationality and impersonal market forces as it might appear at first glance. Relatives, friends, and fictive kin abound and stand ready to make claims on the wares that any vendor has for sale. On many occasions I observed vendors gifting potatoes to their *comadres*, nonkin children being fed by *chicharrón* (fried meat) vendors, and the barter of one item for another—all without any money changing hands. Even more common is the casera relationship, an established and long-term relationship between vendor and buyer in which the vendor may give the buyer a special price, or provide a particularly generous *yapa*[10] (the "bonus" amount), to sweeten the deal. Yapas, though of smaller amounts, may also be offered to non-casera buyers, presumably as a way to lure them to return and become the regular customers on whom most vendors rely for their long-term income.

The vendors of traditional medicines in Challapata differ from those found at the Huari fair in that many of them are regular vendors and, therefore, have more permanence and share more similarities with the practices of urban vendors of traditional medicines. Many of these vendors sell in Challapata almost every Sunday of the year. The twenty Condeña vendors who sell regularly at Challapata clearly see what they do in terms of a "business," rather than as just an annual money-making event (as is the case for some traditional medicine vendors in Huari). Their arrays or inventories are generally much larger and more diverse than those of the more-infrequent vendors. In describing their stands, their inventories, and their practices, these regular vendors emphasize the planning and knowledge that constitutes their status as vendors. Although mothers or sisters may have trained some of them, others picked up the business from neighbors or friends, and they continue to learn by copying the other vendors involved in this pursuit. These vendors also organize their stands in such a way as to cater to the varied needs of larger numbers of customers who seek them out and buy from them.

Individual vendors must be extremely good managers. Doña Eustaquia, for example, relies on the careful management of her stand to yield a small, regular income. As she has several children but no husband, and has little land, her business is a necessary part of her livelihood. Along with the fifty or more herbs in her inventory, she also sells minerals, beans, seeds, and other items that she can knowledgeably combine into particular combinations for cures. Doña Eustaquia sells to those individuals with health problems, and she less frequently assembles offerings that customers take home for use in rituals. In the Challapata market-place, the vendors combine both herbal and ritual preparations, and the line between these two inventories is not as marked as it is in Huari.

---

10. *Yapa* is a Quechua term (from *yapay*, meaning "to give more") that was Hispanicized into *la ñapa*. It was used widely in Hispanic America, and picked up even by traders in Louisiana French Creole society. In New Orleans, it became *lagniappe*, meaning "something given over and above what is purchased or earned." In Bolivia, yapa has become a widespread term, and Spanish speakers sometimes refer to the yapa as the *aumento* ("increase") and talk about it in terms of "completing" a deal. The transaction between caseras is seen as complete when something extra has been added beyond the monetary value, such that an element of reciprocity has entered into the monetary transaction.

Margarita, for one, can prepare an herbal combination for a variety of ailments, or she can sell a ritual mesa that will either be used by the customer herself or be given to a *yatiri* (ritual specialist) who will employ it in a ceremony or cure. She knows the difference between the ingredients in a *mesa negra* and a *mesa blanca* ("black table" and "white table," respectively—one for use to ward off "curses" and the other to promote good luck, health, and prosperity). Margarita has managed to put together a bigger inventory, closer to those offered by big urban vendors. She is aided in her endeavors, and is able to provide such a broad inventory, because she has two sisters who also sell traditional medicines—one is a vendor in Oruro and one works year-round in Cochabamba. Although the items sold by vendors in Challapata most often end up in the homes of individual customers, there also exists trade among vendors (such as between Margarita and her sisters) and the possibility exists that their items will become part of urban inventories through the economic activities of middlemen, as we saw in the case of the remedies purchased at the Huari fair.

For the most part the vendors in Challapata sell to rural customers who come looking for cures, and to those individuals who are particularly interested in obtaining the items that are not available in their home communities. Margarita's expanded inventory, which includes "exotic" lowland plants and ritual ingredients, is attractive to country folk seeking specific products and cures. It is likely that Margarita's customers were spurred to buy an item in the marketplace by a relative or neighbor who said, for example, "What you need for that cough is a little *cola de caballo*" ("horse's tail" or *Equisteum*). In this way, the marketplace provides a number of products that people can buy, take home with them, and incorporate into their home-based system of health care; that is, the marketplace may provide the raw ingredients for a richer array of remedies based in local notions of health, illness, and healing.

In the past, people may have relied on nonmonetary trade networks to provide these items. Today, the marketplace functions as the primary node for serving these needs, as it provides a site where a wide array of plants, not all of them local, can be obtained. Although most of a vendor's transactions in Challapata would be of this sort—between vendor and individual rural customer—in some cases the vendor might sell goods in larger quantities either to a rural customer who is interested in reselling the items in the home community or to a true intermediary who is rounding out an inventory and taking the plants to the city to sell.

How the vendors refer to the items they have for sale also provides a clue about the concepts of healing that are linked to their inventory. Instead of calling them "traditional medicines"—a category used across marketplace venues throughout Bolivia and the term that describes them in urban contexts—the vendors in Challapata call their wares *remedios caseros* ("home remedies"), *remedios* ("remedies"), or simply *medicinas* ("medicines"). In contrast to referring to them as "traditional," the terms that vendors in Challapata use are unmarked, indicating that these medicines are simply *the* cures that most people employ to treat their health problems. Because the local "hierarchy of resort" is such that most problems will be treated at home, remedios are simply the way that people take care of themselves.

In Challapata, one can buy simple pharmaceutical products on the street—items such as aspirin and cough syrup—or one can go to a pharmacy to buy antibiotics and other medicines (prescriptions are optional). However, manufactured pharmaceutical products are sold separately by different vendors than those who sell remedios, and the prices of pharmaceuticals are much higher. Poorer campesinos almost always make recourse to the vendors who sell remedios, unless they have a very grave health problem that they believe cannot be treated with local medicines. In summary, the Challapata market very much services local healing beliefs and forms part of the ethnomedical system, offering an extended and diversified inventory of plants and other items used in treatments. In keeping with this understanding, the home and the marketplace are connected through the use of the term "remedios caseros," and its emphasis on health care from the locus of the home. At the same time, the marketplace is the site of new products and ideas, which eventually become incorporated into "local" health systems, so that local notions of healing are constantly in flux.

BETWEEN FIELD AND CITY: ORURO VENDORS OF TRADITIONAL MEDICINES

The city of Oruro is the capital of the department of the same name, to which Condo belongs. It is also the nearest city to Condo, located approximately three hours away by bus. Oruro is the capital of the contemporary mining region of Bolivia and was once a more prosperous center. Economically depressed today, Oruro can wear a sad and frayed expression—but not during Carnival. Known as the "folkloric capital" of Bolivia, during Carnival week Oruro outdoes itself by presenting a variety of acrobatic dancing troupes, gorgeously costumed dancers, huge marching bands, and playful spectacle.

Because of its relative proximity and amenities, Oruro is an important destination for Condeños and other rural inhabitants who go to the city to buy and sell, to conduct business, occasionally to visit the doctor, and frequently to visit family members. Some Condeños maintain homes in Oruro where, depending on the family, some or all of the family members live year round. For instance, one Condeño family rents and maintains a small second-floor apartment in Oruro for their older children, two of whom are in college. In the shop below, another man from Condo operates a tailor's business with help from his wife, while their children attend school in Oruro. Izíquia's brother and his family, already mentioned, live and work most of the year in Oruro, along with their three young children.

Ongoing ties to Condo are ensured through the land that people continue to oversee in Condo, even while "living" in the city. That is, many people pursue economic or educational activities in Oruro while maintaining some kind of agropastoral livelihood in Condo, whether by splitting time between country and city or by establishing some type of *partidario* ("sharecropping") arrangement. A daily bus service facilitates the constant ebb and flow between the village of

Condo and the city of Oruro. One can take the bus from Condo's plaza (which departs at the bone-chilling hour of 4:30 A.M.) bound for Oruro, arrive there around 7:30 in the morning, spend the day shopping and conducting business, and return to Condo that very afternoon, if one wishes. The number of people traveling between these two destinations has increased slightly over the past twelve years, but overall can be described as steady—every day at least fifteen Condeños make this trip. The strategy in this arrangement is apparent: The livelihoods of particular families may encompass numerous activities, allowing them to weather the economic difficulties of both the subsistence and monetary spheres while making a living. In truth, the reasoning goes beyond "strategy," as this mixture of activities allows families to survive (albeit rarely flourish) under harsh economic conditions.

Among the Condeños who move back and forth between Condo and Oruro are a small group of vendors, some of who sell traditional medicines. Most of these vendors sell in other locations as well. In 1991, 9 of 35 vendors in my intensive sample of Condeños sold in distant locales. The woman who traveled most frequently sold traditional medicines in Huari, Challapata, La Paz, Potosí, Cochabamba, Chile, and Oruro. Traveling to sell (and sometimes to buy) is not a new innovation, but rather a modification of old economic practices. Trading that was conducted during llama caravan trading trips in the past is now accomplished by taking a bus to a market center and selling or bartering wares there. Even two generations back, some Condeños were involved in long-distance trade. Based on the model of llama caravan trading trips, these merchant-campesinos would buy or exchange for an item in one locale, then take the item to a different area (and ecological tier) where they could sell it for cash or trade it for products that they needed.

One common pattern involved taking salt and wool from the high altiplano to the warm lowland valleys, where Condeños could trade these products for corn. Until the last few decades, this sort of trade was accomplished mainly through llama caravan trips. Today, however, many people use public transportation to make the journey and may even sell their items at the other end. This type of trade has its own legacy today in the practices of Condeños who travel to sell their wares in different parts of Bolivia, seeking to diversify their household base as a consequence. Through these kinds of trade patterns, the traditional medicines sold by Condeños are finding a niche in increasingly far-flung marketplaces and reaching ever-greater numbers of people. Because a vendor's inventories bring together medicines from radically different elevations, various ecological niches, and "hot" and "cold" remedies, trade is an important mechanism in bringing the elements together, and it certainly helps keep the Andean pharmacopoeia alive.

Oruro is the most important of Condeños' long-distance market destinations. In colonial times, this city served as a hub of mining activity and commerce, and exerted an economic pull on rural areas such as Condo, albeit to a lesser extent than it affected Potosí. When tin mining was in its heyday (in the mid-1900s), Oruro figured prominently as one location in the circuit of mining centers that Condeño vendors followed. Even more important than its role as a site for occasional vending, however, Oruro is now a gathering place for increasing numbers

Photo by Lynn Sikkink

FIGURE 5.7 Condeña vendors of traditional medicines in their kiosks in Oruro.

of full-time Condeño vendors. As in Cochabamba, some Condeñas have carved out a business niche for themselves by becoming full-time vendors of traditional medicines. These vendors generally occupy one of two locations in Oruro: Either they locate their kiosks[11] within the established marketplace of Fermín Lopez, or they find a spot along the Calle Junin that radiates out from the outdoor market along the railway tracks in central Oruro.

Both market areas have come to include these small enclaves of traditional medicine vendors, who, much like the vendors who work in other sections of the marketplace, group together in the hope of attracting customers to their combined offerings. These vendors self-identify as businesswomen, and although they may still be linked to the agropastoral livelihood of Condo, they endeavor to earn a large portion of their income through their regular vending practices in the Oruro marketplace. Their continued farming activities in Condo provide them with an important subsistence base (and a fallback position in difficult years), even as their ties to the community allow them to provision themselves and their market stands more readily. This is especially true for the traditional medicine vendors who assemble their inventories in part through the items they procure in Condo, through ties with neighbors and kin.

In taking up positions in an urban marketplace, the Oruro vendors adapt their practices, the appearances of their stands, and even their medical advice to cater to new and different customers. In contrast to the ground-level display of mostly herbal remedies offered in Huari and Challapata, the Condeña women who work in an urban setting such as Oruro have set up more permanent stands, resembling

---

11. *Kioscos* are permanent metal stands that can be shut up and locked like cupboards at night. Not only must the vendors buy these stands at the outset, but they must also pay the rental fee that goes along with having a permanent place in the marketplace or street.

in some ways a neighborhood pharmacy, in which their much-diversified wares are displayed in bottles and boxes to tempt the buyer. Here they sell not just the herbs that come from Condo, but also herbs, incenses, and powders that they have carefully collected from other places through purchase and barter. Vendors in Oruro offer a larger selection of medicines for sale as well as many items beyond the common herbal remedies. For instance, they provide many of the ingredients for the offerings called mesas negras, which they can also assemble for customers who request them. The vendors may also offer such items as llama and sheep fetuses, which are important ingredients of the more complicated and complete ritual mesas. In addition, many vendors sell sugar tiles for use in various offerings. Clearly, these vendors offer a wider array of goods than their counterparts in the rural and regional marketplaces, and they pride themselves on their more sophisticated display of traditional medicines, sold from permanent stands.

In the Fermín López Marketplace in Oruro is a small enclave of vendors who sell ingredients for ritual assemblages. They inhabit one aisle in this old indoor marketplace, and are quite centrally located. Almost all of the approximately twenty vendors are from Condo and refer to themselves as Condeñas. They maintain close ties with their rural village, returning to work the land and always traveling home for the fiestas. As a group, they have the unmistakable look of well-organized marketers, and they are: They have established their own syndicate, allowing them to set guidelines for what they sell and the way they sell in their marketing niche. Unlike any other group of medicine vendors I interviewed, these women wear matching attire—light blue crocheted berets and royal blue dusters—that proclaims their status as marketwomen. (It is more common to see prepared food vendors or other groups of marketers dressed in this fashion, especially in La Paz.)

The wares these Oruro vendors sell—q'uwa, sugar tiles (*misterios*), animal fetuses, candies, fat, and alcohol—align them with the inventories of q'uweras in Cochabamba, but their stands do not incorporate any of the medicinal plants or imported items that have come to be included in q'uwera stands in Cochabamba (discussed in Chapter 6). Also, unlike their counterparts on Calle Junin, in a different section of the Oruro marketplace, the Fermín López vendors restrict themselves to ritual ingredients, which they offer in great quantity and wide variety. Like other marketers in urban areas, they engage almost solely in monetary exchange, although vendors exchange products among themselves to some degree. For instance, some of the vendors make their own misterios (sugar tiles) at home, which they then offer to the other vendors in exchange for other merchandise.

The customers of these Condeñas are a cross-section of people from both city and country. Nevertheless, these vendors sell to a more urban clientele than do the vendors on Calle Junin. Anyone who wants to buy a mesa for a ritual of any sort, for example, might buy from the vendors in Fermín López. Often people are interested in buying ingredients to prepare a ritual offering to get their business off to a good start or because they are building a new house. Special ritual assemblages, prepared by these vendors, will provide customers with the proper package for their ceremony. Customers run the gamut from recently arrived migrants to more established urbanites who share similar concerns in ensuring their family's good health or bringing luck to a business.

Central to these stands is the ritual ingredient of q'uwa. Because the vendors rely on q'uwa in almost all of the mesas they prepare, they go through large quantities of this herb. The Condeñas must go to Huari each year to provision themselves with it, and when they do they sell their wares at the annual fair.

Despite the vendors' associations with ritual items and the concurrent healing aspect of healing ceremonies, these vendors are quick to point out that they are not healers, nor do they have any associations with institutions or groups of healers. Instead, they see themselves first and foremost as vendors, and they take pride in their roles as businesswomen.

Many of the traditional medicine vendors from various marketplaces are linked together not only through ties of shared work, but also through kinship. For instance, three sisters from one Condeño family, all of whom are married and have children, sell traditional medicines in different locations. Perhaps not surprisingly, they cite each other as an important source of help in starting out and in maintaining their inventories. Margarita lives in Condo year round, and sells every year in Huari and about once a month in Challapata. She occasionally travels to Oruro to sell at her sister Julia's stand. Julia has a permanent medicine stand in Oruro, where she sells her wares most days of the year. Julia and Margarita help each other by swapping and trading for certain medicines to extend their individual inventories. The third sister, Emiliana, lives year round in Cochabamba, and firmly identifies herself as a full-time vendor. In Cochabamba, like most other vendors, she relies on the selling of mesas and other ritual ingredients such as incense, which people buy to burn in offerings. Taken together, the three sisters illustrate that kinship ties are an important source of economic help in maintaining oneself in the business. They also provide a good example of the various locales in which vendors of traditional medicines ply their trade, and the way in which their ties to urban areas figure into the provisioning of their stands.

In Oruro, Julia (one of the three sisters) has a stand on Calle Junin and is a good example of the particular style of traditional medicine vending in this urban area. Along this street, approximately 35 medicine vendors have formed their own union ("Sindicato de Vendedores de Medicinas Tradicionales"), and 6 of their number are from Condo. This is a high percentage—nearly 17 percent—given that vendors come from a broad surrounding area, and some of them originate from as far away as Potosí. Julia bought a kiosk and started selling in Oruro permanently in 1992. She was aided in this endeavor both by her two sisters and by her mother, who sold traditional medicines in Huari and Challapata when she was still alive.

Julia began her career by helping her mother. She notes that she has been involved in selling traditional medicines her "whole life" but indicates that this business became an even more important source of income after her husband died in 1999—Julia must now support her four children on her own. She is an extremely hard worker. Monday through Saturday, she can be found sitting within her small blue metal stand in Oruro. On Sundays she frequently goes to Challapata, where she sells alongside the other Condeñas in the plaza, most of whom have traveled from Condo, but a few like herself from Oruro. This Sunday trip is one of the reasons she is able to maintain a close association with her sister Margarita and the other Condeños she encounters weekly. At the same time, like other shoppers from Oruro, she avails herself of the lower prices at the Challapata market to purchase food and supplies for her household.

Julia's stand in Oruro itself demonstrates the interface between rural and urban products and ideas. Approximately 50 percent of Julia's wares consists of herbal remedies from the Condo area—of the type that would be sold by Condeñas in the Challapata marketplace. Most of these products come from the altiplano, like the herbs papusa, sasawi, lamphaya, and yareta that one would encounter at the Huari and Challapata fairs. However, Julia also sells medicines from the yungas (lowlands) that she has obtained through barter or purchase. Nearly half of Julia's wares might be categorized as ritual ingredients; they include the q'uwa, sugar tiles, candies, yarn, and alcohol that are used as the main ingredients in assembling mesas. As we can see by her inventory, Julia's business straddles the assembly of herbal remedies that her sister Margarita relies on when selling in Huari, and the ritual ingredients that her sister Emiliana emphasizes in her Cochabamba stand.

This dual selection—herbal remedies and ritual ingredients—caters to the particular customers Julia attracts, who shop in this section of the marketplace. Although some of her clients are urbanites from the city of Oruro, she classifies her customers as mostly *gente campesina*, or peasants from the surrounding countryside who reside in places like Paria, Patacamaya, and Machacamarca (rural villages located within an hour's drive of Oruro). Even when dealing with rural folk, Julia relies on cash sales. Unlike the mix of exchange practices in Challapata, where barter is still quite common, Julia obtains an income by selling her wares. As she explains, in the city one needs money for "everything," unlike the countryside where food and other goods need not be purchased. Therefore, she rarely accepts barter good for her wares, unless the customer is a relative from Condo or offers something she really needs.

Julia obtains the items she has in her inventory through a combination of means, in which her sisters figure prominently. She goes to the annual Huari fair to get both q'uwa and many of the common herbs that are harvested from around Condo. In Huari, she buys sasawi, lamphaya, maranzela, and other herbs. She next buys some items in Oruro, especially the lowlands ingredients that are important in assembling mesas negras (e.g., qalawala, quina, *cristala china*). She sells those items not just in her stand in Oruro, but also at the Huari fair. Clearly, Julia very much relies on Huari as a source of many of her items.

Back at Julia's stand in Oruro, items bought in Huari enter her inventory. Given her diverse wares, she is able to treat many different illnesses and offer items for the various rituals that people seek. Because many of her customers are rural inhabitants, the medicines that she sells are typically used in their particular system of "traditional healing." Most of the herbal remedies bought by people in Oruro are used without the intervention of a healer, but the vendor may instruct the customer about the proper use of the remedy, thereby serving as an ad hoc healer. By comparison, the ritual assemblages that people purchase from the vendor may be taken to their local ritual specialist, in which case the vendor's advice is not as critical. Either way, the vendor's advice serves as a key component of the system of traditional healing practices that most rural Bolivians rely on. Julia mentions rheumatism, kidney conditions, and uterus problems as common complaints for which her customers seek treatment, demonstrating the wide range of ailments about which rural and urban customers complain.

The vending of traditional medicines in Oruro is a microcosm of Oruro's socioeconomic position within Bolivia. Ex-miners, rural migrants, fully established urbanites, and people like Julia whose lives straddle the field and city populate the city of Oruro. Not only do the vendors of traditional medicines cater to this diverse population, but the ingredients and healing practices they assemble also reflect this diversity. In Oruro, people shop for traditional medicines not only because of a long-standing belief in the efficacy of herbs and rituals, but also because it is economically viable to do so. Most people would rather try to take care of their health problems without the intervention of a doctor, especially given the relative costs of the two treatment avenues. As Carlos (an urban curandero) says, "People would rather buy one peso's worth of chamomile than spend 10 pesos on stomach pills" (personal communication, July 19, 2003). Of course, when people stop to purchase chamomile on the Calle Junin in Oruro, they also receive counseling from a sympathetic vendor who offers her specialized advice on its home use.

SUMMARY

The Huari fair is Condo's oldest marketplace venue. Although it is located very close to home (an hour's walk from Condo's plaza), it is regularly used only once a year, when the Huari fair takes place. Nonetheless this venue is important to Condeños as a way to convert medicinal resources into other items needed by the household, whether through barter or by using cash. Huari is also the site from which many medicinal items have found their way into the hands of different people: For individuals ranging from other rural dwellers to middlemen, it has served as a site for procuring and circulating traditional medicines. As the home of an early fair, albeit one that continues to thrive today, it provides a good example of how medicines became economic resources. In particular, it shows us that commercialization is not a new phenomenon.

The Challapata market became important in the region because it is a weekly marketplace and provides year-round vending opportunities. By working in this market, many Condeño vendors are able to earn a steadier income from medicinal wares, a possibility that prompts many of them to turn into specialists in this area. Some vendors become full-time specialists when they move their stands to Oruro or to Cochabamba; the latter marketplace is the subject of Chapter 6. As female vendors move from part-time venues such as Huari, to being full-time specialists in places like Oruro, they become less "traders" and more "healers," a distinction made clear by the ways in which their customers interact with them. The merging of economic necessity with healing practices takes place in these marketplace settings.

Bolivian Traditional Medicines and Urban Commercialization: Medicine Vendors in Cochabamba

INTRODUCTION: FROM LOVE CHARMS TO MEDICINAL TEAS

Tucked away behind the tailors and the fruit sellers of the urban La Cancha marketplace are the vendors of *q'uwas*—herbs, sugar figurines, and confetti, among other items. These items, which are assembled and then burned in offerings to the gods, are considered one feature of the traditional medicine system. Esmeralda has her stand in this small enclave of *Q'uweras* (q'uwa sellers)[1] and occupies a place where her mother's stand was, and her mother's mother before that. Peering into Esmeralda's booth one notices the eclectic mix of medicines, ingredients, and paraphernalia that have come to mark the contemporary wares of traditional medicine vendors in this section of the marketplace. Her wares include not only the varied ingredients for assembling the special offerings for which her class of vendors are named, but also a variety of dried local herbs that will be made into teas by her customers, after consulting with Esmeralda about what she might recommend for their particular ailment.

Accenting this combination of q'uwas and herbs are magic love candles from Brazil; a variety of packaged and bottled herbal remedies, including some of Peruvian or Chilean origin; and sticks of incense. One candle, in the shape of an ear of corn, reminds me of Condeño harvest rituals. Esmeralda tells me it is *para abundancia* ("for abundance"), a notion that links Andean reverence for corn with the imported practice of burning candles to seek specific outcomes. Above Esmeralda's stall, the roof is strung with bird carcasses from the altiplano and the Amazon basin; the bird feathers are useful as charms as well as for the costumes schoolchildren wear during civic parades.

Dark and leathery-looking animal carcasses are another notable feature of Esmeralda's stand, as they are of the stands of other vendors of ritual items. These desiccated animal fetuses are another key ingredient of the ritual assemblages many customers seek. At Esmeralda's stand, customers can choose from llama, sheep, pig, cow, burro, or goat fetuses. She proudly exhibits the full array, and indicates that she can supply any ingredient a shopper seeks. The fetuses at Esmeralda's stand come from either the countryside—from animal miscarriages—or, increasingly, from urban slaughterhouses when pregnant animals are butchered. For a proper offering, adding a fetus to the ritual assemblage is the best way to increase its potency.

Fetuses are expensive, however, and they may be omitted from the ritual by shoppers who can't afford them. These items may be either burned as part of a ritual mesa[2] during the ritual or simply buried, especially during a construction project. Offerings such as these, with the important component of an animal fetus, underlay the foundations of houses and office buildings alike throughout the cities of Bolivia. Although tourists find these items a curiosity, for Bolivians their presence and use is part of everyday life and is not seen as repulsive. Esmeralda explains the uses of the fetuses in ritual from her experience: A llama, like a sheep, is for "luck" and its attendant rituals, but llama fetuses are "better" and consequently more expensive. Both pig and cow fetuses are used for individual healing ceremonies—they are passed over an ill person's body to absorb the ailment and then are burned. Not as commonly used, a burro fetus has a special function—it

---

1. Q'uwa (*Minthostachys glabrescens*) is the aromatic herb that is the central ingredient in the offerings that these vendors have for sale. It is found in most of the preassembled mesas offered for sale by the Q'uweras, and its spicy scent fills the air in this section of the marketplace. The plural of q'uwa—q'uwas—is used to indicate the whole array of ingredients that go into ritual offerings, which is the way the vendors and customers describe it.

2. The definition of *mesa* may be rendered as "prepared offering." The word "mesa" may have been derived from either the Spanish word for "table" or the word *misa*, meaning "mass" (Rösing 1996:276).

ensures success in legal processes and trials. As the Q'uweras explain, the use of a burro fetus turns the opposing lawyer into a "donkey," causing him to lose the case. The presence of the various fetuses illustrates the breadth of ritual assemblages that can be prepared based on items such as those found at Esmeralda's stand, and the contemporary goals of the customers who use them.

The overall inventory of Esmeralda's stand exemplifies the contemporary vendors of ritual items (in Cochabamba, "Q'uweras"), whose wares and business practices are blends of various traditions—that is, hybrids. Other groups of traditional medicine vendors likewise provide goods and services that are rooted in old rituals and cures but change with the times to incorporate new elements. The vendors' arrays of products reflect wider cultural views of Bolivian traditional medicine, which include both utilitarian and spiritual components.

Vendors of herbs and ritual ingredients also provide an alternative to the relatively impersonal sphere of biomedicine. In essence, these traditional medicine vendors offer a personal relationship to their customers by providing information about the beliefs and uses surrounding specific cures and various types of offerings.

Photo by Sarah Linn Gallardo

F I G U R E 6.1 Esmeralda at home in her *Q'uwera* stand. The witch in the foreground pokes fun at those who accuse Q'uweras of practicing witchcraft.

At many of these stands throughout the marketplace, new ideas about healing are promoted through varied business practices alongside old and new cures. Like Esmeralda, many vendors continue to operate the businesses they inherited from parents, thereby bringing a personal continuity to the wares they promote. Thus these vendors occupy a professional niche in Andean traditional medicine that demonstrates its links with the past. At the same time, the simple act of showcasing their wares in the marketplace has led to modifications in the traditional medicines they peddle, especially as the inventory comes into contact with new ideas and products from regional and international sources. Although this "blending" may seem unusual, or "not traditional" from an outsider's perspective, from an insider's perspective the presence of traditional medicines in contemporary marketplaces makes cultural and economic sense. Indeed, there is no contradiction in these practices either for the vendors themselves or for the customers who seek their cures and advice.

Photo by Sarah Linn Gallardo

FIGURE 6.2 Animal fetuses are essential ingredients of ritual offerings, and can be purchased from a *Q'uwera*.

THE COCHABAMBA MARKETPLACE:
LAYOUT AND HISTORY

The marketplace in Cochabamba is the largest in Bolivia, and serves as the central market for the entire country. Today "La Cancha,"[3] as the Cochabamba marketplace is known, is a generic designation for a growing conglomerate of market zones. Based on an in-depth study of this bustling marketplace, Fernando Calderón and Alberto Rivera summarize its importance in the following way: "In La Cancha things are decided. It is the economic heart of Cochabamba and the most genuine expression of the current process of regional commercialization" (1983:13). Not only is the market at the center of Cochabamba city, but it is also the core marketplace of a system of satellite regional fairs and marketplaces, and a crossroads for people and merchandise from different regions of the country (p. 50).

Since Incan times, Cochabamba has been an important provisioning site. Although there were no true marketplaces in the pre-Spanish Andes (Murra 1987), because goods were swapped through an effective system of interzonal trade and reciprocity, Cochabamba and other similar supply centers played an important role in the production and storage of goods destined for other areas during this period. Using a system of forced resettlement, the Incas brought in laborers from other regions, mostly to work the rich agricultural fields of this temperate, mid-altitude valley halfway between the altiplano and the coca-producing lowlands. Cochabamba was an important production area for maize, but also supplied other crops (e.g., potatoes, quinoa) at its higher elevations, and was a rich area for pasturelands (Dandler 1987; R. Jackson 1994; Larson 1988).

In colonial times, under new policies and new forms of forced labor, the valley continued to produce for the populace, most notably supplying food and other useful goods for the growing numbers of silver miners. Although Potosí was the largest city in the Americas in early colonial times, at 14,000 feet there was no agricultural land in its environs sufficient to feed so many workers. Consequently, Potosí relied primarily on Cochabamba to supply goods for the mining enterprise. Marketplaces quickly sprang up in Cochabamba to meet these needs, and buying and selling there began to replace the system of interzonal trade, at least between the monetary economies of Potosí and Cochabamba.

Thus, during the colonial period, the Cochabamba Valley became entrenched as an agricultural supply center; the city of Cochabamba was the hub of this activity. Just as is the case today, Saturday was an important market day for colonial-era residents: "The central marketplace in the region was found on the outskirts of Cochabamba on Saturday mornings" (Larson 1988:202). Focusing on the economic importance of the colonial marketplace and its satellite fairs in the Cochabamba Valley, Larson describes "open-air markets at dawn, swarming with haggling peasants; caravans of llamas and traders trekking down from the western highlands during harvest season to barter in the valley ferias; mule trains loaded

---

3. *La Cancha* is a term that comes from the site's former use as a playing field for soccer—an apt description of its function in the contemporary marketplace.

with sacks of flour en route to Oruro after a good harvest [and] the fluid movement of perishable commodities across the open valleys" (p. 206).

Today "La Cancha" is a designation for several different marketplaces that have essentially grown into one market space as vendors have expanded to occupy the intervening blocks and streets, especially on big market days. The total area covered is between fifteen and twenty city blocks. Contained within this overall "market" are the Calatayud, Aranibar, San Antonio, and La Pampa marketplaces. Rather than the marketplace residing on the outskirts of the city as in colonial times, the residential and commercial zones of contemporary Cochabamba have engulfed the marketplace, and it is now—appropriately—in the heart of the city.

Traditional medicines are sold in various sections of this huge open-air marketplace. La Cancha is certainly not the only place where these medicines can be purchased, however. Some vendors inhabit storefronts that are not part of the marketplace proper, although traditional medicine stands and storefronts are found only in high concentrations in La Cancha marketplace and around it. Other locales radiate out from the marketplace, mostly toward downtown Cochabamba, including the "25 de Mayo" marketplace. Some traditional medicine vendors and *naturistas* (natural medicine doctors) can be found in peripheral residential areas (i.e., in barrios inhabited by new migrants).

From the sixteenth century and well into the Republican period (which began in 1825), there is no evidence that any traditional medicines were sold in the Cochabamba marketplace (Alba 1988). Alba's interviews with elderly residents revealed that even during the early 1900s only one family sold these items; when a few other families began to ply these wares, their merchandise had to be "hidden" and their work was "semi-clandestine" because it was accepted neither by government officials nor by society in general (p. 5). Indeed, Alba claims that these wares were labeled *botica de basura* (garbage medicine) (p. 8). These early vendors sold in the Calatayud market, on what is now the northern edge of the marketplace, among the sellers of charcoal and used clothes. It was not until the 1970s that vendors of traditional medicines began to establish themselves in the section of the marketplace called "La Pampa," which is now thickly populated by Q'uweras like Esmeralda, whose stand was described in the opening paragraphs of this chapter. Alba links both established and itinerant Q'uweras to the Aymara altiplano, because so many of them were from Oruro (p. 13). Many Q'uweras today claim ties to Huari (in the Department of Oruro), but it is clear that now the vendors come from various regions of Bolivia.

Cochabamba provides rich opportunities to examine the interplay of traditional Andean cultural forms and the emergence of new ones. Maintaining its designation as a focal point, crossroads, and economic supply center, the contemporary Cochabamba marketplace continues to serve as a place where people, ideas, and goods meet. In many ways Cochabamba displays a contemporary version of "verticality," John Murra's (1972) notion of the cultural and economic interconnections among people from different altitudinal zones in the Andes.

Murra, a pioneering Andean ethnohistorian, cited several examples of Andean communities that maintained their self-sufficient provisioning by having access to different altitudinal zones and their respective agricultural products. For instance, members of a pre-Inca Aymara group named the Lupaqa resided on the Bolivian altiplano, yet maintained lands in the warm maize-growing region outside its boundaries. Murra called this distributed landholding and agricultural production system an "archipelago." In contemporary times, what was once accomplished through distributed landholdings, reciprocity, or trading trips is accomplished through the marketplace, at least for most transactions. The particular verticality of the Cochabamba marketplace is due to its access to different elevational zones, along with the diverse array of international goods available there. The market is largely separated into different zones characterized by different vendors. An examination of the Cochabamba market also reveals vendors who sell fruit and vegetables from the lowlands, peasants from the Valle Alto (high zones) who sell potatoes and other crops, flower vendors alongside vendors of electronic appliances, and itinerant vendors who sell Brazilian goods; threaded throughout them all—sometimes in their own zones, sometimes in pockets and along sidewalks bordering established market areas—are the vendors of traditional medicines, who compete to make a living in this crowded business venue. The Cochabamba marketplace is, therefore, a kind of concentrated Andean archipelago.

VENDORS AND THEIR MEDICINAL WARES

This chapter examines a particular group of vendors in the city of Cochabamba, all of whom sell traditional medicines, but who vary in the goods and services they offer and the aspects of traditional medicine they cover. There is an increasing diversification within this group of vendors. Likewise, their stands display a set of goods and services that undergo constant change, as well as being a site of interface between rural and urban beliefs, practices, knowledge, and business opportunities.

The blending of traditions in Cochabamba systems of health has been noted by Juan Jose Alba, who uses the term "cultural hybridity" to describe the combination of traditional and biomedical cures, healers, and practices in the region (2000:6). In the marketplace, not only do prospective clients choose between ethnomedical and biomedical health systems, but they also actively mix them in new ways. While it is true that many current health programs at least give lip service to the "articulation" of two health systems, researchers tend to discuss health contexts such as those found in the Andes in terms of "medical pluralism" (e.g., Bastien 1992, Crandon-Malamud 1991), meaning a spectrum of healthcare practices that include different elements and blend biomedicine and traditional medicines. Indeed, the latter depiction might more accurately describe the picture of how rural and urban people take care of their health. Greene (1998) labels this mixture as "intermedicality" and urges medical anthropologists to attend to it when analyzing contemporary healthcare systems.[4]

It is not only rural migrants to the city who use traditional medicine in these constantly changing conditions, but urbanites as well who seek these cures. Many

---

4. Even ritualists working in fairly isolated regions may draw on both systems. Greene (1998), for instance, describes an Aguaruna shaman in Peru who uses a dual diagnosis in his curing sessions, urging his patients to seek injections and further magical treatment.

of these are convinced of the superiority of their ancestors' knowledge and methods. Others mistrust the treatments offered by cosmopolitan doctors or may have had bad experiences with it.

People's health choices and options are filtered through the setting of the marketplace, which is a center of supply and demand for goods and services, and where traditional medicine sections are run mainly by women.[5] Many people make use of the marketplace to find out what is available to treat their particular ailment, and to consult with an herb vendor about what to use and how to do so. Customers who want to know what is good for a cough may ask the vendor, or they may even consult with other customers. Customers may consult a natural medicine doctor for help with a more complex set of symptoms, and the naturista may diagnose the problem through conversation, or even by a short examination if the naturista has an office (usually on one of the city blocks surrounding the marketplace). (The practices of naturistas are considered in more detail in Chapter 8.) The marketplace offers new and potent products, too—rather than buying domestic cat's claw (a very popular remedy for many ailments), a customer may choose the more exotic "Hindu" cat's claw, which is of Peruvian origin and is packaged in Chile.

The available options, along with the sheer number of people who come and go from the marketplace, demonstrate how important the Cochabamba site is in terms of health care. The marketplace functions on one level like a multifaceted pharmacy because of the dazzling array of products—from chamomile to cancer cures, and from herbal asthma-relievers to antibiotics. Given that healing services are offered up alongside these products, however, it is more accurate to compare it with old-fashioned pharmacies, where the pharmacist presided as the dispenser of both cures and medical advice. But here the analogy runs out, because the marketplace boasts other possibilities that would never have been found in an old European pharmacy. Along with the herbal remedies that one would expect to find in a system of traditional medicines, one also finds all the ingredients for assembling offerings to use in various rituals, such as Esmeralda sells. Mostly the mesas will be burned in a variety of locations and for a variety of purposes, and the vendors in the marketplace help to explain it all, educating customers and assembling the ingredients.

Medicinal products are thus offered along with a service. At a minimum, vendors describe the uses of the products; in other cases, they function as healers or ritualists. This is also the case for other products and in other settings—in general, marketwomen are adept at providing time-saving or informational services to customers (e.g., Babb 1989, Chiñas 1992, Clark 1994). The value added to traditional medicines by vendors includes their knowledge and suggestions, and perhaps assembly of the proper combination of elements. Q'uweras combine sugar tiles, aromatic herbs, brightly colored candies, llama fat, coca leaves, confetti, and sometimes a dried animal fetus (which adds potency) into a neat package, ready for the particular ritual the customer seeks. In buying this pre-assembled offering, buyers purchase a service along with the ingredients, which they may extend by hiring the vendor to help with the ritual at home. In

5. For more on the Andean marketplace and women, see the following sources: Babb 1989; Buechler 1997; Buechler and Buechler 1996; McKee 1997; Seligmann 1989, 1993; Weismantel 1988, 2001.

considering the work of traditional medicine vendors, therefore, we need to take into account the specialized nature of the services they offer. Their specialized knowledge and advice provide a healing value to the product that is important to their customers.

In the city, traditional medicines are actively marketed as "traditional," illuminating further the interface between countryside and city. For example, many intermediaries from the city shop at the rural Huari fair (described in Chapter 5), where once a year large quantities of traditional herbs and other remedies are offered for sale. The Cochabamba Q'uweras also replenish their stocks at the Huari fair, as q'uwa, the main ingredient in their inventories, is sold cheaply and in abundance in Huari. Many Cochabamba vendors rely on yearly trips to Huari as a way to restock their stands cheaply and effectively, but the connection also allows them to renew a link they have with a more "authentic" source of these cures.

In Cochabamba, traditional medicine vendors run the gamut from individuals who operate more established storefront businesses to itinerant healers selling their wares. The remainder of this chapter examines both the array of traditional medicines in the marketplace and their particular inventories of medicine, allowing a glimpse into the diversity of practices and surrounding traditional medicines. Although healers such as naturistas sometimes work out of the marketplace, the discussion in this chapter is confined to those people who call themselves vendors (*vendedores*), and who in turn downplay the healing knowledge with which they are sometimes well equipped. Examining a cross-section of vendors in Cochabamba, I explore the promotion, vending, and use of traditional medicines as it is revealed in marketplace settings.

The data described here were gathered through a combination of direct observation and interviews. I observed vendors at work in their stands in the marketplace, and I interviewed them about their marketing practices and beliefs regarding traditional medicine. My sample includes fifteen vendors in Cochabamba, some of whom I worked with extensively. These data are supplemented with observations from their customers, and I draw on comparisons with Bolivian vendors of traditional medicines from other locales. The vendors are classified into four groups: (1) traditional medicine vendors from San Pedro de Condo (Condeñas); (2) vendors of fresh medicinal herbs; (3) the Q'uweras of La Pampa, and (4) businesspeople promoting their natural medicine cottage industries. Exploring how individual vendors got started in the business, how they procure their products and from whom, who their clients are and what kinds of problems they most commonly treat, and how they would characterize the knowledge they have about traditional medicine provides insight into the variety of businesses, including how each type construes the category of traditional medicines, and how vendors go about making a living.

After providing some brief descriptions to introduce the four groups of marketplace vendors from whom I collected data, the practices and beliefs of the various vendors are analyzed for what they reveal about the nature of the rural/urban interface, and how notions of healing and healing services differ in the marketplace setting. In terms of the link to the countryside, vendors may serve as "brokers" between urban and rural spheres, but in the process they mold the category of traditional medicines to their ends and take it in new directions. From a historical vantage point, healing has not traditionally been associated with the marketplace. So what happens when it *is* linked to marketplace products and the practices of vendors? Vendors attempt to reconcile this tension in interesting ways, by both running a business and operating from a position that takes morals and religious beliefs into account.

RURAL–URBAN INTERFACES: MARKETWOMEN AND MEDICINAL WARES

Marketwomen, as emblematic of an urban class of *cholas* who have ties to rural communities but are unique entrepreneurs, have been described as cultural brokers between the rural and urban spheres (Babb 1989, Seligmann 1989, 1993). The term "chola" is uniquely tied to marketwomen in the Bolivian Andes, where it is often used to label a merchant class of women who signal their status by wearing full skirts, fancy blouses and shawls, and either bowler or straw hats. Marketwomen do not often call themselves "cholas," and it should be noted that the term is a broad category usually applied by outsiders. (See also de la Cadena 1995.) The term "chola," as well as the way marketwomen dress and present themselves, has a long history, being rooted in processes of racial and class formation in Bolivia (Barragán 1992). In Bolivia, a common modification to the term chola is *cholita*, which people claim is "softer."[6] The widespread public presence of marketwomen/cholas across the Andes provides a screen on which many caricatures are played—they have been portrayed as nationalist symbols, archetypal mothers, sexually degenerate, or witches, depending on the viewer and his or her interpretation (Weismantel 2001).

Organized into subgroups within the marketplace, marketwomen's solidarity along gender, class, "racial," and occupation lines has allowed them a degree of power in the political realm as well. Concerned with documenting Andean women's historical roles, Laura Gotkowitz demonstrates how a group of marketwomen, known as Las Hijas del Pueblo, influenced the celebration of Cochabamba war heroines, recasting them as "humble market women" (2000:229). Perhaps due to the very real political power that cholitas sometimes wield, the contemporary image of them has been celebrated, sexualized, politicized, and appropriated by male politicians in various instances (Albro 2000). The image of the tough, nononsense, "saucy," and sometimes very well-off cholita-businesswoman is one that is commented on throughout popular Bolivian society.[7] Although not all of the vendors I discuss are female, this notion of the marketplace—as a site of brokerage between urban and rural spheres and people—is heavily influenced by the preponderance of female marketers and their image as cholitas. Many of the vendors

---

6. A diminutive of "chola" that is not used derogatorily in the way "chola" or "cholo" may be, "cholita" is used to refer to an urban mestiza with rural roots in modern-day Bolivia. By contrast, in 1765 it was associated solely with domestic workers (Barragán 1992:111). In contemporary times, the term "cholita" might not only "soften" the designation, but also seek to disempower the status associated with the women who bear this label.

7. This topic is analyzed in detail by Weismantel (2001), especially for Ecuador and Peru.

serve as intermediaries in a business sense, in that their wares come from rural suppliers with whom they have a social and economic relationship. Most vendors also have personal links to the countryside and relatives living there, and they interact with a wide array of customers, many of them closely tied to rural traditions.

Condeñas

My introduction to the Cochabamba marketplace came through Condeña vendors of traditional medicines. Having heard from villagers in Condo that some of their relatives sold medicines in Cochabamba, I originally traveled to the city to conduct a quick survey of vendors from my rural home. In 1995 I found them relatively quickly, but the next year I stumbled around the maze of the streets that make up the marketplace. Thinking I would be able to feel my way there—after all I had been there the year before—I wandered for a long while before finding their particular block. The approximately seven Condeña vendors situated there (among other vendors and storefronts) and their locations on the sidewalk along that short city block have remained almost constant from 1995 to 2002. Though part of a sprawling scene of vendors, these women are physically somewhat peripheral to the marketplace—they spread their wares on the sidewalk, and occupy a space outside and across the street from the established Calatayud Market.

These particular rural vendors represent a small segment of women from Condo who have used commerce as a way to supplement their agricultural livelihood.[8] During tin's heyday, many Condeñas sold merchandise such as food and medicine in mining centers. When the mining centers declined after the collapse of tin prices in the 1980s, the Cochabamba marketplace became a more popular destination. The Condeña vendors in Cochabamba typically got their start at the Huari and Challapata fairs, but recently some women have also traveled to many other locations: Potosí, Oruro, Santa Cruz, border towns (on the border of Bolivia and either Argentina or Brazil), and Cochabamba.

Of the overall group of traditional medicine vendors considered here, Condeñas are the most directly linked to the countryside. These women are recent migrants and usually dress like the altiplano women that they are, but they also blend into the crowds of more urbanized merchants who sell flowers, cheese, or general housewares on the same block as the Condeñas. Like the Cuzqueña vendors that Seligmann (1989) calls "in-between," they bridge the rural and urban worlds by offering altiplano herbs alongside a small selection of preassembled offerings (mesas) that are ready to be burned in supplication to the gods for a variety of purposes, and that are sought after by Cochabambinos.

From their location in the Cochabamba marketplace, Condeña vendors sell to whoever approaches them. Although the shoppers and passersby are a cross-section of Cochabamba society, the people who buy from the Condeñas tend to be either recent migrants (like the Condeñas themselves) or lower-class urbanites

---

8. These families often keep one foot in the country and one foot in the city, using their meager urban income to pay for agricultural items, for instance. Equipment, oxen, and other household goods will be bought with the money earned from these activities. These urban income earners are also likely to sponsor fiestas, as they can use their cash income to this end.

looking for a good bargain in the wares—the Condeñas who sell here offer their wares at reduced prices relative to women who sell mesas in the permanent stalls of the enclosed marketplaces. Their identities as rural women from the altiplano, which is easily discerned by their bowler hats and longer skirts (skirt lengths are shorter in Cochabamba), mark them as knowledgeable sources of information and healing advice, and these women subtly encourage and utilize these stereotypes. Their authority arises from the perception of them as businesswomen with healing knowledge, if not "healers." Several of these vendors claimed to know "many things that doctors do not." Although ten to twenty years ago Condeñas were more widely lauded for their knowledge of herbs and ailments, competition for customers and the presence of many new vendors and healers have diminished Condeñas' hold on this market niche. Some of the Condeñas who work in Cochabamba, however, have expanded their venues by traveling to sell traditional medicines—going to the more distant Huari fair, and also to Cochabamba's neighboring markets in Punata and Sacaba, for example. At those locales, they may still prescribe medicines and give advice.

Condeñas provision their stands by cultivating and maintaining their ties to rural areas. They return to Condo to attend at least one fiesta each year[9] and also appear in Condo when they travel to the Huari fair. The Condeña vendors from Cochabamba go to Huari to buy q'uwa, to trade with other Condeñas for other herbs, and, in some cases, to collect herbs themselves for their stands. At the same time they bring along the ingredients for mesas negras, which they offer for sale at the Huari fair. Many of the ingredients for these mesas come from the lowlands but are readily available in Cochabamba.

Herbalists

Across the street from the Condeñas in the Mercado Calatayud are the vendors of fresh herbs ('herbalists'), whose wares must be resupplied almost daily. In 2000 there were just two—Sara and Catalina—and their two adjacent stands both complemented and competed with each other. Sara has a good location and an airier atmosphere than the more crowded stalls of the Q'uweras in La Pampa. She has quite a few regular *caseras* (clients), but given the presence of her neighbor-vendor who sells the same plants and products that she does, Sara must compete for customers. Both vendors, however, benefit from the presence of a naturista just a block away who often refers customers to the herbalists when he prescribes the fresh plants his patients need to supplement his treatments.

Comparing her stand to those of other herbalists, Sara calls hers *más surtido* ("more varied"). She considers her business to be more stable than those of vendors such as the Condeñas because she has built up a steady clientele who rely on her and buy from her on a regular basis. Her contention appears to be apt from observation: I observed eighteen customers approach Sara's stand in a one-hour

---

9. Migrants such as these sponsor fiestas much more frequently than Condeños who live in the village year round, because migrants have more funds. For instance, Eliana, a Condeña vendor in Cochabamba, told me that she and her family had sponsored the fiesta of San Andrés the previous year in grand style.

FIGURE 6.3   A corner of Sara's stand, showing the fresh plants on display.

period, and fifteen of them purchased something from her. By contrast, one of the Condeña vendors had just one or two sales in an hour on a similar day.

Sara has been selling at this location for approximately fifteen years. Although she learned her trade mostly from her mother, she also learns from her customers, an important component of *medicina popular* ("medicine of the people"). Her herbs—chamomile, aloe vera, plantago, eucalyptus, and mint, among many others—are piled in big mounds around the perimeter of her stall, which is a permanent metal kiosk within the confines of the marketplace that can be locked up at night. (The marketplace is guarded at night by private security guards.) The twenty to thirty fresh plants she offers for sale are the most visible wares, but in the interior of her stand Sara also has dried plants, packets of teas and herbal preparations, and even a telephone that shoppers can pay to use.

Sara calls out to passersby who seem to be eyeing the herbs—"Sí, caballero? Que le vendo, reina?" ("Yes, sir? What can I sell you, Queen?") She signals a degree of respect as she speaks to her potential customers in this way—in general her customers come from the middle class, and she defers to them. Occasionally an upper-class client or tourist wanders by, typically owing to her location on the edge of the marketplace closest to the city's main plaza, and even Quechua-speaking peasants may come her way.

Photo by Lynn Sikkink

F I G U R E 6.4 Catalina's stand, offering fresh herbs for sale.

The herbalists provision themselves a little differently than do Condeña vendors. Sara and Catalina rely on their rural suppliers—campesina plant collectors—to supply their wares. They must buy plants on almost a daily basis because their customers look for freshness above all else when considering which herbs to buy. Sara may occasionally buy from other itinerant vendors, but mainly she has long-term relationships with particular wholesale vendors. These wholesale plant vendors are mostly women—Sara buys from very few men. The cottage industry representatives of prepared medicines (from companies such as Coincoca) also come around every three to four months; these distributors are mostly men.

Q'uweras

As described at the opening of this chapter, Q'uweras sell from permanent kiosks within the marketplace proper, like the vendors of fresh herbs. In contrast, however, the Q'uweras occupy a regular zone in La Pampa where some twenty-five to thirty vendors sell similar wares. Although the Q'uwera section is large and established, it is not visible. The Q'uweras are tucked away between tailors, condiment sellers, and coca vendors within a maze of aisles. To find them the first time, one needs to be determined, and to be willing to ask directions several times.

Photo by Lynn Sikkink

FIGURE 6.5 *Q'uwera* section of La Cancha marketplace.

The individual stands are cluttered with an eclectic mix of products along with household items, illustrating the "marketplace as home" look.

Esmeralda, whose stand was described earlier (see Figure 6.1), grew up in the Q'uwera section of the marketplace; her mother was a vendor there, as was her grandmother. Her grandmother didn't have a proper stand—she sold dried plants and ingredients for mesas in the Mercado Calatayud, where she displayed them on the ground, just as the Condeñas do today.[10] Esmeralda's mother acquired a spot in La Pampa and focused her selling on charcoal (used in the braziers in which people burn their ritual offerings). On the side she also sold mesas. Esmeralda inherited both the market space and her mother's caseras, and she has been selling in the marketplace for approximately thirty years.

Esmeralda's stand is a three-part arrangement, which reflects the chronological progression through her wares: first the charcoal stand of her mother; second her own large stand, filled with mesas and their ingredients; and third the "new wing" consisting of dried herbs and natural medicine products, which reflects the influence and work of her daughter. Esmeralda's daughter Maribel, following in her mother's footsteps, had a stand nearby in La Pampa until she began to study natural medicine at the local institute, at which point she opened up her own shop on a street along the far edge of the marketplace. Esmeralda sells the q'uwas that this section of the marketplace is named for, but she likes to be able to offer the other traditional medicines and cures, as well as the charcoal her customers buy on the same shopping trips as the mesa ingredients.

---

10. Esmeralda's story illustrates the life cycle of vending through the generations as it moves from a more itinerant stage to the acquisition of a permanent stand. This process may take place in a shorter span of time, too. Nevertheless, although Condeñas may dream of this possibility, it is unlikely they will be able to afford it.

Photo by Sarah Linn Gallardo

F I G U R E 6.6 Plate of cake and fake money.

At Esmeralda's stand in Cochabamba, the customer first encounters stacks of prepared mesas, on which are balanced particularly elaborate offerings containing large sugar-figurines of the houses, cars, and frogs that are used in supplications (houses and cars are frequently sought; frogs indicate a general request made to the "Earth Mother" or *Pachamama*).[11] Beyond the mesas and surrounding them are the ingredients Esmeralda uses in assembling the offerings or that she adds at the time of the ritual: small stamped tiles, various candies, yellow Scotch broom flowers, rosemary, cinnamon, yellow and black incense, copal, llama fat, wine, and cane alcohol. These items, along with the prepared mesas, occupy approximately 80 percent of her stand. Alongside them, she offers a variety of packages of herbal mixes for various ailments, as well as incense and charms. Amidst her splendid array of wares is a telephone, a television set (usually on), and stools for herself, her family members, or visitors. Adding to the home-like quality of her stand, Esmeralda

---

11. Esmeralda prepares many kinds of mesas: "white," "black," "for the souls," for "luck," and for "glory"—the last aimed at Catholic saints whose representations are included in the stamped tiles. All of these mesas can be modified and customized to individual needs.

shares snacks and meals with those assembled, and takes care of a niece's baby who is often be found there, sleeping in a quiet corner.

To replenish the wares they sell, Q'uweras would not need to travel very far, as they are targets of traditional medicine middlemen. However, as a means of controlling the quality of their products and keeping costs down, Q'uweras do sometimes travel to buy material for their inventory, and to sell at the same time. For example, Esmeralda goes to the Huari fair as often as she can, particularly because q'uwa is so cheap there.

Q'uwa is the foundation and key ingredient of many ritual assemblages, which is why the vendors who specialize in ritual ingredients in Cochabamba are metonymically referred to as Q'uweras. Because q'uwa's fragrance adds a special aroma to the burnt offerings it accents, it is sometimes even referred to as "incense." The gods for whom burnt offerings are intended appreciate its pleasant scent.[12] Because the bulk of q'uwa sold in the marketplace in Cochabamba comes from Chile and enters Bolivia at the Huari fair, it is an important part of the particular assemblages that originate on the southern altiplano and radiate into other areas of Bolivia, such as Oruro, Cochabamba, and, to a lesser extent, Villazón.

The trade of q'uwa through the Condo region began a few generations back, and some Condeños took advantage of their location in this exchange trajectory, becoming q'uwa merchants. Natalio told me how his grandfather was a *comerciante* (merchant) of q'uwa. The grandfather traveled to Chile to buy q'uwa, which he took to Potosí to sell. Instead of then buying goods in Potosí (which would be a more common trading pattern), he used the money to buy more q'uwa in Chile and to continue the cycle of buying and selling. Natalio remembers that his grandfather brought back food from Chile for the household when he made his buying trips there: "My grandparents fed themselves from Chile. They ate flour, corn, and olives from there." Today, the q'uwa in Huari is transported across the salt flats in Bolivia, where it can be brought in as *contrabanda* that is not taxed. Q'uweras are vitally interested in this trade, attempting to get q'uwa as close to its source as possible. In 2000 Esmeralda did not go to the Huari fair—"because of the crisis," she said—but it is the main trip that she and other Q'uweras set their sights on in a given year.

Q'uweras' customers are more likely to be urbanites than the other visitors to the Cochabamba vendors, and middle- and even upper-class people who would probably not buy their wares from the Condeña vendors. These customers seek out the more established and comfortable business places of the marketplace, while at the same time attempting to "buy into" the ritual knowledge that Q'uweras are believed to possess. The daily pace of business is slower at the Q'uweras' stands than

---

12. Different varieties of q'uwa are used on the altiplano, depending on the type of mesa and the availability of certain kinds of plants. Fernández Juárez (1995:233 and personal communication, March 5, 2003) indicates that in Omasuyos, Ingavi, and the city of La Paz, *q'uwa wira* ("red q'uwa") is the preferred variety for mesas dedicated to the *achachilas* ("ancestors" or divinities of sacred places) or *Pachamama* ("Earth Mother"). For black mesas, *q'ili q'uwa* or *t'ika q'uwa* ("flower q'uwa") are preferred. In general, q'uwa is sought as the basis for many mesas—in La Paz and El Alto, ritual assemblages are called *q'uwachas* or *q'uwachada*, which emphasizes the essential importance of q'uwa in the mix, and the fact that the other ingredients are built on this core item, which represents the main ingredient of the offering.

at the herbalists' stands, except at certain times of the year when demand is great, such as at Carnival, when many people buy mesas for special libations (*ch'allas*).

Cottage Industries

Cottage industries based on traditional medicines sell their products in the form of pills, extracts, or syrups, catering to a more sophisticated clientele who are interested in herbal cures in a newer, more pharmaceutical form. Two companies based in Cochabamba provide further examples of the range of vendors of traditional medicine. One company, Aleph, has several storefronts in Cochabamba and distributes its wares throughout Bolivia. Its products include a large number of dried, packaged herbs—most of them meant to be used as herbal teas—and a line of popular cosmetics, based on plant extracts. Oriana, one of the founders, explained to me that her company was based on the belief in Bolivian customs and traditions, and that it had resurrected the "recipes"[13] in storage at the city's oldest pharmacy to begin experimentation. This business is obviously very different in scale from the vendors in the marketplace, but is operated nonetheless as a family business that employs workers to help in production, distribution, and sales. This cottage industry is not only home based in a production sense, but also in its business ethos—drawing on old recipes, and based in the tradition of herbal remedies. In summary, the business promotes itself as supplying the family lore of traditional medicine, albeit on a larger scale.

A second cottage industry, Coincoca, is also based in Cochabamba, although the father of the current owner founded it in the lowlands. Marlena picked up her father's ideas and business when he died, and has successfully managed Coincoca ever since, despite many obstacles. She is a successful middle-class businesswoman, though she describes herself as "coming from poverty." Coincoca products are based on coca extract, as Marlena's father believed fervently in the curative powers of coca, and the products are combined with Andean medicinal plants.[14] Coincoca is run out of Marlena's house, and she manages it almost single-handedly.

Coincoca's products are geared toward the sorts of ailments that naturistas commonly treat, such as diabetes, prostate problems, and "nerves." One of its most popular products is actually a potion for dieters called *jarabe antiobésico* ("anti-obesity syrup"). A product such as cough syrup costs approximately half of what a pharmaceutical cough syrup goes for at the drugstore, so Marlena considers her products "economical." Unlike Aleph, Coincoca does not have its own storefronts. Its products can be found in venues ranging from Sara's herbalist stand to some of the many national pharmacies, which now sell "natural products" alongside their biomedical pharmaceuticals.

---

13. *Receta* in Spanish also means "prescription." In this case, "recipe" seems nearer Oriana's meaning. These recipes give instructions for making medicines and cosmetics, which Oriana claims are based on European traditions maintained by women, but probably incorporate many Bolivian plants and notions of healing as well.

14. Coca, the main ingredient in all Coincoca products, is considered by Bolivians to have medicinal qualities alongside its use as a stimulant. It is generally not sold in medicine stands, but rather at the stands of coca vendors who specialize in its sale. (See Chapter 7 for an examination of coca and coca medicines.)

F I G U R E 6.7   Some of Coincoca's products, packaged for a variety of ailments.

In general, these cottage industries illustrate a point made by Dandler: Given current economic conditions and the strategies people must adopt to support the family, it is not always possible to differentiate between the economy of the domestic unit and the business (1987:650). In contrast to the other types of vendors found in the Cochabamba marketplace, the founders of the cottage industries are more business oriented, presenting themselves as entrepreneurs. Making prepared medicines from traditional medicines is a fairly new business niche. Thus, unlike some of the other vendors already described, these entrepreneurs got into the business by breaking with the past. One of the founders had a successful career in television reporting prior to her entry into the business; her husband did have experience in business, however.

Interestingly, although these businesses are new to them, their owners emphasize that they are helping to rescue past knowledge and traditions by selling herbal products. They do so by studying the ancient lore of traditional medicines (through books and by contact with country folk). In a similar vein, one entrepreneur has been involved in a building restoration project (of a colonial hacienda) while launching a line of new traditional medicines. That their herb suppliers are peasants from the countryside (mostly women), who regularly come to the hacienda gates selling their wares, underscores the marked class difference in their positions, and harkens back to older class structures that persist in modern-day Bolivia.

The people who buy the products distributed by Coincoca and Aleph are middle- to upper-class Bolivians, as the prices for these items are higher than for unprocessed herbs. The cottage-industry products also target more "urban" ailments, such as diabetes, cancer, high blood pressure, and heart problems. At Coincoca, Marlena prides herself on offering her products at affordable prices, however. She describes her customers as people of the upper middle class, to whom she sells mainly through distributors and representatives. Likewise, some of the herbs for sale at Aleph are within the reach of poorer people, although in general the company's stores cater to people with more money. They offer, for instance, spa-like facial treatments and cosmetic consultation.

HEALING AND THE MORALITY OF MARKETPLACE EXCHANGE

Because of the system of values and beliefs in which traditional medicines are embedded, selling traditional medicines in the marketplace is very different from selling bananas or shoes. In their book *Money and the Morality of Exchange* (1989), Jonathan Parry and Maurice Bloch argue that although all systems make it possible for people to pursue monetary gain in an honorable way, these activities are subordinate to goals of long-term reproduction within particular cultural contexts. Cultures ultimately convert monetary exchange into something that is socially meaningful, and the articulation between monetary and nonmonetary exchanges is culturally defined.

In Bolivia (as elsewhere), the commercialization of healing, through the vending of products and services in the marketplace, has converted what was once a nonmonetary activity into something to be shopped for, bargained over, and consumed. Instead of simply transforming traditional medicines into simple commerce, however, vendors of traditional medicines maintain aspects of the moral economy of healing. They do so by displaying the rural and home origins of products. For instance, vendors emphasize these aspects by calling their products "home remedies" and providing homey advice about how to use them, evoking images of a sphere where reciprocity and emotional concerns are more important than money. Morality is enacted in the marketplace exchanges through the beliefs of both vendors and customers about the sources of health and well-being, and their desires to heal and be healed. That is, although the vendors sell remedies and explain their uses, the cures are part of a moral or religious system to which the vendor, the customer, or both adhere.

In part, traditional medicine works for people because they perceive it to be a potent product of the past, with a higher moral foundation than biomedicine. Traditional medicine is based in Andean beliefs about Pachamama, sacred geography, deities, and the efficacy of rituals to heal people. This medical system also has roots in beliefs about the body and hot and cold systems (Foster 1994). The sale of traditional medicines in urban settings relies on and makes use of these belief systems, yet also transforms the beliefs in the process. For instance, cardo santo (*Argemone mexicana*) is referred to as an "ancient remedy" by one business-woman, but is used as an ingredient in a "cerebral tea" for students and professionals who require a stimulant. In all of the case studies of the vendors presented in this chapter, we see the link between Andean beliefs and new, yet still "traditional" medicine products.

Condeñas have found an economic niche in the sale of traditional medicines in the Cochabamba marketplace, albeit a very modest one. To compete in this growing market, they rely on their links with relatives in the countryside and their own ability to collect plants in their rural home as a way to make a living in this business. In contrast, the rural connections they apply to utilitarian ends are viewed quite differently by their customers. Condeñas are recognized as women from the altiplano, which gives them a position of authority and implies they have a connection to the ancestors who used traditional medicine. In being associated with rural beliefs and authenticity, Condeñas gain a slight moral authority (and foothold) in their section of the marketplace.

The vendors of fresh herbs take a different route to their knowledge. They learn from those around them (including their mothers, who often got them started), and they study on their own. For instance, Sara reads booklets about herbal medicine and offers these booklets for sale as well. Although she is interested in the classes in natural medicine offered at a nearby institute, she hasn't pursued this study. Her neighbor, Catalina, claimed to know all the information already—"I know it by heart"—and felt no need to take courses. Sara gains her edge through being a hard worker who has a flair for selling—she talks her customers through the sales and she waylays the "window shoppers." One customer told me how much she appreciates Sara, because Sara "knows so much"—which is why this customer has bought from her for years. Both Sara and Catalina often sell to the customers sent their way by the naturistas. They provide a wonderful service for people who believe in the healing power of plants. Engaging each other or me in conversation at Sara's stand, customers offer up short testimonials for natural remedies. Gesturing to Sara's piles of plants, one man said, "With this, there's no need to go to the doctor." In this way the customers share many of the beliefs ascribed to the vendors of traditional medicines; there is a shared assumption in the efficacy of the cures, and in their inherent goodness.

In contrast to the services of Condeña vendors and the vendors of fresh medicines, Q'uweras offer ritual services to their clients. These customers may pay for them to perform a ritual using the mesas and q'uwas that they sell, and in this way the Q'uweras augment their sales. In Esmeralda's case, her abilities as a ritualist come to her through her family genealogy of vending ritual ingredients. During the week of Carnival, when Cochabambinos perform libations and burn offerings for their homes, offices, businesses, new lots, vehicles, and market stalls, Q'uweras are called upon to help perform the rituals. The first Fridays of the month are considered auspicious days for offerings and, therefore, are a busy time for sales. Thus the "value added" to the Q'uweras' products not only is couched in terms of possible services, but also acknowledges that through their knowledge of the ingredients the vendors add a more authentic touch—a legitimizing quality that helps to make the mesas more effective in the eyes of their customers. While many Q'uweras are now permanent residents of Cochabamba, they—like the Condeñas—are associated with an altiplano background; in fact, some even come from villages close to Condo. Consequently, they provide a direct link to rural traditions.

The founders of cottage industries have a different relationship to traditional medicine. As urbanites with urban families, they view traditional medicine as a legacy of their "ancestors." They perceive the past use of traditional medicines as a kind of "golden age." These businesspeople see that some of that knowledge has been "lost" and suggest that they are in the process of "recovering" it. The story of Coincoca, for instance, is intertwined with Marlena's and her father's position as Christians and their beliefs in the healing qualities of coca. In describing her products, Marlena talks about coca as the "sacred leaf" of the Incas and expresses nostalgia about a past that she hopes to honor with her products. She also discusses contemporary misperceptions of coca, which were responsible for eradication programs she perceives as unjust, and hopes that Bolivians in general will regain an appreciation for coca's curative powers.

The founder of Coincoca sets her work within the context of her religious beliefs. Marlena's work, in her own mind, is based in something of a contradiction. At first, she could not resolve her Christian beliefs with the use of coca, which is condemned by church and state because it is the source of cocaine. Although she hasn't completely reconciled the use of coca as a healing plant with her Christian beliefs, she has become a fervent advocate. Discussing her work, she "witnesses" for coca by campaigning for its acceptance. Her faith is an integral part of her work, rather than a separate facet of her personality and lifestyle.

SUMMARY

The sale of traditional medicines in the Cochabamba marketplace is a relatively recent phenomenon. Even in the 1900s, these medicines were not widely accepted in public places, and thus their public sale grew out of more clandestine marketplace operations. In more recent times, the vendors of traditional medicines in the Cochabamba marketplace have become specialized, in that they sell particular ingredients or items that are part of a larger inventory. Some vendors emphasize fresh plants, some peddle ritual items, and some bring items from their rural homes into the bustling urban marketplace, as is the case with some Condeña vendors. Nonetheless, all of the stands are "blends" of some sort in that they are new arrangements of traditional medicines. While the exchange relationship between seller and buyer may be less personal than most interactions found in rural marketplaces, the vendors of traditional medicines still draw on the moral quality of their products in that they form part of a larger traditional healthcare system. The vendors perceive that they are not selling mere products, but items that will help cure illness. Consequently, they position themselves as healing authorities— for instance, through their link to rural identities. Although their work is unquestionably economic, most vendors have a sense of being called to perform the work they do, which allies them with the work of healers.

7

Coca, Coca Medicines, and the Dilemma of Coca in the Andes and Beyond

INTRODUCTION: COCA AS DRUG/COCA AS SACRED

Coca leaf provides a case study for examining how a traditional medicine and, in this instance, "sacred leaf" has been transformed into different commercial products with vastly different meanings and uses. The case study of coca illustrates how the flow of ideas and meanings between resource center, traditional user, and consumer has linked Andean rural and urban areas in specific ways. Additionally, the exploitation of coca as a resource has linked the Andes with the Western world in conflictive commercial ties. Although the story of coca commercialization has many chapters, not all of them implicated in the current "war on drugs," in contemporary times a growing array of coca-based consumer products has become available for sale in Andean marketplaces and pharmacies, paralleling coca's use as the raw material for the drug market.

The appeal of the new (legal) coca-based products is linked to their traditional uses in Andean medical practices. For instance, the popularity of a product such as coca toothpaste draws on ethnomedical beliefs in the benefits of coca to the teeth and gums. Similarly, a variety of coca medicines have become quite common owing to coca's multiple uses as a digestive, stimulant, headache reliever, blood-fortifier, and so on. Coca-based cough syrups, tonics, vitamins, and "anti-obesity" potions are readily available for sale in the open-air marketplaces of Bolivia, but can also be purchased from some conventional pharmacies. This history, which stretches back to the 1800s, illustrates the changing ecology of coca leaf, the appropriation of medical ideas and products, and the production of new and hybrid treatments. In the early 1900s, for example, coca greatly surpassed other agricultural products (including coffee, corn, and cocoa) as the leading export item in Bolivia (Soux 1993:37).

As a way to begin the exploration of coca's use in new commercial products, it is useful to examine its principal dichotomy: at home in traditional Andean contexts, and as the source of an illegal drug. The chasm between these two realms was brought home to me upon my first return from the Andes, when I brought home a small bag of coca leaf. On my entry through U.S. customs in Miami, I noticed that the customs inspector seemed to be able smell its presence with his hands. He opened my duffle bag, went straight to its buried heart, opened one plastic bag, and then pulled out another that contained a small bundle of coca leaves, a souvenir from my one-year stay in Cuzco, Peru. It was my first trip to South America, and I had gone as an exchange student. During my stay I had lived with a large extended Peruvian family and attended the small university in Cuzco, where I studied Inca archaeology, rural sociology, and anthropology. The experience launched my long fascination with Andean culture—but that day in the airport, I was sweating my immediate fate.

I knew even then that it was illegal to bring coca leaves into the country. The crime didn't carry the same weight as transporting cocaine, but it wasn't allowed—even coca tea bags could not be imported—and at that naive age I wasn't sure what might happen to me for breaking import laws. The customs official asked me what I intended to do with the leaves. I nervously answered that I had wanted to make tea, to share "mate de coca" with my family in Minnesota. At that point he smiled, adding that coca was good for stomach problems and that his grandmother swore by it. It turned out that he was Colombian by birth, and had grown up knowing about the medicinal virtues of coca. "It's great for altitude sickness," I added, "and headaches." He nodded and we ritually exchanged an abbreviated list of the benefits of coca, as I warmed to the topic with relief. Not only did he let me go, but he repacked the coca leaves for me, apparently assured that they would be made into tea and not processed for the potential minute quantity of cocaine contained therein. Although I felt very lucky, and my mother later commented (with some exasperation), "You kids seem to be protected by a guardian angel," I suspect that this was not an unusual scene.

Americans routinely bring back coca from their travels to Peru, Ecuador, and Bolivia, most often in tea bags that hardly fit the ominous description of "controlled substance." Although they may be warned against this practice, there are probably thousands of boxes of coca leaf tea sitting in cupboards around the country. Most Americans, however, due to the U.S. government's "war on drugs," equate the plant with cocaine. Even though the Drug Enforcement Agency (DEA) and other international organizations now recognize that coca use is harmless, the International Narcotics Convention refused Bolivia's request in 1992 to strike it from its list of prohibited substances (Mayer 2002:194).

When I teach my Introduction to Anthropology course, my students read an ethnographic account about coca and culture in the Andes (Allen 1988). Trying to head off their knowing looks (and occasional nervous sniggers) when it comes to coca use, I begin with a lecture that explains the difference between coca and cocaine (which includes a footnote about the difference between coca and cocoa, too!). I tell them that coca provides a "pick-me-up" for chewers, along with small amounts of vitamins and minerals that enhance the diets of many Andeans, besides its being an important part of Andean social and ritual life.

Coca might have continued to live alongside tea leaves and coffee beans in popular usage and history had it not been for the isolation of the alkaloid cocaine from its juice in 1860. In fact, the coca leaf contains fourteen alkaloids, and some evidence shows that the fourteenth alkaloid—cocaine—is destroyed by the chewer's saliva (Burchard 1976). Some of coca's other effective alkaloids are responsible for the slight numbness in the mouth and boost in energy that coca-chewers experience.

Even after hearing this information from their professor, however, not all of my students are convinced, a measure of the insidious nature of the drug war's rhetoric in the United States. I want my students to see that coca use has another, entirely different face. I discovered this fact myself in my anthropological field-work in the Andes.

Ten years after the incident in the Miami airport, I had once again returned to the Andes to conduct doctoral research for my degree in cultural anthropology. I was living on the southern altiplano of Bolivia, in an arid region on the same latitude with the Atacama Desert and some 300 kilometers due west of it. "Conducting anthropological fieldwork" eluded me most days, however, as some of my colleagues also admit about their fieldwork. Ethnographic research seemed to hinge on small flashes of understanding that came from just being there, and which provided direction for future research.

One of these flashes came the first time I entered the Catholic church on the eve of a Saint's Day. The interior of Condo's rustic colonial church was painted several shades of vivid blue and pink, and on this night it was ablaze with candles, placed there by congregants. San Pedro, the town's patron saint, was at the head of this Catholic display. People entered and sat quietly, either on the tiled floor in front of the saints or in the pews beyond. It was a cold winter night in June, and inside the drafty church we were all bundled up. From beneath layers of clothing, people began to produce coca bags and to offer small handfuls to the other people assembled. Having been forewarned, I too took out a small bag of coca and of-fered it to my neighbors. At first, through this immediate reciprocity, the amount in my bag stayed roughly the same. Gradually, we all began to "chew" our coca (actually it is "sucked," as only the juice of the leaves is swallowed). As the worshipers circulated their coca, they also began smoking cigarettes and passing around small bottles of alcohol.

This scenario does not at first convey the solemnity of the religious occasion. In reality, all of this activity was carried out in the spirit of an offering: The smoke rises to the saints and gods, the alcohol is sprinkled on the ground for Pachamama (the "Earth Mother"), and, eventually, the spent coca quid is tossed on the floor as an offering. Instead of a party-like atmosphere (though some of the alcohol is also drunk), people for the most part are quiet and in prayer. Coca is shared with the other participants and shared with the gods in a social act that draws all together. Although it does not seem to be a particularly Catholic scene, this event depicts the unique form Catholicism takes in this part of Latin America: part Catholicism brought from Spain, part Andean nature worship. For one of the church's worshipers this syncretism is not experienced as two strata from totally distinct belief systems, but rather as a seamless meaningful whole. That coca has a place in these Andean Catholic rituals attests to its enduring role in social and religious activities. In this context, coca is sacred.

From the double vantage points of the Miami airport and the rural Bolivian church, we see that coca is simultaneously a "drug" and an important element of traditional Andean culture. There is no way to reconcile these two perspectives, as one comes from a position that views coca only as the raw material for cocaine and the other from a tradition in which coca is considered "divine" and a "gift from the gods." Nevertheless, it is worthwhile to keep in mind coca's origins and the myriad ways it has been used over the long span of Andean history (and prehistory). Coca's use within Andean society today is also in flux—its medicinal qualities are being refashioned and commercialized, in direct opposition to the rhetoric that translates coca into "cocaine." In Bolivia, traditional medicine cottage industries employ coca as an ingredient in an array of products for the modern consumer. The sale of these coca products in pharmaceuticals within a country like Bolivia might be the key to coca's future acceptance by a wider audience, including the international community.

COCA IN THE ANDEAN COUNTRYSIDE:
TRADITIONAL USES OF COCA

The scientific name for coca, *Erythroxylum coca L.*, is based on the common name by which it is called throughout the Andes. "Coca" is more accurately rendered as "kuka" or sometimes "kuka kuka" (e.g., Ayala Loayza 1988; De Lucca and Zalles 1992; Huidobro Bellido 1986) because of its pronunciation in Quechua or Aymara.

Coca has myriad uses, many of which overlap. Foremost among them, coca has a time-honored place as an ingredient in the medical system, both as a medicine and as an ingredient of ritual, ranging from general rituals to those dealing specifically with health. Coca's medicinal uses have always been somewhat secondary to its uses in ritual or as a stimulant, or perhaps it is more accurate to say that its medicinal uses are part and parcel of its other uses. When coca is chewed, its juices are said to help stomachaches, diarrhea, and chilblains (De Lucca and Zalles, 1992:161). Topically, it is applied to the temples as treatment for headaches or "air" (*aire*, a common folk illness throughout Latin America); alternatively, the leaves can be steeped in alcohol and used as a rub for rheumatism (De Lucca and Zalles, 1992).

In the southern altiplano community of San Pedro de Condo, coca use is neither as prevalent as it is in certain parts of the Andes (such as in the yungas where coca is grown—see Spedding 2005) nor as restricted as it is in very isolated regions where coca is a scarce commodity. Coca is, however, an integral part of life, and it plays a special role during both rituals and fiestas.[1] Its use throughout much of Andean social life, and in so many different contexts, has led anthropologists to characterize coca as a "leitmotif" of culture in general in the Andes (Allen 1988). Looking at one rural community on the southern altiplano, it is easy to discern that coca has an important role to play in many aspects of daily life. As in other parts of the Andes, in Condo coca has three principal uses: in ritual, in work, and in medicine.[2]

An average coca leaf chewer uses approximately one ounce of coca per day (Morales 1989:13). Coca leaves may be carried in small woven pouches, called

Photo by Lynn Sikkink

F I G U R E 7.1 At a ceremony in Condo, during which the staffs of office are passed from the old authority to the new one, coca is a quid in the mouth of all participants. The small bags people carry also contain coca leaves.

1. As stated by one Aymara healer: "La coca es el sello de todos nuestros pactos, el auto sacramental de todas nuestras fiestas, el manjar de todas nuestras bodas, el consuelo de todos nuestros duelos y tristezas, la salva de todas nuestras alegrías" ("Coca is the stamp on all our pacts, the sacramental vehicle of all our fiestas, the special dish of all our weddings, the consolation of all our griefs and sadness, the start of all our joys") (P"axsi Limachi, 1983).

2. This division is not absolute, obviously. For example, people use coca ritually at the beginning of the planting season, when fields are "opened" for sowing. Here, its uses in work and in ritual intertwine.

ch'uspas, or in folded cloths, pockets, or plastic bags. Coca chewing may be simple or part of an elaborate ritual, solitary or social, but in general requires at a minimum a meditative moment and certain ritualized steps. In the same way that food or any other gift is received from another person, coca will be taken with two hands—to hold out only one hand would be disrespectful.

The coca-chewer settles in, and begins by selecting coca leaves, one by one. Holding the leaves between the fingers, the chewer often makes a small blessing or prayer, murmuring an incantation to God, the Earth Mother, a patron saint, or local deities and places. The blessing is said over the leaves, a practice sometimes referred to as *phukuy* ("blowing") in Quechua, and described by Catherine Allen (1988) and Edumundo Morales (1989). Allen (1988) notes that in the community of Sonqo, Peru, chewers frequently make a tripartite incantation, invoking places from abstract to near—for instance, beginning with the Earth Mother, followed by a mention of Sonqo, and ending with the name of local shrine of importance to the particular individual.

Before the coca is chewed, the stems are removed from the leaves; the soft parts of the leaves are then tucked into the cheek to form a quid or bolus. When the leaves are adequately dampened within the mouth, the chewer may add *llipta* ("lime") or anything else suitably alkaline, sometimes even bicarbonate of soda. Llipta is a homemade product that is obtained by first burning quinoa stalks, plantain, or other plants and then forming the residual ash into balls. The addition of llipta to the quid aids in the release of the alkaloids.

Hurtado (1995) explains what happens next: "A few minutes later, there is an intense anesthetic effect on the mucosa next to the bolus and also in the cheeks, throat and tongue. It is certain that the ingestion of the juice exerts an anesthetic effect on the lower intestinal tract and at the systemic level." The green alkaloid juice is swallowed, and when it is gone, the quid can be renewed with more coca leaves and more lime. Eventually the quid is discarded, and the chewer begins anew.

When I first arrived to do fieldwork in Condo, I was visited by an old *yatiri* (a ritual specialist—literally "he who knows") who insisted on reading my coca leaves. In this role the yatiri acts as a diviner, by "throwing" the leaves—depending on their arrangement and color, the yatiri is able to glean facts about one's future. To do so, Don Fermín came to my house, spread a small cloth on the ground in front of him, and on its surface began to toss the leaves, blending them into the picture that would reveal my fate. In my case he foresaw me having to do things twice—a prediction that later rang true as I stayed into my second year of fieldwork, rechecking data.

Ritual specialists throughout Bolivia and the Andes use coca to "read" the problems of the client or patient and to find a way to help the individual; in this way, coca serves as a transmitter and as an assistant to the ritual specialist (Allen 1988, Fernández Juárez 1999). The use of coca in divination of all sorts is important to people in all walks of life and backgrounds, and even today it is possible to have one's coca read in the streets of La Paz, Oruro, or Cochabamba. The person who comes to the ritual specialist may wish to know the reason for an illness or inquire into a different problem. People may want to have their coca

FIGURE 7.2 "Famous Healer" sign from Cochabamba marketplace: the coca leaves with the husband's and wife's names on them indicate that they are adept at reading coca leaves and diagnosing problems.

read for very specific and utilitarian reasons. For instance, the señora with whom I lived in the countryside had her coca leaves read several times after her house was robbed, as a way to discern the identity and location of the thieves.

Another way that coca is used ritually is in various sorts of offerings. It has a place of honor in some mesas (ritual assemblages), such as the mesa for Pachamama or the ritual mesa "para Gloria" (supplication for protection of the sky; Martínez 1987). For the Pachamama mesa, the coca leaves are carefully selected and "stood on their feet" around the edge of the offering like a border. Each coca leaf may contain a special request from the supplicant to the Pachamama (Fernández 1997:153). By comparison, the Gloria mesa brings together certain smells, tastes, and visual cues of ritual importance (Martínez 1987). In Condo, the local yatiri Don Fermín also used coca in a mesa he prepared for me to bring "luck." Both coca leaves and q'uwa were used in the preparation of the mesa and were burned as a *despacho* ("send off"/offering) after the ingredients had been assembled and we had given the proper libations. The exact arrangements of the ritual assemblages vary from place to place and are partly determined by the individual who prepares them.

In general, coca's role is to link the supplicant to the gods by using specifically chosen leaves to convey messages and ask for help. During the preparation of a ritual assemblage, which will be burned at the end of the ceremony, the participants also share coca and chew it together. They understand that just as people chew coca and enjoy it, so will the gods (Allen 1988). In sharing coca together, the human actors also express and model reciprocity as reciprocity is desired between humans and gods as well.

Coca's importance in work is well documented. Because it is a stimulant, coca helps people work longer and more readily, curbing their fatigue, hunger, and thirst. While working, some coca-chewers even go without a mid-day meal, preferring instead to continue to chew coca.[3] This plant's widespread use as an aid during hard labor probably dates back to the colonial era, when it was used extensively and intensively by the miners who worked long and difficult shifts underground, especially in the mines in city of Potosí, and later in the provinces of Potosí and Oruro (Gironda Cabrera 2000). Not only did miners chew coca, but they also offered coca and cigarettes to the guardian of their mine shafts (the uncle [*Tío*], also a devil figure), whose aid they sought in the highly dangerous situations involved in working far underground. The practice of leaving offerings to the Tío continued into the modern mining era (Nash 1979), and spread more widely to all forms of labor.

During agricultural work in Condo, some workers chew coca, while others do not. Nevertheless, it is considered as important to offer coca as it is to provide a good meal to those neighbors and relatives who are helping out, or to the hired help. The distribution of coca, and sometimes cigarettes and alcohol, may be a precisely calculated part of the relationship between the farmer seeking help and those helping out (Mayer 2002:178).

In comparison with coca's use in ritual and in work, its use as a medicine is less well documented. However, it is important to understand that its use in ritual is often related to health concerns, so any absolute distinction between ritual and medicine is an artificial one for this plant. As a medicine that is administered to a patient, coca has a number of applications: It may be chewed, drunk in tea, eaten in its charred form, used externally to "cleanse" a patient, or applied as a poultice (Alba and Tarifa 1993:284). Coca is considered to be good for the digestion, and some evidence suggests that it helps Andean people digest the prodigious quantities of potatoes they consume (Burchard 1978). It may also have a positive effect on the heart, nervous system, and circulatory system (Gironda Cabrera 2000:37). Although rural Andeans do not necessarily cite these precise effects, they do use coca for stomach problems and to "cleanse the blood"—prescriptions that hint at parallels with the biomedical claims made by

---

3. Obviously, coca does not replace food over the long term. The old arguments that coca-chewers are malnourished because they prefer coca have been disproved (see the rebuttals in Allen 1988 and Mayer 2002). Coca has been shown to be an effective dietary supplement, however, so it does have some nutritional value (Plowman 1984).

authors such as Gironda Cabrera (2000) and earlier sources beginning with Mortimer (1901).

In Condo, coca is used in tea, albeit sparingly, because it is expensive.[4] One leaf stuck to each temple marks a person as suffering from a headache. Coca is also used locally to ward off altitude sickness for those who ascend to the high valleys to pasture animals or look for medicinal herbs—and the quids may be left at the *apachetas* (rock cairns) that mark high mountain passes and the places where gods reside. From this example, we see coca's simultaneous use as a medicine, an aid to work, and a ritual offering to the gods.

Coca Medicines in Bolivia

Coca's ubiquitous use in the countryside, and the numerous ways in which people employ it, makes it a good candidate for an urban herbal remedy. Perhaps not surprisingly, in responding to the public's desire for new forms of old medicines, Andean cottage industries have begun to sell traditional medicines like coca in the form of pharmaceutical-like products. Several new Bolivian companies have sprung up that mass-produce their medicines for a clientele that is fascinated by the blend of old and new medicines and the chance to take care of their own health problems. For instance, maca, a highland tuber known for its multiple uses, is now marketed as the "Andean Viagra" because of its ability to combat prostate problems and its claims to enhance "sexual potency." A customer convinced of the efficacy of products such as maca is now able to take his dose of traditional medicine in a modern capsule, syrup, or tonic.[5]

This phenomenon is not altogether new, but rather is part of the long history of exchange and appropriation of medical ideas and products, and the production of hybrid treatments. This chapter focuses particularly on the use of coca in these hybrid treatments, for two reasons: (1) Coca has long been used to treat a great variety of ailments, and (2) the simple coca leaf has played such a huge role in medical and entrepreneurial history, and has an ongoing impact on world politics. Alongside selling coca leaf tea (which is a popular remedy even among tourists, as a way to combat altitude sickness), Bolivian cottage industries make use of coca extract as a basis for some of their remedies. One company—Coincoca—has even based its entire line of products on the blending of coca extract with various herbs. This company serves as a good example of the use of old medicines in new contexts, and it provides a good point of departure for a closer look at coca in its many historical forms and as an ingredient in a number of wide-ranging products.

Although coca leaf has most commonly been chewed by Andean farmers, herders, and travelers, it is also frequently made into a tea, a method of preparation that dates back centuries. Today coca has become more than a quid in the mouth of a rural dweller or a tea that tourists drink for altitude sickness: It is employed

---

4. To give an idea of its relative value in the marketplace, a pound of coca costs three times as much as a pound of mutton (1999 market prices, from Challapata and Oruro).

5. Today products such as maca and coca leaf tea can be purchased via the Web, which contributes to the internationalization of these sales and the corresponding medical ideas.

explicitly as an herbal cure for a host of ailments, including in some applications based on the standard rural cures outlined earlier. Also, as coca has moved from chew to prepared medicine, the health claims attached to it have moved from the more general to the specific. From the general claims emerging from its use in the countryside as an energy-booster and a suppressant of hunger and thirst, coca has been transformed into a remedy for chronic fatigue, sexual impotency, anemia, and depression. It is also used as a diet drug and an "anti-aging" compound. In prepared pharmaceutical-like concoctions, this plant is used in everything from cough syrups to weight reduction pills.

Some healers, who still adhere to traditional uses of coca and decry its commercialization as a cure-all, criticize the touting of coca as a panacea for all ailments. Says Dr. María Asturias, "People now claim that both maca and coca can cure everything—but it's not like that. We should be using them for their traditional purposes" (personal communication, June 25, 2002).

Coincoca (more formally, Coca Industrialization Company) is a Cochabamba-based company that is today run by the daughter of its founder, a man who was for most of his life an officer in the Bolivian military.[6] Marlena's father became convinced of the curative properties of coca by reading about it and by engaging in a process of empirical observation. Initially, he noticed that the farmers in his region who chewed coca were healthier; later, he began to advocate that everyone drink coca tea as a daily dietary supplement. In 1968 a Peace Corps volunteer left Marlena's father the classic tome *History of Coca* by W. Golden Mortimer (1901), a book that details coca's interesting history and persuasively advocates its widespread use. Coincoca finally got off the ground in 1987–1988 as a response to national initiatives for alternative uses for coca, as a way to counter the coca eradication campaigns.[7] The company's first products entered the market in 1989.

When Marlena discusses her father's conviction that he could mass-produce coca medicines, she admits that she thought him crazy at first. After Marlena read about coca and the scientific studies surrounding it, however, she came to describe it as the "sacred leaf" (as in the time of the Incas) and "powerful." She began to agree with her father that coca was both a food and a medicine, and together they perceived that their new company could be a vehicle to provide coca to people throughout Bolivia, and eventually (she hopes) to people in other countries. Marlena criticizes people who fail to understand the power of coca and who disparage it as a "drug plant." "It is so much more," she says. "How wonderful it would be if Bolivians would value their culture and say, 'Why did our ancestors use coca and call it the sacred leaf?'

---

6. This company was briefly described in Chapter 6 as an example of a traditional medicine cottage industry.

7. In 1961, President Paz Estenssoro's Uncía Convention called for a 25-year program to gradually reduce and eradicate coca leaf growing and harvesting operations. Subsequent administrations have continued and broadened these campaigns. In 1988, Law 1008 targeted the eradication of "illicit" coca (Gironda Cabrera 2000). In 2000, for instance, the government claimed to have eradicated 90 percent of the entire coca crop. Since then, the pace and tenor of demonstrations by coca growers (*cocaleros*) has intensified. Evo Morales, the 2002 pro-coca presidential candidate, lost the presidency by a slim margin, attesting to the degree of support behind this political bloc. Currently President, he has been able to press for many of his reforms, including better alternatives to coca eradication. Instead of focusing on the drug business, Morales sees the U.S.–Bolivian war on drugs as a war on the Quechua and Aymara people (Finnegan 2003:51).

Perhaps then we would use it as a food source and medicine, and help to solve the world's hunger problems." By providing coca in palatable forms to urbanites, Coincoca has played a role in helping to create a positive atmosphere for the acceptance of coca's contemporary place in the medical realm.

Coincoca today produces an astonishing array of products, which it distributes throughout Bolivia, and particularly in Cochabamba and Santa Cruz (see Figure 6.7 in Chapter 6). Many Bolivian pharmacies feature the products prominently. For example, if you ask for a cough syrup in a mainstream pharmacy in downtown Cochabamba, it is quite likely that you will be offered Coincoca's particular mix (including the ingredients coca, eucalyptus, and wira-wira, among others). Some of Coincoca's most popular products are its cough syrup, an " slimming" syrup, a detoxifier that is marketed as a "vesicular" product, and a tonic that fortifies the kidneys. The products are offered at prices below those of standard pharmaceuticals; for instance, the cough syrup sells at less than half the price of its pharmaceutical counterpart.

COCA WINE

One Coincoca product that sells less well, but is of interest to the discussion of old medicines used in new ways, is coca wine. This mix of an inexpensive red wine and coca extract is a conscious imitation of the famous Vin Mariani ("Mariani Wine") that was produced throughout the late 1800s and early 1900s and sold in Europe with wild success due to in part to its impressive marketing campaign. Vin Mariani may be held up as a particularly good example—and an early one—of the power of endorsements. It was promoted by doctors, two popes, and Sigmund Freud, and was used by Ulysses Grant at the end of his life to alleviate the pain of the throat cancer that eventually killed him. Scientists, musicians, and businessmen alike praised it. Angelo Mariani collected these endorsements, along with his commentary on the medicinal power of coca leaf, into wonderful little books that helped give Vin Mariani the scientific and social seal of approval that drove his sales. (See Mariani 1892, 1902, Mariani & Company 1896.) Mariani was an entrepreneur who came from a long line of doctors and chemists; he became an expert on the coca plant and its varieties, which he tested in his own Andean greenhouses.

Combining the particularly French ingredient of Bordeaux wine with a carefully expressed extract of coca (from the specific varieties of coca that he had tested and approved), Mariani (1892) produced a powerful and delicious stimulant with medical applications. His initial intent was to produce a medicinal tonic, but the wine soon became a very popular beverage in Europe, especially among those who suffered from a "fatigued and overweak body and brain." Thus the original recipe combined the pleasure of a good drink with the qualities of an energy tonic.[8] One enthusiastic doctor proclaimed, "Serum of Eternal Youth, you may stay in hiding from the research of microbiologists, now that we have Vin

8. In keeping with the makers of other proprietary medicines of the times, Mariani kept his recipe a secret. In 1886, a chemist reported that Vin Mariani contained 0.12 grains of cocaine per fluid ounce (Pendergrast 1993).

Mariani" (cited in Mariani 1902:26). Another endorsement noted, "Vin Mariani is an excellent tonic, an exquisite medicine; my children appreciate it also" (p. 28).

Vin Mariani's market success exceeded all expectations: The beverage was eventually produced in locations as exotic as France and Geneva, Alexandria (Egypt) and Saigon (Pendergrast, 1993:24). Its worldwide diffusion was aided greatly by the publication of Angelo Mariani's books—half empirical data to teach his customers about coca and half advertising for his "remedy par excellence." The combined commercial and literary aspects of Mariani's books had the effect of introducing coca to a huge number of people in non-Andean world, and creating an appreciation for this "ancient herbal remedy." Vin Mariani began to be prescribed throughout Europe in 1863, before cocaine was isolated from coca leaves. W. Golden Mortimer, whose *History of Coca* educated generations about coca and the history of the Incas, even dedicated his book to Angelo Mariani: "A Recognized Exponent of the 'Divine Plant' and the First to Render Coca Available to the World." Mariani, in turn, cites Golden's work.

FROM COCA WINE TO COCA-COLA

Because of its enormous commercial success, the combination of wine and coca extract was a much-imitated pharmaceutical product and tonic drink. Recognizing the threat to his business posed by the large number of imitators, Mariani was compelled to warn the public against them, claiming that the knock-offs were "disagreeable to the taste" and "without efficacy," and even "caused nausea, vomiting, etc." (Mariani & Company 1896:4). In this same publication, Mariani notes that six manufacturing druggists in New York City alone produced a coca wine preparation.

The most successful imitator in the United States was actually John Pemberton, who produced and sold "French Wine Coca." He claimed to have improved on the general formula by adding African kola nuts, "pure grape wine," and the dried leaf of *Turnera diffusa* (considered a tonic and aphrodisiac). Like Mariani, Pemberton advertised his coca wine as a curative for nervous disorders, digestive disturbances, and impotency (Pendergrast 1993:26).[9] His coca preparation sold well, especially in his hometown of Atlanta, but this success was short-lived due to the onset of Prohibition. Before the alcohol ban associated with Prohibition was imposed in Atlanta in -1908 Pemberton had begun experimenting with a "temperance drink" to take the place of his French Wine Coca. To make a palatable product, he substituted essential oils, sugar, and carbonation for the wine (p. 29). As a result of his work, Coca-Cola, with its tightly guarded "secret formula," was born.

In the transformation of Coca-Cola into the 99 percent sugar syrup drink of today, alcohol was removed before the cocaine. In 1903, due to a growing public

---

9. One advertisement reads, "Americans are the most nervous people in the world....All who are suffering from any nervous complaints we commend to use that wonderful and delightful remedy, French Wine Coca, infallible in curing all who are afflicted with any nerve trouble, dyspepsia, mental and physical exhaustion, sick headache, neuralgia, etc." (cited in Pendergrast, 1993:26–27).

outcry over cocaine and its effects, the coca flavoring in the drink was "decocainized." This "drug-free" version of the coca element of Coca-Cola is today supplied by the Stepan Company of Maywood, New Jersey, which imports 175,000 kilograms (175 metric tons) of coca leaves annually, turning some of them into the cocaine that ends up in legal medical products, and the rest into the decocainized flavor essence that Coca-Cola representatives say "adds to the flavor profile" (Miller 1994).[10]

The Coca-Cola Company does not like to dwell on this particular ingredient of its famous "secret formula"; indeed, it is mostly known through its connection with the early coca wines and the name Coca-Cola, which modern executives must surely wish they could disavow. The company solves the problem of Coke's association with coca by keeping quiet on this point, and by continuing to emphasize the secrecy of the formula.[11] When the "New Coke" formula came out in 1985, it contained no decocainized coca leaf, partly because President Ronald Reagan's plans to eradicate coca made company officials nervous about the future availability of this ingredient. However, the public's response to the new formula, and its nostalgia for the old, had company officials scrambling to return to the "original" formula (Pendergrast 1993:355). Although coca is only a minor ingredient, it would seem that discerning customers noticed its removal from the overall flavor profile.

A new coca drink, called KDrink, is currently being marketed in Peru as an energy drink—a kind of "health food" version of Coca-Cola. The combination of coca extract and the claims that it is natural and thus good for consumers has it "flying off the shelves" (Forero 2004).

COKE VERSUS COCA: ORIGIN MYTHS

Coca-Cola is distributed in more than 185 countries, making it the most widely distributed product on earth. Given this position at the vanguard of globalization and colonization, it is interesting to compare its origins (and origin myths) with those of the coca leaf itself. The Coca-Cola Company has fought to keep its image squeaky clean, and over the years has even distanced itself from the drink's origins as a medicine, when it was sold as a "valuable brain tonic and a cure for all nervous affections—Sick Head-Ache, Neuralgia, Hysteria, Melancholy, etc." (advertisement cited it Pendergrast 1993:33). Today, guides in the Coca-Cola Museum assert that Coca-Cola never had any cocaine in it (p. 9).

In contrast to the revisionist origin myths promoted by the Coca-Cola Company, in some Andean versions of the origin of coca, the leaf was given to Andean

---

10. Coca leaves may be a minor ingredient in Coca-Cola, but their early addition may have been essential to the product's success. Metzger (1998) claims that Coke's "conception and early acceptance were due largely to the cocaine content."

11. To maintain its supply, the Stepan Company must cooperate with the Drug Enforcement Agency. The company has its own network of agents in Peru and Bolivia and gets coca leaves from the same sources that supply the Colombian drug cartels (Miller 1994): "When a shipment arrives in the U.S., a high-security convoy of trucks ferries the leaves from the docks of Manhattan to Maywood, where it is greeted by a rifle-toting guard. After production, armored cars leave the building loaded with barrels of high-quality cocaine."

people as a way to help them withstand the pain and suffering ushered in by white colonizers. As a remedy bestowed by their god, coca was intended to allow indigenous people to "numb" their pain and "withstand fatigue.... the juice of these plants will be the best narcotic for the immense pain of your souls" (Gironda Cabrera 2000:29). In these accounts, coca would mean "strength and life" for the native Andean people; in contrast, in the hands of the white race it would be a "repugnant and degenerating vice ... causing idiocy and madness" (Ibid.).

COCA MEDICINES AND CHANGING PERCEPTIONS OF HEALTH

This brief history of the use of coca in nineteenth-century medicines, tonic drinks, and Coca-Cola serves as a backdrop for the modern coca preparations produced in Bolivia by small cottage industries. Building on notions of these beverages as being "medicinal" in nature, some of Coincoca's products target new "diseases" such as obesity, depression, and alcoholism. The founders of Coincoca also know the history of the commercialization of coca as an energy drink. That kind of commercial success may be out of reach of a small Bolivian cottage industry, but it is still capable of bringing to market a large array of coca products.

The pamphlets that Coincoca distributes to promote its products are jampacked with both scientific information about the biochemistry of coca and descriptions of the various products. The pamphlet lists the fourteen alkaloids present in the coca leaf and notes the presence of the vitamins A, B_1, B_2, C, E, thiamine, niacin, and riboflavin, calling the coca plant "the most complete plant in the universe." The claims for the extract of coca, on which most of the products are based, state that, depending on the dosage, it can help to "open the appetite and make one sleepy"; in higher dosages, coca is purported to "suppress the appetite and sleep." It is a perfect "painkiller for toothaches," but it is also "ideal for hypertension" (Coincoca promotional pamphlet).

Coincoca's tonic called Cocamiel is a combination of coca extract and honey. A very popular product called Cocaestet is prescribed as a dieting aid. In combination with the coca extract, Cocaestet contains a number of common Andean herbs that are considered to help burn fat, suppress the appetite, and slim down. The promotion of this "anti-obesity" syrup points to the new values placed on "thinness" by the urban population (women and men), and indicates a new context and meaning for an old medicine. Although thinness is not valued in a similar fashion in the countryside, where being round and "substantial" is considered a mark of good health and beauty, contemporary urbanites believe that plumpness is unattractive and unhealthy.

The coca wine made by the Bolivian company is referred to as *el Vino Mariani* (Mariani Wine) in its informational pamphlet, in a self-conscious attempt to draw on the 100-year-old success achieved by the original Vin Mariani and perhaps its European associations. In that all of Coincoca's products combine a coca extract with other ingredients, the wine serves as a kind of prototype for this cottage industry, and Marlena refers to it with enthusiasm.[12] In her own library, Marlena has a copy of Angelo Mariani's *Coca and Its Therapeutic Application*, originally published in 1892. It is ironic that a coca medicine intended for Bolivian consumption is likened to a popular European medicine that has not been used for almost 100 years, and that this is apparently so in part because no similar success stories exist for local products.

The ways in which the modern coca wine is to be used are a cross between some of the claims made for the original Vin Mariani and traditional uses of coca, especially as a tea. The use of coca wine is specified in Coincoca's promotional literature for instances when an individual

> is depressed or suffers from apathy, lack of appetite, low blood pressure, or when one faints a lot. It is a cardiac tonic that regulates the action of the heart; it also tones the vocal cords and fortifies the larynx. The wine is also good for strenuous activities, whether these are mental or physical, including sports. It aids in staying awake until late hours. For colds or flu one can drink coca wine hot like a toddy, with chamomile, eucalyptus, wira-wira, cardosanto, and lime. To eliminate undesirable microorganisms, boil the wine with papaya and squash seeds and drink it with lime for one to three days, preferably at night (Coincoca promotional pamphlet, 2000).

The modern-day wine's uses as a heart tonic, to fortify the vocal cords, and as a boost for strenuous activities echo claims made for the original Vin Mariani. When Coincoca's wine is heated with Andean traditional herbs (chamomile, eucalyptus, wira-wira, and cardosanto), the result is a basic prescription used to treat colds. In conjunction with papaya or squash seeds, it serves as a vehicle for the seeds, which are considered an effective purgative/remedy for internal parasites. Along with providing a good idea of the breadth of coca's medicinal uses, these general prescriptions indicate the degree to which coca use is based on a blend of old and new ideas about traditional medicine.[13] In rural areas, coca has generally been used for specific illnesses such as gastrointestinal ailments and those having to do with "blood" or "air"—both of which can affect one's digestive tract. Conversely, contemporary promoters of coca note its quality as a panacea: It can be used to treat altitude sickness, arthritis, stomach ulcers, typhoid fever, tuberculosis, colic, asthma, pneumonia, high cholesterol, dental cavities, and obesity, among other conditions (Gironda Cabrera 2000:37).

Coca wine by itself is also touted for treating depression, loss of appetite, apathy, low blood pressure, and fainting. Within traditional Andean notions of

---

12. Modern recipes for coca wine reveal its similarities to Mariani wine and a convergence between "wine" and "elixir." The following recipes come from P''axsi Limachi (1983). Coca wine: 120 grams coca leaves, 160 grams alcohol, 600 grams hot water, 180 grams sugar, 240 grams wine. Elixir: 60 grams powdered coca leaves, 120 grams alcohol, 500 grams white wine, 350 grams simple syrup, water. Steep leaves for twelve hours in alcohol, add wine and steep for eight days. Pass through cheesecloth and squeeze, add the liquid to the syrup/sugar. Add water to make one liter.

13. Coca leaf tea can now be purchased through Web-based companies. It is touted as a treatment for blood pressure, altitude sickness, gastrointestinal ailments, and motion sickness—all of which are older applications of coca leaf. Newer claims include its use as "a fast-acting antidepressant medication," as a coffee substitute, and as an adjunct to programs of weight reduction and physical fitness (PERUherbals.com).

healing, these issues are not considered so much physical or mental problems as spiritual ones. They are ailments generally associated with *susto* ("fright") or with *mancharisqa* ("soul loss," Quechua). Although these two ailments are sometimes considered equivalent, the condition of mancharisqa may also be considered "broader" or "more serious" (Carlos, personal communication, June 6, 2002). However, people who are prone to susto may be candidates for the more chronic condition of mancharisqa.

Susto is often cited as an example of a "culture-bound illness" in the literature on medical anthropology (McElroy and Townsend 1996). It affects certain segments of the population (poorer, more marginalized) more frequently and signals that the victim is spiritually vulnerable (Baer 2003). Susto can affect children or adults. Its symptoms can vary by age or individual, but generally cause people to feel weak and listless. People with susto become pale, and they experience appetite loss and sleep problems. They are also able to identify a particular experience when they were frightened—an experience such as an accident, a fall, exposure to harmful wind or air, or an encounter with some kind of malignant spirit (usually at night). As a result of these experiences, the soul becomes separated from the body, which saps the energy of susto-sufferers and sickens them.

On one hand, susto and mancharisqa could be characterized as "problems of low energy or physical weakness," thereby using a general description and putting them into a cross-cultural framework. When I discussed the concept of "energy" with an urban *curandero* (a healer who has roots in rural healing but a broad knowledge of cross-cultural healing practices himself), he noted that the concept of energy exists in Andean healing, but takes other forms. He then proceeded to talk mainly about the *ajayu* and the *ánimo*, words that roughly translate as "soul" or "spirit" and are used in Aymara and Quechua, respectively. These concepts are very important in terms of health: By being frightened or encountering malignant spirits or forces, a person's spirit or soul can become separated from the body, which will cause the person to sicken and even die in extreme cases.[14] In these instances, a ritual healer must call back the person's soul, and attempt to reunite it with the body. Very often the healer is successful in this endeavor, so that it is uncommon to die from susto.

Both patients and healers understand that this kind of illness is untreatable by a biomedical doctor or through the use of pharmaceuticals. Instead, it must be treated ritually, by calling back the person's soul during a specific ritual, including the use of use of bells and voices to bring the spirit back. The use of certain plants may accompany the ritual. In treating this illness, the healer may employ coca, but generally coca is used as a way to diagnose the illness and not as an herb that is prescribed medicinally for susto. In some cases, coca may be used externally with other ingredients, as a way to draw out the fright and remove it from the patient (Alba and Tarifa 1993:284). A good healer is able to change the condition of "fright" through a variety of means: The spirit can be returned to the person; it

---

14. One biomedical doctor, trained in natural medicine, agrees with the curandero's assessment. The concept of "energy" is subsumed in the concepts of *ajayu*, so that the loss of one's soul through susto requires its return. Fright can also be caused by a *mal energía* ("bad energy").

also may be a case of a "diminished" spirit that needs to be "fixed, augmented, or fortified" through ritual practices (Carlos, personal communication, June 22, 2002).

On the other hand, the condition of soul loss can be avoided altogether if one is strong. One healer states, "If we have strong blood and a strong soul, we won't be affected" (cited in Alba and Tarifa 1993). Thus the key is for the person to maintain a strong and positive state and for the healer to help in this respect, before, during, and after episodes of susto or mancharisqa.

That pharmaceutical-like products now exist to combat some of the symptoms associated with susto indicates that this condition is being perceived differently by some of the populace, in part through the intervention of manufacturers of traditional medicines. Converting the illness of susto (or mancharisqa, in some Andean contexts) to its component symptoms, and increasingly using words such as "depression," "low energy," or "mental exhaustion" to describe its effects, patients are brought into the hybrid medical world of Andean medicine: The particular Andean health problems remain (albeit somewhat transformed), but are described with new names and may be treated with new medicines, should the patient choose this course of action. That is, in attacking the "depression" aspect of the illness, a patient may focus on treating it, instead of the more general problem of soul loss, which would require the intervention of a ritual specialist. "Depression" can be treated with herbal remedies, whereas "mancharisqa" cannot.

In the case of coca wine, Coincoca also touts it as a tonic that regulates the action of the heart (see the picture of *Vino de Coca* in the center of Figure 6.7). From the perspective of traditional Andean medicine, this capability is important because it will lead to the "strong blood" that keeps one's soul from separating from the body. Claims for this medicine also state that it will help people who must engage in vigorous physical activity and keep late hours (when the chances for susto are greater). Clearly, the appeal of coca wine is made as broad as possible, speaking both to people who may believe in and experience susto/mancharisqa, and to those who may believe in concepts of low energy and blood fortification. Both of these ideas would resonate with most Andean people, including those who live firmly in the urban sphere with its accompanying belief system surrounding health.

Similar to other traditional medicine businesses in urban settings, the coca-based cottage industry Coincoca has found its niche in the immediate healing it offers to people. The products the company provides allow people to self-diagnose and self-medicate, a quality that is associated with several of the other traditional medicine businesses and vendors connected to the marketplace. Coincoca's owner, Marlena, emphasizes that her products are effective and inexpensive because they don't require a trip to the doctor (or to any healer, traditional or otherwise). In conversation with me, she called one of her favorite remedies "a star." It is such an indispensable part of her array of healing products that she calls it "the little doctor in my house." With its help and the other natural products she uses, she had not taken her children to the doctor for more than twelve years. Marlena firmly believes in natural medicine (or what people in the United States might term "alternative medicine"),[15] so this self-help program appeals to her especially on this level. At the same time, she also believes that the products are beneficial in that they save her customers a great deal of money by allowing them to take care of their own health problems without going to the doctor. For instance, depression can be treated with Coincoca products, similar to the use of St. John's wort in the United States and Europe. This treatment regimen also means that people who have a better understanding of health concepts and types of ailments will feel more comfortable taking an independent course of action. If they do no, they will consult with the available naturopaths.

Working in a parallel fashion to traditional medicine cottage industries, naturopaths usually offer their services in conjunction with a line of products that they sometimes manufacture in their own kitchens. Alternatively, they may serve as representatives for products that they buy from national or international distributors, oftentimes drawing together products from several companies.

COCA PRODUCTION AND COCA ERADICATION

Because coca is an "Andean" item that grows in the tropical valleys that descend from the Andes proper, it has been an important trade item since humans' earliest presence in the region. The yungas region of Bolivia, where coca has long been grown and whose crop is still considered to be in the "traditional" (as opposed to "illicit") production zone, has seen Aymara occupation since around A.D. 1200. Before that time, there is evidence of some Tiwanaku presence (A.D. 400–1145), and later dominance by the Incas (A.D. 1438–1532), who used the area as a "penal colony" and forced the farmers to send half of their production to the Inca state (Spedding 2005).

In pre-Hispanic times, coca circulated less formally from family to family and from zone to zone through a general system of interzonal barter and exchange (Murra 1987). By contrast, during colonial times, when the demand for coca leaf from mining centers increased dramatically, communities in the yungas became independent of highland control and distributed their products through the marketplace (Ibid.). Haciendas were the main commercial producers until 1953, when agrarian reform broke their political control and shifted power to the hands of small peasant producers, a pattern that continues today (Léons and Sanabria 1997).

Although intense demand for coca leaf from mining centers subsided with the collapse of the mining economy in Bolivia, the demand for coca leaf from the general populace continued. Eventually, the drug market both filled the void left by the mining centers and further increased demand for coca. Nevertheless, it is inaccurate to assume that the entire supply of coca leaf now goes to the production of cocaine and the drug trade. Rural marketplaces and even the most

---

15. Marlena's belief in natural medicine goes well beyond her business practice. She continues to study natural medicine at the Natural Medicine Institute in Cochabamba, and is in training to be a full-fledged naturista, or naturopath. The link between "natural medicine" is an interesting example of the hybridization of medical beliefs and cosmology. (See Chapter 6 for a discussion of natural medicine and its place in the overall system of traditional medicine.)

isolated stores in the Andean countryside sell coca leaf, and rural dwellers seek it for work, medicine, divination, and ritual assemblages, and as a reciprocal gift offered to others during fiestas. Rather than purchasing it with money, highland dwellers may obtain coca through long-distance trading trips. Corn and coca are two of the important trade items sought by the residents of the altiplano region surrounding Lake Poopó, and these items are procured by offering wool, chuño (freeze-dried potatoes), and dried llama meat in exchange (Molina Rivera 1986, West 1981).

Until 1995, Bolivia was the second largest producer of coca leaf. Currently Colombia is the biggest producer, followed by Peru, with Bolivia now occupying third place. For a country with such a small population and lack of modern infrastructure, it is amazing that Bolivia ranks as the third biggest producer of anything, much less coca. Some 50,000 hectares are planted annually in coca (2000 estimate), and in 1994 approximately 6.2 percent of the country's gross national product (GNP) was attributable to coca income (Léons and Sanabria, 1997:17–20). Although it is difficult to construct accurate estimates because much of the money runs through unofficial channels, Léons and Sanabria suggest that approximately 10 percent of the work force receives part of its income from "drug-related activities" (p. 18). Money from the illegal production of coca and cocaine circulates in the Bolivian economy and helps to stabilize it (p. 2). This picture of an economy dependent on the production and circulation of coca and its derived products provides some perspective on the Bolivian government's half-hearted efforts to work with the DEA to curb the production and circulation of coca.

Cocaine is produced illegally in a series of steps, each of which requires obtaining and applying toxic chemicals, exploiting peasant labor, paying bribes, and in other ways entering into an underground and illegal economy. Morales (1989) has extensively researched the complex pattern of cocaine production in Peru. The following account is condensed from his observations of the practices, workers, smuggling routes, and other ethnographic details relating to the cocaine economy.

There are basically two steps in the process of refining coca leaves into high-quality ("street") cocaine: (1) the preparation of coca paste and (2) refining of the coca paste (*pasta básica*) into cocaine. Generally these processes are separated by time and place and are usually undertaken by different groups of people.

Coca paste is generally manufactured in areas where coca is grown in the Andean lowlands (referred to as "green mines"), in isolated locales that are difficult to police. A big pit is built, either out of cement or more simply with wood poles and plastic sheeting (the latter type of pit is more portable and less incriminating). The four chemical agents required—sulfuric acid, calcium oxide ("lime"), kerosene, and sodium carbonate—must be obtained in large quantities through illegal channels and are sometimes carried in by the same "burros" (human carriers) who will later transport the coca paste.

One expert "mixer" and two to five other workers oversee the preparation of the paste. The mixer directs the pit to be filled with water, to which the coca leaves and sulfuric acid are added. The leaves are soaked for twelve to eighteen hours. Laborers (*pisacocas*) then stomp the leaves for about an hour, producing a liquid called *caldo* ("broth"). The caldo is decanted, and in the next pit calcium oxide is used to render the alkaloid "soup." The "soup" is then mixed with kerosene, and water and sulfuric acid are again employed. Sodium carbonate is added to the solution, and a whitish substance—the paste—forms at the bottom of this final container. This *pasta básica* is squeezed through fine cloth to remove the water and then dried. "At the end of the preparation, thousands of gallons of polluted water are drained into streams and rivers" (Morales 1989:77).

For many years, coca paste was necessarily transported to Colombia's production facilities, where it was then transformed into cocaine. Today, some cocaine is produced in Peru and Bolivia, and smuggled directly to the United States. Unlike the production of coca paste, which is presided over by poorer peasants from the lowlands, much of the second stage of production is undertaken by middle-class entrepreneurs who run the operation out of their own kitchens. Approximately three to four kilos of coca paste are needed to make one kilo of cocaine. In the "hot" procedure, kitchen distillers are used. The "cold" method is also quite common, largely because it requires less sophisticated equipment.

In the first step of the refining process, the coca paste is crumbled and diluted in acetone, and the fluid is decanted. In the second step, hot water is added to separate the acetone, leaving the alkaloids to condense at the bottom. This substance is forced through a press, after which it is considered "washed coca paste" or "base." Two separate solutions—using acetone, ether, and hydrochloric acid in different combinations—are poured (with the paste) into a separate vessel, finally producing a crystalline substance (*cristal*). Electricity is used to dry the final product, which comprises export-quality cocaine hydrochlorine powder. In the 1980s, this powder could be sold on the market for between $7,000 and $10,000 per kilo (Morales 1989: Chapter 4).

Morales (1989) characterizes the two steps of this process as converting the "white gold ore" into "white gold." Used along with the many mining metaphors employed by the participants in this manufacturing process are cooking terms, such as "broth," "soup," and the use of hot and cold processing in kitchens. Like many of the cottage industries offering contemporary traditional medicines in places like Cochabamba, the processing of coca paste and cocaine is perceived as an artisan-style industry in which family members may participate together, and the product is turned out is small batches. In an ironic twist, cocaine production in Bolivia is a "model of appropriate technology" (Léons and Sanabria 1997:16). It is also evident that this industry is particularly open to corruption and vice, and is a source of real temptation because of the enormous profits that can be made. For instance, a trucker who uses a small fraction of his load capacity to transport coca paste into the city (hidden amid his bananas, yucca, and other legal items) can make six times his monthly income in one trip. Hence a vast network of people becomes part of the illegal economy, with most of them participating in very small ways.

Suggestions about how to control the circulation and use of coca have ranged from eradication of "excess" coca leaf, to providing incentives for voluntary eradication, to encouraging alternative crop development, to "Opción Zero"—total eradication of all coca in the main growing region in a six-year period at an estimated cost of $200 million (Dubberly 1995). Substitution programs, aimed at finding crops that will provide "alternative production" options for peasant farmers, have proved largely unsuccessful, which means that "voluntary" eradication has also failed. The substitute crops that have been attempted—coffee, fruit, macadamia nuts, soybeans, and cacao—have never matched the hardiness and productivity of coca. Another problem is that suggestions for alternative crops have been based on ecological characteristics rather than economic considerations, without market research or, in fact, any plan for how and to whom the crops are to be sold.

Adapted perfectly to the slopes leading toward the Amazon Basin, coca can be harvested three times a year for thirty years at a stretch before replanting is necessary. Although coca production requires a lot of initial labor to build terraces and plant the coca bushes, once planted coca is fairly self-sufficient. Plants that begin from seed will blossom after approximately five months, and can be cropped after one and a half years. Unlike coffee, coca flourishes in poor soils (Spedding 1994:38). It is not susceptible to most diseases, and it has a much higher market value than other crops (Morales 1989:57). It is no wonder it is so difficult to convince farmers to grow something else. Even when they do make such an attempt, they sometimes switch back to their beloved coca crop.

Some of the coca that traditional farmers produce is undoubtedly funneled into the drug trade, but producers are hardly becoming rich from it. Approximately $700 worth of coca is converted into one kilo of cocaine, which in turn has a street value of $150,000 (Léons and Sanabria 1997:42). Obviously the cocaine producers, the drug runners, and the dealers on the street are the ones in line to reap the windfall in this scenario, not the Bolivian coca farmers.

Coca substitution and eradication programs sponsored by the United States not only threaten the livelihood of poor peasant farmers, but also weaken the place of coca in the traditional life of Andean people. Traditional medical and spiritual uses of coca are threatened by the ongoing confusion between coca and cocaine. Gironda Cabrera accuses the United States of swaying national and international public opinion by deliberately confounding coca with cocaine and coca producers with drug traffickers (2000:89). Beginning in 1923, the question was put to Bolivian officials (in that year by the Secretary of the League of Nations): Were Bolivians producing cocaine for export? (p. 83). The authorities answered no and dutifully reported their coca leaf production (75,000 *quintales* per year), which was intended for the following uses: (1) for internal ("traditional") use, (2) to supply legal production of pharmaceutical cocaine, and (3) as the raw material for Coca-Cola flavoring. Indeed, cocaine was not manufactured within the borders of Bolivia until relatively recently, and only then as an "unintended consequence" of the drug war in Colombia, which effectively displaced some cocaine factories from Colombia to the Bolivian (and Peruvian) Amazon.

As cocaine production centers grew in isolated areas of the Bolivian Amazon, more people migrated to the "illegal coca-growing" Chapare area of lowland Bolivia because of trends related to unemployment, lack of agricultural opportunities, and the depopulation of mining centers (Léons and Sanabria, 1997:14). Some highlanders come for part-time work on coca plantations or to work in cocaine production. Thus the coca market has offered a wage labor opportunity for altiplano residents that functions to subsidize their traditional economy. Peasants may work as coca stompers in the first stage of coca production, during which their feet are dyed bright green by the coca juice. Through these unorthodox activities, some laborers are able to further their own "traditional" highland goals. Zorn (1997), for example, describes how some temporary migrants from communities in the province of Potosí use the cash they earn to create new versions of ethnic dress on their return to their home community.

To be sure, the activities of cocaine producers and suppliers in Bolivia have their negative social and environmental effects, and coca production is not altogether a positive boost to the Bolivian economy.[16] Nevertheless, the activities of those who seek to eradicate it are more destructive yet. Unfortunately, most Bolivian and Peruvian peasants have gotten caught in between the politics of the drug war and their search for a better way of life (Mayer 2002). Even after years of massive eradication programs in Bolivia (such as that initiated in 2000), the supply of cocaine to the rest of the world has not been stanched, or even reduced.

The laws that regulate coca production and sale have become increasingly punitive, to the point that they threaten the civil and human rights of Bolivian citizens. The issue of coca production, industrialization, and penalties was one plank of the platform that gained Evo Morales the presidency in 2005. On the one hand, the ongoing debate surrounding coca production has led to a better understanding of the place of traditional coca use, for which the law ostensibly makes allowances. On the other hand, the crackdown on alleged illegal coca activities brought about the militarization of the Chapare region of Bolivia (where the "illicit" coca production supposedly resides) and attendant human rights abuses, including unfair imprisonment, confiscation of property, and even death.

A good example of the problems accompanying the Bolivian-level "war on drugs" is the 1988 anti-narcotics legislation known as Law 1008 (or, in its longer form, "The Coca and Controlled Substance Law"). Law 1008 grew out of the Reagan administration's promotion of the war on drugs and was written with the assistance of the U.S. Agency for International Development (Dubberly 1995). The law allowed for only 12,000 hectares of coca production to satisfy traditional use (mainly coca leaf chewing and tea), but called for the eradication of coca produced beyond this area and in places identified as "excess and transitional." To implement the law's objectives, Controlled Substance Courts, separate from the regular judicial system, were established. The original idea was that having such special courts would expedite the hearing of these cases; in practice, it led to denial of due process, presumption of guilt, and harsh sentences (Dubberly 1995). As a consequence, Bolivia's prisons are now filled with "narco-offenders," most of whom are poor, and an outcry has arisen over the system's trampling of human rights. As Farthing (1997) points out, the accompanying social and political effects have been to enhance police corruption by boosting the power of the police, and to magnify the already considerable inequalities that exist in the Bolivian justice

---

16. Bolivia depends as no other country on the drug money that comes from the sale of part of its coca crop. Although it is difficult to calculate the amount exactly, in 1990 the drug money it generated amounted to an estimated $1 billion—a substantial portion of the Bolivian GNP (Gironda Cabrera 2000:285). Because this illicit trade is controlled by relatively few people, so that the money does not circulate evenly (some of it leaves the country), the cocaine business is not as lucrative an "industry" as it might seem at first glance. Nonetheless, Gironda Cabrera estimates that perhaps 50,000 families (approximately 200,000 people) owe their livelihoods directly to this "culture of cocaine" (2000:284).

system, as detainees are invariably poor people who have a hard time arguing their cases and winning their release.

A key to solving at least part of the problem surrounding coca production and eradication lies in the expanded use of coca in medicine, especially in new medicines produced by cottage industries in larger volumes. The more alternative uses found for the coca plant itself, the more coca that can be produced under the label of "traditional production and consumption," which would benefit both farmers and entrepreneurs.

According to Marlena, the director of Coincoca, her company is "covered by Law 1008." In 2000, the company was able to buy the coca it needed for its products quite easily because at that point its volume was not huge. Marlena was able to purchase approximately 10,000 kilograms per year (200 *cargas*—each carga is 100 pounds) without difficulty, but would face problems if she sought to buy much more to produce in larger quantities. To open a market for Coincoca's products in Europe, and especially in France or the Netherlands (a proposition that Marlena has explored), Marlena would need to assure investors that the company could continue to obtain sufficient quantities of coca leaf. Perhaps not surprisingly, investors are concerned about the exact volume of coca that Coincoca will be able to use annually in its production, and about the effects that the coca eradication programs will have on the company's prospects. As Marlena says, "They [foreign investors] are not going to invest, say, four or five million dollars if coca is going to be eradicated and become scarce."[17] This is a far different picture from the heady days when Angelo Mariani was producing his wine and was assured of a steady supply of coca—but then he was operating long before the days of the drug trade and drug war, when cocaine had a wider legitimate medical use.

Given that the Andean population does live in the midst of a drug war, what can be done to offset the problems of balancing legitimate uses with the violence and corruption associated with the drug trade? Enrique Mayer, an economic anthropologist who has conducted extensive fieldwork in Peru, offers a number of suggestions for strengthening the position of coca in the Andean world and beyond (2002:192–194):

- Expanding the groups that consume coca. Mayer's discussion focuses on urbanites in South America, but could also include the international clientele for alternative medicines.
- Joining the international natural foods and medicines market.
- Eliminating international restrictions.

These three suggestions are interrelated in important ways, and I would like to suggest ways that they might be expanded in light of my foregoing discussion.

---

17. Marlena was also quoted in a *New York Times* article about the potential for exporting coca drinks. She said, "To export, oh, that would be such a big dream. That would be something anyone who produces coca products would want" (Forero 2004).

Photo by Sarah Linn Gallardo

F I G U R E 7.3 Legal production and commercialization of coca leaf, here being transported to interior markets. Either it will be sold to coca-chewers, or processed into legal coca products.

First, by aggressively marketing coca products (along with other traditional medicine products) in country, new customers are created within the Bolivian populace and beyond.[18] The existence of a strong domestic product and companies to promote it will create opportunities for market expansion through export as well as provide much-needed jobs. Many international visitors to the Andes are interested in the availability of herbal remedies, and some are seeking cures for various ailments. The Internet can help to bring products to new customers beyond the national market as well. Coca is a potential source for an expanding market to cater to those interested in traditional cures and medicines.

The natural foods and medicines market is a booming business and provides real opportunities—the spread of products such as Echinacea, kava kava, ginseng, and *Ginkgo biloba* indicate the huge demand for such products. It is a logical place to market coca products. As vendors promote the products as traditional medicines, however, they must be careful to protect the rights of the original users of these medicines against corporate interests. This issue is steeped in controversy

---

18. Coca consumption appears to be on the rise in Andean households. Says Gironda Cabrera, "Converted into all types of products, especially medicinal ones, coca has entered into many [urban] homes" (2000:424).

concerning who has the rights to use which kinds of knowledge and to profit from it; it is considered at length in Chapter 9.

In spreading coca use beyond the Andes, the biggest obstacle is the current restriction placed on coca. Even though the DEA and other international organizations now recognize that the use of the coca leaf itself is harmless, the International Narcotics Convention refused Bolivia's request in 1992 to strike it from its list of prohibited substances (Mayer 2002:194). This refusal to remove coca from the list of official narcotics undoubtedly relates to the continued, and willful, confusion between coca and cocaine. As long as this restriction persists, coca cannot be exported to many countries.

In truth, those fighting the drug war would benefit from the move to promote alternative uses of coca, as the coca crop might be diverted from its illicit use in cocaine production to traditional uses such as those found in the medicine market. Furthermore, now that the interests of the coca growers are much better represented in the Bolivian politics with the advent of Evo Morales's new administration, the door is open for a redirection of the debate over coca production versus coca eradication. There is great hope that Morales's call to further industrialize coca, through the launch of even more legal coca products, will help farmers, traders, and entrepreneurs alike.

SUMMARY

The case of coca stands as an example of how a simple leaf that has applications in traditional medicine can be made to serve many different uses over time, and how these uses may end up at cross-purposes with one another. Coca's original Andean use as a central component of rituals, social contracts, and agricultural work continues today, as evidenced by its incorporation in many facets of rural life. Because coca had important uses in Andean traditional medicine, it was noted and examined by outsiders who were interested in introducing new products to the west. The trajectory of coca from leaf, to Mariani Wine, to Coca-Cola indicates the distance a medicinal item can travel, and the distant applications it can assume, when it is manipulated by outsiders with new interests, related to health and otherwise. Coca's denatured essence still lives on in Coca-Cola, although this historical fact has been masked by the economic enterprise of its parent company.

The coca leaf's other trajectory—as the raw material from which cocaine is crystallized—is a distinctly different road that has been marked by danger and controversy. Originally accepted as a legitimate pharmaceutical, and still used so today in specific applications, cocaine has been transformed from a nineteenth-century over-the-counter drug to which a few people (including Sigmund Freud) were addicted, to an unregulated street drug that affects the lives of many and is accompanied by criminal activity. In the long campaign against cocaine, the coca leaf has become an unwitting victim, and the traditional uses of coca have been ignored by the anti-drug campaigners. Traditional uses of coca as the leaf in Andean chew and tea, as well as new uses of it in legitimate products, are threatened by programs that seek to simply eradicate coca, without taking its traditional and medicinal applications in the lives of Andean people into account.

The example of coca leaf provides us with insight into not only the workings of traditional medicines, but also the very different and unforeseen forms they can take in the contemporary world. Interestingly, it continues to be used in multiple ways, thereby serving as a complex illustration of the commercialization arc of traditional medicines.

8

Natural Medicine and Naturopaths in Bolivia: A New Twist on Traditional Medicine

> More than a science, Naturismo is a pattern of life that shows us
> how to obey natural laws that emanate from Mother Nature....
> Naturismo is the science of health, liberty, and happiness. If we
> wish to be free of illness, social problems, exploitation, hunger,
> war, fear, and other problems, we must insist on returning
> to nature, the generative force of life.
> —EXCERPT FROM *NATURALEZA Y SALUD,*
> A BOOKLET FOR SALE AT A COCHABAMBA SHOP
> THAT SELLS NATURAL MEDICINE PRODUCTS

NATURISMO AND NATURISTAS IN
CONTEMPORARY BOLIVIA

In Bolivia and other Latin American countries, the use and promotion of "natural medicine" (*medicina natural*) is also referred to as *naturismo*. On the one hand, it is closely aligned with traditional medicine in that naturismo draws on some of the same cures from local traditional medicine, and claims its authority as emerging from the ancient practices of Bolivian ancestors. On the other hand, the concept of natural medicine draws from global sources of health care, making it a particularly good example of a hybrid system. Unlike the case with coca leaf and coca medicines, with natural medicine the flow of ideas and practices is into Bolivia. Practitioners may emphasize links to Bolivian traditional medicine or global alternative medicine, but generally natural medicine is an outgrowth of the processes of commercialization.

Of course, natural medicine sellers realize a commercial benefit from tracing naturismo to traditional sources. A spokeswoman for one Bolivian cottage industry, based in natural medicine, said that the initial idea of the company she runs with her husband was to "rescue medicinal plants for the welfare of the population." A pamphlet for sale from a vendor of fresh plants (the vendors discussed in Chapter 6) describes the approach as "alternative medicine" and calls for the defense of traditional medicine plant species that may be in danger of extinction because of ecological degradation or the loss of knowledge about their use. One biomedical doctor working in a very isolated area during her internship became converted to the approach of natural medicine, first "out of necessity" (because the biomedical clinic's resources were so limited),[1] but later because she appreciated its broad scope. She also recognized that the relationship between the patient and the doctor could be "more fluid" in this setting, incorporating an exchange of ideas about how to treat the problem.

In contrast, traditional medicine healers see a sharp distinction between natural medicine and traditional medicine, and perceive that commercialized natural medicine may harm the practice of traditional medicine. One urban healer with whom I spoke was very careful to differentiate natural medicine from traditional medicine. He called natural medicine a "branch" of traditional medicine—one much more influenced by "European ideas" than "authentic Andean" traditional medicine. Concurring with the notion that natural medicine is a derivative of traditional medicine, Dr. María Asturias characterizes natural medicine as being overly commercialized and endangering the system of traditional medicine, which in her estimation is distinct from the traditional medicine practiced "non-commercially" in the countryside. In the commercial sphere, natural medicine certainly functions as an opportunistic hybrid in terms of what it offers to customers. From a variety of sources, such as the practitioners of natural medicine and their

---

1. Biomedical doctors who spend a year doing a rural internship face the challenge of working with very limited resources, along with the discrepancy between what they have learned in medical school and the way in which rural folk deal with health issues. In the case of Dr. Asturias (quoted above), the experience led to her conversion to "alternative methods" and a reliance on the traditional medicine that rural inhabitants practice.

customers, pamphlets for sale to the populace, and the institutes of natural medicine, it is clear that natural medicine incorporates ideas from non-Andean traditions, simultaneously promoting itself as the healthy alternative to biomedicine.

Natural medicine practitioners proffer a different option for patients; they claim that modern health problems can be best addressed through the application of natural medicine. For instance, prostate problems are a major area of concern for *naturistas* (naturopaths or natural medicine "doctors"), along with the prevention of breast cancer, dandruff, high blood pressure, baldness, and stress. Naturistas are concerned with all the afflictions that people experience, but emphasize the ways in which natural remedies can be used to combat the ills of modern living. One naturista insinuated that I must know a lot about these ailments, being from the United States where life is full of pressure and strain, provoking numerous cases of *nervios* ("nerves"). An article in a publication from an organization of traditional and natural medicine healers tackles the issue of *estrés* (stress) by noting that these days many people suffer from it beginning in childhood (*Revista Amauta*), mostly due to the perils of urban life.

Natural medicine treatments range from those emphasizing "health" to those focusing on appearance or "beauty." One naturista in Cochabamba specifically advertises his services as promoting *Salud y Belleza* ("Health and Beauty"). The products that he sells at a kiosk outside his office range from wheat germ and vitamins, to lotions and toothpaste. He also offers at least fifty different varieties of dried plants to be made into medicinal teas.

Aleph, one of the natural medicine cottage industries in Cochabamba, had three retail stores in the city of Cochabamba in 2000. Customers can choose from a variety of dried plants and special teas for many ailments, along with getting facials, purchasing tonics to help hair growth, and even experimenting with "slimming" treatments. Aleph's advertisements of *Tratamientos Naturales Unisex* ("Natural Treatments, Unisex") send a clear message that these products are not just for women, even though the company's customers are predominately female. Underscoring the medical claims made by the firm, the shop attendants at the Aleph stores wear white lab coats (like pharmacists or doctors) but the atmosphere in the Aleph stores is one of an upscale spa.

Nutrition is also a key element of the work of natural medicine doctors. Although they may sell natural medicine treatments (often formulated as pills and powders), naturistas typically provide advice on what their patients should and should not eat—in other words, their advice is aimed at providing a complete health regimen for those who seek it. They ask their patients to make major changes in their lifestyles, including giving up alcohol and caffeine or at least reducing their intake. Healthy diets are a key component of naturistas' advice, as they frequently deal with urban clients who may eat a larger number of processed foods with a higher content of fat, salt, and sugar, which the naturistas claim undermines the medical treatments they employ for the illness or health problem experienced by their particular customers. Indeed, many of their clients are concerned about their excess weight.

One well-known naturista in Cochabamba always provides nutritional advice along with his natural remedies. He recommends eating lots of grains (for instance, oatmeal with soy milk for breakfast) and consuming fruits and vegetables at every meal. Eating papaya or drinking its juice is a recommended snack. This naturista's list of "prohibited" items aligns his nutrition regimen with natural medicine as practiced in many developed countries. On the list of things to avoid are red meat, processed meat (sausages, hot dogs), cheese, coffee, tea, chocolate, alcoholic drinks, cigarettes, vinegar, fried food, noodles and white bread, excess sugar, jam, soda pop, fats, spicy foods, and drugs.

The health system advocated by naturistas encompasses more than a promotion of health, beauty, and diet, however. From the practitioners' perspective, it is a philosophy—a way of life. Grover Crespo, the director of the Institute of Traditional Medicines in Cochabamba, says that naturismo is "a way of living naturally in the world and in communion with the water, sun, air, and energies." He considers naturismo to be branch of traditional medicine, because traditional medicine "encompasses the whole" (i.e., it is the general category containing plant- and tradition-based cures). Carlos, a curandero who works within the system of traditional medicine, rather than natural medicine, claims, "Naturismo is more academic, but traditional medicine is based on oral tradition."

Although the two systems share many similarities, especially in their use of the same plants from the Andean pharmacopoeia, they differ in the extent to which ritual is incorporated in the healing process. A healer such as Carlos, who has a heritage of traditional medicine, is a ritualist as well as a medical healer. He believes that omitting the ritual aspect of healing means an erasure of Andean tradition, and that naturismo alone is not sufficient for all ailments. Even practitioners who are not ritualists themselves decry the absence of ritual in natural medicine treatments, and believe that Andean healing is incomplete without ritual practice (M. Angulo, personal communication, June 25, 2002).

Reflecting the basic differences between natural and traditional medicines, within the ranks of healers who have organized themselves through organizations such as the Institute of Traditional Medicine in Cochabamba, there is an ongoing clash between naturistas and curanderos. There is a move for naturistas to create their own organization or society, and this split is currently becoming more apparent at the level of the healers themselves. For patients and customers, however, the distinctions are probably less clear.

In the past twenty years or so, traditional and natural medicines have gained popularity in urban areas, and with this popularity has come greater visibility at the governmental level. SOBOMETRA is the Sociedad Boliviana de Medicina Tradicional (Bolivian Society for Traditional Medicine). Aided by the mandate from the World Health Organization (WHO) at its Alma Ata Conference in 1978, which stated that traditional medicine should be incorporated into local health care, the Bolivian society was founded in 1984 as an institution that "organizes, orients, empowers, and protects the therapists that practice Native Medicine and Alternative Natural Medicine." Established by Supreme Resolution #198771, SOBOMETRA is charged with the task of "rescuing, establishing, practicing, and diffusing the knowledge and medical arts of the different indigenous cultures" of Bolivia, and attempting to "elevate the level and quality of health care" available to all Bolivians.

Since SOBOMETRA was recognized nationally, it has opened branch offices (*filiales*) in various locales, including one in Cochabamba. Those natural medicine practitioners who are able to do so seek affiliation with SOBOMETRA and become members. The organization's certification process is aimed at recognizing specialists in two broad categories: (1) "therapists" (healers) and (2) "agents" (vendors) of traditional or natural medicines. Included in the rank of healers are both curanderos (*yatiris* or *kolliris* in Aymara and Quechua, respectively) and naturistas. Thus SOBOMETRA makes a distinction between healers and vendors, though this distinction is blurred by the activities of naturistas such as Jorge who practice healing and sell products in the marketplace.

SOBOMETRA has the greatest presence in La Paz, where it was founded, though each Bolivian department now has its own office. These subsidiary offices differ from one another in that each reflects the local variations in traditional medicine found within its region. For instance, the Santa Cruz branch is supposedly based on traditional medicine practices of lowland groups, rather than Andean traditions. However, some SOBOMETRA members have noted that the society is dominated by the powerful Kallawaya healers (from the Charazani area of the Department of La Paz), and claim that SOBOMETRA is not truly representative of the variety of healers and healing traditions found in Bolivia. Others bemoan the lack of organization at the national level, which sometimes keeps people from knowing that alternative therapies are widely available. Nonetheless, at this point SOBOMETRA functions as the umbrella organization for traditional medicine in Bolivia, and it has gained national recognition in doing so.

One of SOBOMETRA's charges is to register the "therapists" (*terapeutas*)[2] who work in the countryside and it the city. To become registered, the therapists/healers must pass an exam. Based on their exam results, they are classified as belonging in one of these categories: (1) traditional medicine healer or naturista—category A; (2) naturista—category B; or (3) specialty healer (for instance, ritualist, curandero, or bonesetter). Taking the exam and becoming registered in one of these categories is important for the healers themselves, who gain authority by being registered with SOBOMETRA and can then advertise their credentials. In reality, the exam that SOBOMETRA administers may provide a classification that is at odds with what the practitioner actually does. For instance, it may classify a person as being a "ritual specialist" when that individual considers this work to be only one aspect of his or her healing practice.

The Institute of Traditional Medicines in Cochabamba is loosely affiliated with SOBOMETRA but currently serves to train those who work with natural medicine, or naturismo. That distinction reflects the fact that curanderos (yatiris, jampiris) are by definition those who have hereditary knowledge and are generally trained in the countryside in an apprentice-like process. In contrast, healers with urban backgrounds might aspire to heal people naturally (with herbs, nutrition, and the application of natural living regimens, as outlined earlier), but they must

---

2. *Terapeuta* is used as a general term for traditional medicine healers in this context. It conveys the idea that both curanderos (traditional medicine healers) and naturistas (natural medicine doctors) are included.

be instructed in this school of thought and its associated practices. Naturistas, therefore, require formal training to arrive at their positions as healers. The Institute of Traditional Medicines fulfills this purpose.

The first course of instruction at the Institute of Traditional Medicines provides the students with general knowledge about plants and skills in using herbal remedies, describes how medicinal plants are used, and specifies the illnesses to which they are applied. Upon the successful completion of this course, students are given the title of "Terapeuta." A yearlong program may be taken next, comprising a series of courses in biology, pathology, laboratory analysis, diagnosis, massage, and other relevant topics. Only students who excel in the first course are allowed to continue the official training. At the end of the year, and after passing the tests, a student is given the title of "Médico Naturista" (natural medicine doctor). After this, short courses are offered so that naturistas can continue to increase their knowledge while sharing their learning with one another.

The most well-known naturistas in and around Cochabamba are those who teach and study at the Institute of Traditional Medicines. Many local natural medicine doctors in Cochabamba have attended courses at the Institute, and many are working toward the goal of becoming full-fledged naturopaths complete with certificates. Among the group of naturistas I came to know, both Maribel and Marlena had been attending courses at the Institute and were completing formal study to earn degrees in natural medicine. Both perceive that being in natural medicine commerce is not enough—their credentials as official naturistas will enhance their businesses, and the process of learning more about natural medicine is personally fulfilling to both of them.

The presence of SOBOMETRA in Bolivia allows for an overarching organization to which various practitioners can belong; the group also runs workshops for those wishing to know more about traditional medicine practice. In this way, it helps to disseminate valuable information and bring people together. Unfortunately, problems sometimes arise as the result of the government's inconsistent support of SOBOMETRA and a general lack of infrastructure. Although the Ministry of Health has promoted SOBOMETRA since the organization was established by law, thus leaving the door open for alternative health practice, solid funding has been lacking. Therefore, the group is unable to bring together a true synthesis of biomedical practice and traditional medicine.

For example, during a workshop on tuberculosis (TB), which was sponsored by both the Ministry of Health and SOBOMETRA,[3] participants complained that the exchange of ideas was "asymmetrical"—that is, the biomedical doctors sought only some complementary practices (the use of certain traditional medicines to boost the immune system) that they could promote alongside the standard biomedical regimen (an array of antibiotics, administered in a monitored situation). Biomedical doctors also hope to train natural medicine doctors to identify patients with TB, who they will then send to the biomedical "specialists." Because

---

3. The workshop was titled "Tuberculosis: Complementary Actions Between Andean Traditional Medicine, and Health Services for Its Control" (June 15, 2002).

of the powerful position occupied by biomedicine, called "authoritative medicine" by Jordan and Davies-Floyd (1992), some of the workshop participants charged that the dialog was part of a pattern of "borrowing" by biomedical practitioners, without fully valuing what alternative practitioners have to offer. One biomedical doctor confided that she has yet to see these exchanges go beyond "simple dialogs, and theory." At this particular TB workshop, the tension between practitioners of biomedicine and natural medicine was readily evident, though they shared a common rhetoric and perception that there was ample ground for "complementarity" and for cooperation.

Naturismo is taught and learned in a school-like setting, unlike Andean healing in the countryside, which is transmitted orally from person to person. For this reason, curanderos criticize naturismo as being divorced from Andean cosmology and lacking the social orientation of traditional healing. Seen from this perspective, naturismo is purely "academic." The curandero Carlos, for example, sees a need and a use for this type of medicine, but is troubled that a naturista knows little about the incorporation of ritual techniques in healing, and that the healing techniques employed are not based in a religious system, aside from a belief in the power of nature. Many naturistas do not have a firm grounding in Andean cosmology, nor necessarily practice it themselves. For instance, two very important roles for curanderos in rural areas are to diagnose health problems using coca, and to perform rituals that will help cure the patient alongside the patient's family. Naturistas do not perform rituals, but rather are involved only in the "physical" side of healing through the use of food, herbal preparations, and healthy living advice. Carlos argues that much of this advice is reasonable but ignores spiritual aspects of healing, making the treatments not altogether efficacious.

Carlos and Dr. Asturias (a biomedical doctor with training in traditional medicine) also argue that the loss of the spiritual aspects of healing has come about through naturismo's association with commerce. Carlos explains that migrants to the city looking for business opportunities are drawn into the commercialization of natural medicine. They are looking for "something that will sell"; they need to make a living. Secondarily they might seek knowledge in this area, especially as a way to improve their businesses and advance their economic goals. Dr. Asturias believes that at times this commercialization threatens traditional medicine, rather than promoting it. In her view, traditional medicine is threatened by not taking care of it—it should be "rescued" and recorded carefully, and returned to the rural folk whose ancestors used it.

Most consumers of natural medicine and traditional medicine see the two branches as components of the same system. In the eyes of healing experts, however, they represent different options that offer different treatments and results. The remainder of this chapter considers four case studies, to demonstrate how natural medicine is purveyed through commercial enterprises in the city of Cochabamba. The case studies also illuminate the important link between commerce and natural medicine, which in turn is changing the shape of how people perceive traditional medicine in general, and the ways in which it is practiced.

COMMERCE AND HEALING: THE MARKETPLACE
SERVICES OF A NATURAL MEDICINE DOCTOR

The name of Jorge's natural medicine business is *Kiosco El Gran Médico* ("The Great Doctor's Kiosk"). Located at one of the busiest intersections in the Cochabamba marketplace, his stand's visibility and the sheer traffic that flows by this busy corner give Jorge a claim to this title. The name also indicates the kind of services to be found here: Jorge will offer medical advice as a *naturista*, and his customers will be able to purchase a number of products that promote *salud, nutrición, y fortaleza* ("health, nutrition, and strength") as promised by his advertisements. Jorge is both a healer and a businessman. He is also a good talker, as required by his profession and his daily interactions with a cross-section of the populace of Cochabamba.

On the first day I met Jorge, I noted his emphasis on religion; he discussed the power of herbs alongside his faith in God. Describing himself as a Christian, he

FIGURE 8.1 Jorge's Kiosk.

speaks fervently of the power of medicinal plants, and harkens back to biblical times when "people lived 600, 700, even 900 years." In his account, people began to have health problems when they left behind their "natural lifestyle" and began to eat a poor diet. Jorge sees his work as a healer as one of helping people return to a better way of life. To achieve this goal, he prescribes not only herbal medicines (*fitoterápia*), but also a healthy diet, steam baths (*hidroterápia*), and mineral poultices (*geoterápia*). This broad-ranging health system is what characterizes his brand of naturismo, and Jorge's work and business are excellent examples of the way this system operates to provide health care to people interested in the health benefits it promises.

Jorge's reputation and business location have drawn in a large clientele, and he has become an important leader within the group of local naturistas, especially those working out of the marketplace—in 2000, he was the Director of Natural Medicines for the Department of Cochabamba. Jorge is also active in union organizing within the marketplace and has been the leader of the marketplace sellers' union for many years. And he is a trailblazer—his practice was an early one in the marketplace and helped pave the way for other natural medicine doctors and related vendors to sell their products successfully to the Cochabamba populace.

When I first met Jorge and his wife Cristina, they were warm and welcoming after hearing who I was and learning about my interest in studying the sale and use of traditional medicines. Even though their cramped space left little spare room to maneuver, they allowed me to sit on one of the folding chairs set up for waiting customers (and people often did have to wait for a consultation) and to observe the stream of customers seeking advice, while I simultaneously took in the constant swirl of activity on the market street outside their striped awning. Whenever a short break in the activity occurred, we conversed. On one of these occasions, in between chatting with Jorge and Cristina, I specifically recorded the customers and other market folk who came and went. The following description provides a snapshot of the activity in this stand in a one-hour period, indicating the popularity of the stand, while providing a glimpse into the commerce of natural medicine. The day I recorded these observations was a Tuesday, and my visit took place during mid-morning, so it was not a particularly busy period at their stand. Nonetheless a steady stream of people poured in and out of Jorge's kiosk, as usual.

One man, a naturista himself, came to the stand at the beginning of this period to discuss some business matters with Jorge, including a plan for organizing a meeting of naturistas from the area. Their talk dealt with how to get more people involved—they bemoaned the lack of collaboration among members of the group.

Interrupting their heated discussion, a Quechua-speaking woman came by with some fresh herbs she tried to sell to Jorge. He respectfully replied to her in Quechua. Although he was not interested in purchasing her wares, he told her where to find the vendors of fresh herbs, to see if they would buy the plants from her.

After a pause in the activity, and after Jorge's naturista colleague had also departed, a forty-five-year-old middle-class woman came in complaining of pain in her upper back and shoulders. Jorge diagnosed a "lung problem," and sold her a whole set of medicines to take, including garlic tablets, cough syrup, herbal tea packets, *propolis* (from bees), and *sangre de grado* ("dragon's blood"—a red sap from the Amazonian tree *Croton lecheri*).[4] Speaking carefully and repeating himself so that his customer would remember, he took about fifteen minutes to explain how to take the medicines, what her diet should consist of, and how she should prepare the vapor baths to ease the immediate pain and facilitate the healing process. Jorge also handed the customer one of his informational sheets on which much of the diet advice is printed. On it he scribbled some further notes—a kind of medical prescription. At one point the woman seemed to balk at the price of the medicines (about $15 for everything), but Jorge assured her that it was all "guaranteed," and stated that she could return the product for a refund if she wasn't satisfied.

While Jorge was waiting on this woman and selling her his natural medicine products, another Quechua-speaking campesino approached the stand, somewhat cautiously. Jorge waited on him next, speaking with the sixty-year-old man in Quechua about his health problem, which he diagnosed as prostate related. From his shop's shelves, he took down a bottle of pills, which he sold the man for approximately $5. Jorge did not sell this customer anything else or speak to him about diet, but he did describe to the man the special steam baths he should take and the herb teas he should drink, made using common plants. The implication was that this individual would already have a better diet as he lived in the countryside, and that the man would have the herbs available to him in their natural state, in contrast to his previous customer.

Before the next customer arrived, there was a lull in the stand's activity. Outside on the city street, itinerant vendors passed by, shoppers flowed along in a steady stream toward La Cancha, and traffic pulsated. The next customer, a forty-year-old, tall upper-class man, confidently approached the stand. He came for help with a "pulmonary problem" and was sold a bottle of pills. This man had been at the stand before, and he knew what he needed because he had already purchased the pills at least once before. He left after he made his purchase; very few words were exchanged.

Several minutes later, the next customer, a fifty-year-old middle-class woman, remarked that she had come on the advice of her daughter. She complained of bad breath. Jorge prescribed the same medicines for her "lung problems" as he had for the first middle-class woman (who was also diagnosed as suffering from lung problems), along with some herbal preparations.[5]

As Jorge was speaking with this woman, the next customer arrived and waited restlessly just at the edge of the stand. She was a young woman, approximately twenty-five years old. Jorge's wife Cristina waited on her as by then Jorge had

---

4. *Sangre de grado/drago* ("dragon's blood") and its myriad uses within Bolivian natural medicine regimes are described later in this chapter.

5. On a different day, when I had asked Jorge to prescribe something for the ongoing sinus problems I was experiencing, he diagnosed my condition as "sinusitis" but prescribed the basic medicines for "lung problems" that he used for two customers in this period of observation. In keeping with the basic principles of naturismo, which shares elements of Chinese medicine, the organism is composed of five major systems: the heart, stomach, liver, lungs, and kidneys. As a consequence, any problem having to do with the respiratory system is diagnosed as a "lung problem."

departed to talk to someone about selling some land (a country lot, outside Co-chabamba). Diagnosing the problem herself, this young customer complained of "liver problems." She explained that one side of her abdomen hurt, especially when she bent there. Cristina asked if something had upset her lately (a state of mind that is considered to cause liver ailments); the young woman said yes, that she had been depressed over the death of her boyfriend. When Cristina told her the price of the medicine that Cristina felt would help the alleged liver problems, the young woman hesitated, then responded that she would have to consult with her husband about the medicine's cost. She then departed without buying any-thing. This exchange left Cristina shaking her head, trying to understand a young married woman's grief over a deceased boyfriend. Cristina went on to tell me that she has heard every kind of complaint and story in her line of work, and that many ailments cannot be cured with medicines.

Before I left the kiosk to visit vendors in other parts of the marketplace, the police came through on an inspection tour of this section of the marketplace, and noted down the name of Jorge's stand for their paperwork. This is a routine procedure to keep track of old and new stands. Cristina said the police were doing a "census" while also checking up on the vendors, who are required to pay rent on their stands. According to Cristina, the police had begun "keeping track of people" in an effort to clean up the marketplace, because many kids in this area of Cochabamba had become involved in glue sniffing. One of Cristina's nieces had become a glue addict and has never been the same since, even though she quit using the inhalants.

This description of an hour in the life of a natural medicine stand in the marketplace captures some important elements of naturismo. First, it shows nat-ural medicine's dual aspects: Naturismo is almost always practiced as a healing/medical system alongside the commercialization of various products that are aimed at bringing about the healing in question. Jorge's business takes the form of a kiosk, or a market "stand," but his presence within it as a natural medicine doctor gives the interactions there the quality of a medical consultation. His diagnoses emerge from the verbal descriptions of health ailments given by his customers, but in 2002 he was also in the process of opening up a consulting room (*consultorio*) that would be very similar to those used by medical doctors when examining their patients. Jorge hoped to increase this aspect of his work while continuing to sell health products.

The wide cross-section of patients who came to the stand on this day is also typical, demonstrating the diversity of natural medicine's followers even in this short sketch. From Quechua-speaking campesinos to upper-class clients, natural treatments appeal to a diverse group of people. The appeal for the campesino is the medicines' modern appearance; urban customers appreciate their natural origins. Even my presence was representative of a certain type of clientele—Jorge reports that many foreigners come to him seeking cures for ailments ranging from asthma to cancer to "nerves" (*nervios*). Jorge has quite a few customers he describes as "moneyed" or upper class. Although a broad cross-section of people may consult with him, the ones who are most likely to buy his products and return to buy more are those who are economically well off. A charge of 100 bolivianos (around

$15 in 2000) is not a small amount to Bolivians; indeed, for most people this sum represents a substantial cash outlay. It is certainly possible to visit the doctor (or at least some doctors) for the same amount of money, so the popularity of Jorge's treatments is not necessarily due to its cost alone. Rather, many of his customers like the well-rounded advice on health and diet that Jorge gives them, the natural products, and the fact that health care remains more in their own hands than when they visit the doctor.

DRAGON'S BLOOD, COMMERCIALIZATION, AND NATURISMO

One of Jorge's key ingredients is dragon's blood, or *sangre de drago*.[6] Jorge claims he was the first person in Bolivia to use dragon's blood as a commercial medicine, beginning in 1983. According to Jorge, a Peruvian, Dr. Carrasco, used this in-gredient before him as a "regenerator." This doctor administered it in tiny doses, combining it with distilled water in a homeopathic manner. Likewise, Jorge began by using it by drops. He now has increased the dosage, after seeing that it is effective in much higher amounts.

Jorge claims that dragon's blood has amazing curative powers. He says, "It cures more than 200 illnesses." Many other naturistas now prescribe it as a cure-all for topical and internal use. Following this logic, in Jorge's treatment regimen, he regularly prescribes dragon's blood to patients with various sorts of illnesses. Taken internally, it is used as laxative or as a treatment for diarrhea (depending on dosage). It is also used to treat irregular vaginal discharge. When used topically, the claims for it range from an ointment for wounds to a blemish remover. In general, dragon's blood is considered an excellent topical treatment for all sorts of skin problems. It is also reputed to be an excellent healer of ulcers and piles, especially if taken with particular herbs. Dragon's blood is also administered as an astringent for diarrhea.

The plant that Jorge uses and that is found throughout Bolivian marketplaces is native to the area, but the sobriquet "dragon's blood" may actually be an Old World transplant. Dragon's blood is a name bestowed on the red resin that comes from a variety of plants. The early Greeks, Romans, and Arabs all believed that dragon's blood had medicinal properties, and the ancient Greek physician and botanist Dioscorides, in his classic text *De Materia Medica*, described its healing powers.

The chief source of dragon's blood in ancient times was *Dracaena cinnabari*, a tree in the agave family. Another species that produces dragon's blood is *Dracaena draco*, which is found in the Canary Islands and East Indies. Dragon's blood was used as a source for varnish in the eighteenth century by violin makers; later it was used in photoengraving. Today the most common source of

---

6. Sangre de grado (*Croton lecheri* or *Croton charaguensis*), is a euphorb, common in tropical and subtropical regions of the world (De Lucca and Zalles 1992:113). When this particular *Croton* tree is cut, the latex (some call it "sap" or "resin") runs out with the color and consistency of blood, which is the source of its colorful name.

Photo by Sarah Linn Gallardo

F I G U R E 8.2   Sign in marketplace listing a combination of ailments and remedies. Note that Sangre de Grado ("Dragon's Blood") is listed, toward the bottom.

the resin, as it is employed in medicinal preparations as well as in dyes, comes from *Daemomorops draco*, also known as "dragon's blood palm." This particular palm is indigenous to Sumatra, though similar species are found in Malaysia and Borneo. The same palm, also known as *Calamus draco*, is now found in the New World, and used in the traditional medicine of the greater Southwest United States. In a new twist, it is sometimes called *sangre de venado* ("stag's blood") in reference to a real rather than a mythical beast (Curtin and Moore 1947:162). Spanish New Mexicans buy the dried red resin in traditional medicine pharmacies and use it variously in the treatment of paralysis, *aire*, or even employ it in love magic (p. 162).

The "dragon's blood" used in South America is from the *Croton lecheri*[7] tree and has become a popular commercial herbal remedy in the past decade especially. The tree grows from ten to twenty meters high, and has mottled bark and large heart-shaped, bright green leaves (Taylor 1998:198). The genus *Croton* is rich in alkaloids, and many of its 750 species are used as sources of medicines, especially purgatives and tonics (p. 198). Although its use in South America dates back at least several centuries (Loza-Balsa 1995), this plant's fame has spread through its incorporation into natural medicine treatments and new commercial preparations. The dragon's blood tree is found in ten Latin American countries, and it has been widely used for medicinal purposes by a

---

7. Other species of *Croton*, such as *charaguensis* and *roborensis*, are also called dragon's blood, and are used in similar ways (De Lucca and Zalles, 1992).

number of indigenous groups in the lowlands areas. Bernabé Cobo (1653) described its curative powers in the 1600s as a plant used by indigenous groups in Mexico, Peru, and Ecuador. Calancha (1638) also mentions it in his writings, although we cannot be sure that the particular plant these chroniclers mention is the *Croton lecheri* of today. The name does indicate a familiarity with the plant in the Old World, however.

Croton's contemporary and ubiquitous presence in Andean marketplaces and as an ingredient in a wide array of prepared medicines is largely due to recent efforts to commercialize it. Although it is used mainly as a topical treatment for healing wounds and irritations, and to treat herpes lesions and sore muscles, it has been used internally for a vast array of illnesses, including diarrhea, respiratory infections, symptoms of cold and flu, tonsillitis, rheumatism, enhancement of fertility, contraception, hemorrhoids, and tuberculosis (Conte 1996, King 1996).

The plant extract known as dragon's blood has been further developed as a modern pharmaceutical. Shaman Pharmaceuticals began its testing of *Croton lecheri* in the company's early days of operation (early 1990s). Shaman isolated an antiviral fraction from the latex, which it tested as a treatment for genital herpes and respiratory problems (Clapp and Crook, 2002). Eventually the developers shifted their focus to an oral formulation for the treatment of diarrhea. When Shaman became a "botanical supplement" company, renamed Shaman Botanicals in 1998,[8] it continued to test and use dragon's blood in its formulas, especially in the product called "Normal Stool Formula." The company recommends this herbal medicine for any type of diarrhea, but especially when the condition is chronic. In its press releases, Shaman claims that dragon's blood is an effective treatment for HIV-positive patients who suffer from chronic diarrhea. In preparation for large-scale exploitation of *Croton lecheri*, Shaman has also actively promoted research on the ecology, production, and sustainable management of *Croton*, and has attempted reforestation programs in Latin America intended to guarantee a sustainable harvest of this plant (Clapp and Crook 2002).

WILSON: NEW OPPORTUNITIES IN THE CITY

Unlike the case involving Jorge, who is a businessman and a healer, this next case study illustrates the work of a vendor who is not a naturista and is not affiliated with any healing tradition, old or new. Wilson's family migrated to Cochabamba in 1985 from the Siglo XX mine in Oruro. At that time the mining industry was in sharp decline, and the mining centers were full of unemployed miners. In the

8. Shaman Pharmaceuticals, founded in 1989, is a well-known example of a company that tried to buck the exploitative bioprospecting model, by remunerating the people and communities with which they worked. The firm had a "vision of collaborating with the rainforests' indigenous people as part of a sophisticated drug discovery and development process of modern Western medicine" (quoted in Clapp and Crook 2002). Shaman's bankruptcy ultimately led the company into the nutritional supplement market. Its failure as a pharmaceutical company should be seen in light of the financial difficulties of drug development rather than as a failure of the collaborative model of drug discovery (Clapp and Crook 2002).

early half of the 1980s, Bolivia experienced runaway inflation followed by economic "shock" programs that led to massive unemployment. Roughly 45,000 jobs were terminated in the mining sector and public administration (Farthing 1991). Fanning out from the mining centers, people began the process of searching for new employment opportunities, eventually arriving in cities like La Paz and Cochabamba, and finding their way into the informal economy. Wilson's family is a classic example of the fate experienced by the "relocalized miners" within Bolivia. Although the government claimed to be involved in "relocating" them into new job sectors, high unemployment in Bolivia precluded this outcome; instead, ex-miners scrambled to find jobs on their own. Lacking secure employment, they were pushed into the city, along with many other rural migrants who came from agricultural regions. Relocalized miners generally have the advantage in that they speak Spanish and have received specific job training, but in the city the miners and their families end up in a variety of service or informal sector jobs, similar to what happens to agricultural workers.

As in other "relocalized" families, it was the children in Wilson's family who had to support the parents. Wilson is one of seven children. Because their parents were unable to find secure work, each sibling began in turn to work in various occupations. Wilson and his older brother, who were the eldest boys in the family, started out by working for the natural remedies company called Coincoca.[9] There they learned about the properties and commerce of traditional medicines from their work with the family who runs this cottage industry. As Wilson explains, his brother was good at business, and after several years decided to open his own kiosk selling natural medicines (around 1994), including some of his own products that he concocted at home. The brother based some of his formulas on those of Coincoca, but he also experimented and came up with his own recipes. He was also interested in natural medicine, so he studied books describing products like bee pollen, royal jelly, and brewer's yeast—products that he planned to sell at the stand.

At their stand, the brothers began to sell products from a variety of sources, including the local distributors of natural medicines, one of which was Coincoca. At their small kiosk, which is located on a busy street at the edge of the Calatayud Market (where the vendors of fresh herbal remedies and the naturista Jorge also have their stands), the pair began to offer an appealing array of natural medicine pharmaceuticals, a few packaged herbs, coca toothpaste, bee products, and a coffee substitute drink. Their partnership was cut short when Wilson's brother died in a motorcycle accident at 29 years of age; Wilson now runs the stand on his own, maintaining it in the way his brother did when he was alive. The stand had just opened when his brother died, and Wilson talks about keeping his brother's "dream alive." Wilson's brother had actually studied natural medicine in preparation for making the products, but Wilson has not, and feels that he does not have the time or the inclination for it. He considers himself to be a businessman. Because his brother had built up a clientele before his death, Wilson is able to keep the business running and provide his wares to "all classes

---

9. See Chapters 6 and 7 for more on Coincoca.

of people"—rich, middle class, poor, peasants, everybody. He has quite a few *caseros* (regular clients).

Wilson's case illustrates how the commerce of traditional medicine represents a business opportunity for migrants to the city, and might serve as a source of income even without the underpinnings of beliefs in and training surrounding the natural medicine system. Wilson is an example of an individual who runs a natural remedies stand without having much background in naturismo, and without demonstrating much interest in studying to become a naturista himself. In this way he differs from the other case studies explored here, in which the subjects do have a strong desire to become knowledgeable in natural medicine as well as aspiring to sell the products.

MARIBEL: FROM Q'UWERA TO NATURISTA

Maribel was eighteen years old when she got her own stand and began selling q'uwas just around the corner from her mother's stand in the marketplace.[10] She had worked with her mother since she was a young girl and knew the business of selling ritual ingredients through her experience assisting her mother and speaking to a variety of customers. When she got a separate locale, her mother helped her by equipping Maribel with the goods and the know-how to run this kind of business. But right from the beginning Maribel favored the plants and herbal remedies that she could offer to her customers over the line of ritual items that her mother had always sold. Even at a young age Maribel was an excellent businesswoman, and she was the first of the Q'uweras to include herbal remedies at her stand in this section of the marketplace, in a place where only ritual items had been sold before.

When Maribel entered this line of work, right away she noticed her neighbor-vendors watching what she was up to ("*Había miramiento*," she said—"There was envy"), and knew they were noting the new customers whom she brought in with the herbal remedies. Some of Maribel's customers bought small quantities of dried herbs; others bought by the kilo and even by the *arroba* (1 arroba = 25 pounds). The people who came to buy in such large quantities were mostly naturistas, and they purchased the plants to make their own herbal preparations, which they would then prescribe to customers or sell at their own businesses. As a result of this exchange, Maribel began to have contact with naturismo and to learn from her customers how to use and administer herbal remedies.[11] As Maribel's business grew, the other vendors began to copy her by incorporating herbal remedies into their inventories. This shift in focus took place around 1995. Little by little, more vendors began to offer herbs at the Q'uwera stands at La Cancha. Today, in fact, many Q'uweras' stands sell a combination of plants and ritual items—not unlike the stands of the vendors in Oruro on Calle Junín.

---

10. The Cochabamba Q'uweras (i.e., ritual ingredient vendors) are described in detail in Chapter 6.

11. Although she feels that she has a background in natural medicine from her upbringing around medicines, and through the teachings of her mother and grandmother, Maribel did not obtain any formal training in naturismo until later.

Nonetheless, it is interesting that so many people see the selling of ritual items and herbal remedies as separate undertakings, and that the vendors themselves have specialized in one or the other until very recently with the introduction of "combination" stands such as Maribel's.

Maribel has the mind of an entrepreneur, so once again she began looking for a new business opportunity. In 1999, she opened a storefront on a busy street just off the marketplace. Her new business is located approximately three blocks away from her mother's stand in the Q'uwera section of La Cancha, but a long enough distance away from the other sellers whom she had begun to see as competition. One of the things that Maribel most appreciates about her new location is that she is "alone"—that is, in a location where she is not surrounded by neighbors who sell similar items ("*Quería alejarme,*" she said—"I wanted to distance myself"). She also loves having her own space and filling it with the fragrant herbs that shoppers sometimes are able to smell before they see them. "It is the aroma that attracts people," she told me.[12]

Once in this new location, Maribel began to sell dried herbs in much larger quantities, along with a whole series of bottled pills and syrups made by natural medicine companies. She also started her own line of products, manufacturing small envelopes of powdered herbs that sell well not just at her store but throughout the city. She also began to make and sell her own syrups, essences, and oils. In this way, her new business evolved to incorporate elements of a cottage industry (or micro-enterprise). The inventory in her store is huge, and includes rows upon rows of dried herbs alongside pharmacy-like cases that are stocked with prepared natural medicines from many different companies. Maribel also sells ointments and lotions, herbal teas (in teabags), bee pollen and royal jelly, wheat germ and brewer's yeast, soaps, pamphlets, and vitamins. Only twenty-five years old at the time of opening her shop, Maribel is a naturista, a successful businesswoman, and a mother, and she has the shop with the largest inventory of natural medicines in the city of Cochabamba.

To manufacture the numerous herbal preparations she sells in small envelopes, and to obtain the bulk quantities of herbs she offers, Maribel relies on a network of purveyors who bring her the fresh plants. These suppliers comprise a network of women with whom she has formed a working relationship. Generally peasants from around Cochabamba, these individuals come from Punata, Capinota, and Tiquipaya (villages relatively close to the city of Cochabamba). At first Maribel collected the plants herself, but she wasn't able to keep up with her business and the necessary volume of plant collecting, so she started to ask the women who bring herbs to sell wholesale from the countryside to get the plants for her. Specifically, she asked them to bring dried plants in large quantities.[13] When the purveyors saw that she needed such a large volume, some women started to work

---

12. Maribel's customers are a mix of people who mainly live in the city. In Maribel's opinion, people from the countryside are stronger and healthier. When they get sick, the illness is usually not as serious as those experienced by city dwellers.

13. Maribel had to "teach" the purveyors with whom she worked to wash the plants and to dry them in the shade (so they would come to her in good condition).

Photo by Lynn Sikkink

FIGURE 8.3 The natural medicine offerings at Maribel's store.

together and pool what they could collect to provide Maribel with the amount
she needed.

In 2000, Maribel was buying as much as 60 arrobas[14] of dried plants per week,
which she received at a corn mill in Cochabamba that had agreed to grind her
plants on Thursdays. At one point she received plants on both Mondays and
Thursdays, but the chaos and volume became too great; now she concentrates this
activity on only one day. At the mill, Maribel separates out the plants that she will
sell individually in bins in her store or on a wholesale basis. The rest of the plants
are ground up to be used as ingredients in her herbal preparations.

Not all of the plants are intended for Maribel's use in the shop. She also has
clients (who buy both the bulk dried plants and the preparations) in Santa Cruz, La
Paz, and even Yacuiba (a frontier town on the border with Argentina). She does
business with them over the phone, and sends their orders out via bus line. Thus
one of her many entrepreneurial activities is acting as a wholesaler of medicinal
herbs that come from the environs of Cochabamba.

---

14. One *arroba* is equivalent to approximately 25 pounds, so this is a huge plant volume, which is able to supply many herbal
preparations.

ALEPH: FROM PHARMACY TO TRADITIONAL
MEDICINE COTTAGE INDUSTRY

Oriana and her husband Freddy started their business with Freddy's cousin as a partnership. They started from nothing, without knowing much about traditional medicines. What they knew, collectively, was business—and they saw a promising opportunity in the rich resources of medicinal plants and knowledge about herbal remedies available in Cochabamba.

Freddy's cousin was the son of the pharmacist from the Farmacia Boliviana, the oldest and most prestigious pharmacy in Cochabamba. In the pharmacy's old records, the partners found ancient "recipes" (formulas) that were used to make cosmetics, and they began experimenting with them. According to Oriana, these "recipes" were handed down by the colonial señoras of the eighteenth and nineteenth centuries, who brought the ideas from Spain, Italy, and Germany. Once in Cochabamba, the formulas were modified to incorporate local ingredients and herbs. Gradually the partners—who named their new company Aleph—began to make lotions, shampoos, facial products, and other items that were based on the old formulas, but modified to better suit the current market and its contemporary customers.

As they worked with these cosmetic formulas, Aleph's founders also became interested in herbal remedies. Soon they began assembling packets of medicinal teas and other products to be sold at their stores. In contrast to the European formulas for making beauty products, Aleph's herbal preparations are perceived as originating in ancient Bolivian indigenous traditions. Oriana explains that these are time-honored traditions, dating from a period when people knew how to take care of themselves *naturalmente* ("naturally").

During Aleph's early years of operation, Oriana's husband Freddy was in charge of organizing the production of the medicines, organizing the stores themselves, and finding purveyors of the medicinal plants Aleph would need for its products. Freddy continued in this role even after his cousin left the business, though he delegated laboratory procedures to the staff that he hired, which included a pharmacist to oversee the preparations of the products themselves. Oriana always had a supporting role in the business, but her role expanded after the cousin-partner left the business, and as her duties became more established. Oriana describes herself as a business partner and a manager. As such, she has taken a much more active role as overseer of the business operations in the past few years, especially since her husband began pursuing his engineering career, which requires him to do a lot of traveling.

The products sold by the Aleph team are varied and include a line of cosmetics, such as a cleansing cream for the face, as well as body oils, shampoos, deodorant, and athlete's foot powder. In terms of their medicinal remedies, they offer products that appeal to their upscale clientele: slimming tonics, a hemorrhoid preparation, and teas for diabetes, nerves, menstrual regulation, and use as a "sexual regenerator." Aleph's products appeal to an urban audience. Indeed, although the company sells a wide array of medicinal preparations, its cosmetics remain the main product line. Clients who come in for a cosmetic application such as a facial may follow it up with the purchase of some beauty products, as well as buying something from the line of herbal remedies to complement the treatment they receive at Aleph.

The Aleph business is truly a cottage industry: The products are made at home, and family members are involved in their manufacture. In contrast to the image of brewing potions in a cramped kitchen, this family's facility is located on the site of a rural estate (an old hacienda), where the walled colonial compound affords them ample room for separate buildings dedicated to the manufacture of their products. Aleph's owners have also been able to hire a small contingent of workers, so that the family can pursue other activities.

Oriana emphasizes that the production process entails everything being done "by hand" and likens it to "handicraft" production, which is "rustic." This description underlines the homey quality of the products, and the fact that they are based on traditions that come from Europe as well as traditions that are indigenous to Bolivia. Aleph also demonstrates a more international marketing sensibility, recognizing that artisanal rustic products are considered very fashionable today.

The family's production facility includes a laboratory, quality control room, packaging room, and storage area. The plants themselves are kept in a separate storage facility that includes a drying area and a plant preparation room. Surrounding these two separate wings of the facility are gardens, where some of the medicinal plants used in the Aleph products are grown in fragrant garden plots. On the grounds of this colonial hacienda, where animals and agricultural plots were once tended by the peasant laborers, a new class of workers sees to the production of contemporary products based on the traditional medicines of the colonial past, transformed to fit the needs of the current market.

The customers who patronize Aleph's stores are mostly upper-class women, unlike the majority of the clients who frequent the various traditional medicine stands in the marketplace. The soothing ambience of Aleph and the service provided by the company's middle-class female assistants make this a comfortable place for upper-class women, who mainly come for help with beauty treatments and products. Middle-class women may also find a special cosmetic here that allows them to feel that they are pampering themselves by participating in the upper-class world of natural beauty products and treatments. Nonetheless, it is interesting to note that a common request at the Aleph outlets is for the "menstrual regulator," which is sought by women who fear they are pregnant and come looking for an abortifacient. This particular herbal product, which other women sometimes seek at traditional medicine stands throughout the city of Cochabamba, is also sought at Aleph, oftentimes by young girls of lower-class backgrounds.

Thus Aleph boasts a somewhat mixed clientele, who seek a variety of treatments ranging from herbal preparations to beauty products. Although Oriana does not study naturismo, she sees herself as participating in this system of health, by making natural products available to her clients.

Photo by Lynn Sikkink

F I G U R E 8.4   Exterior of Aleph store.

SUMMARY

Naturistas in Bolivia, who can be roughly likened to the "naturopaths" found in alternative medicine, have carved out a niche for themselves in urban venues. Similar to the Cochabamba vendors of traditional medicines described in Chapter 6, they have links to what is perceived to be "authentic Andean traditional medicine," although naturistas emphasize the commercial aspects of their businesses. From offering natural medicine consulting services in the marketplace (as in the case of Jorge's stand), to having a store that caters to the natural medicine crowd (such as Maribel's business), to operating a cottage industry (as illustrated by Aleph, which has grown to include several storefronts), naturismo offers an attractive opportunity to a number of business-minded folks.

More so than the traditional medicine vendors described in earlier chapters, naturistas offer an array of "exotic" natural medicines such as Echinacea, St. John's wort, and various vitamins and minerals in prepared medicines. At the same time, they may employ a "local" (albeit Amazonian) cure such as dragon's blood as an important cure, albeit in a variety of new preparations, casting it as a panacea for urban ailments.

Naturistas may not have direct ties to rural lifestyles (they likely grew up in the city themselves), but they still draw on Andean tradition as an anchor for their practices. Many of them invoke the God of modern Protestant religion as being a healing source as well. As they increasingly use and commercialize Bolivian plant resources, the question of ownership—specifically, who benefits from the sale of these products—has become ever more important. The commercialization of traditional medicines on a countrywide and international level is the topic of the next chapter.

9

Traditional Medicines and Intellectual Property Rights

INTRODUCTION: A CASE OF CONFLICTING CLAIMS

The article in the Bolivian newspaper *Los Tiempos* is titled "Pirates of Life" ("Piratas de la Vida," MacLean 2000). Exploring the controversy over the use of plants and other resources ("Bolivia's patrimony") by foreign companies, especially pharmaceutical companies, the article discusses several cases of biological resources assayed by companies in search of new products and patents. One of these cases involves wira-wira (*Achyroline satureioides*),[1] a plant offered in herbalists' stands throughout Bolivia as a cure for lung and respiratory problems. Wira-wira is recognized and used by people throughout Bolivia, and it is sold in Bolivian marketplaces everywhere. The story in the newspaper claims that wira-wira is being explored as an AIDS (acquired immune deficiency syndrome) drug and that

---

1. Wira-wira is an aromatic annual herb with small white and yellow flowers and leaves that are serrated. When it is dried, wira-wira has the pale appearance of straw due to the white flowers and the pale hair that spans the surface of the plant. The leaves and flowers are the parts employed in medicinal infusions. Several varieties of wira-wira exist, among them the distinct genera of *Gnaphalium* sp. and *Achyroline satureioides*. These varieties are similar in appearance and in the intensity with which they are identified and used as herbal remedies.

at least one of its biologically active components has been patented by a U.S. company.

Known by different common names (the Raintree Nutrition Database lists sixteen such labels), wira-wira is known and used throughout South America. In Brazil, for instance, it is called *macela* and is used for a large number of ailments, including gastric problems, epilepsy, rheumatism, and menstrual pain. In Venezuela, it is used to treat diabetes, as an emmenagogue (menstrual flow stimulator), and to overcome impotency (Raintree Nutrition Database 2003).

In Bolivia and Peru, wira-wira is a well-known treatment for upper respiratory tract infections, especially those involving the chest, lungs, and throat (Lira 1985:162–163). This native plant has a long history of use in the Andes. In fact, wira-wira is mentioned in Contreras y Valverde's (1650) early colonial manuscript describing Cuzco and its characteristics. In the 1600s, it was one of the herbs used by María Ticlla as mentioned in witchcraft proceedings against her when she was accused of *hechizera* ("sorcery")—locally she was recognized as a healer but considered a witch by colonial authorities (Griffiths 1996:100).

In contemporary times, wira-wira has been the most commonly used cold remedy on the dry and colder southern altiplano. Wira-wira's common Bolivian use as a cough remedy and for bronchitis reflects the fact that these ailments are persistent health problems related to high-altitude living. Other uses of this herb, such as its use as a menstrual regulator and a treatment for diabetes, are also known in parts of Bolivia and Peru, and point to its other applications.

That wira-wira is mostly used to treat lung diseases in Bolivia may be related to the large number of viral diseases that may afflict this organ system (Abdel-Malek et al. 1996). Wira-wira has been subject to much phytochemial research; its component properties have been identified and isolated, and explorations have focused on its various local ethnobotanical usages (e.g., Abdel-Malek et al. 1996; Gugliucci and Menini 2002; Santos, Ripoll, Nardi, and Bassani 1999). This attention, in turn, has led to its promotion as an important herbal remedy by companies such as Raintree. Wira-wira is also claimed to be effective against tuberculosis, probably because it has an ability to boost the immune system—a property that aligns it with its proposed use as a treatment for AIDS patients.

The story about biopiracy and wira-wira in the Bolivian newspaper was similar to one I had heard from a Bolivian vendor of traditional medicines. In discussing the consequences of an expanding market in traditional medicines, the vendor claimed that "tons" of the wira-wira plant were being removed from Bolivia because of its potential as an AIDS drug, and she feared that the plant would become extinct. "Then we will have to buy our wira-wira from the United States," she said. A medical doctor also told a related story. She worried that because wira-wira is a wild plant and, therefore, not easily replaced, a day may come when it grows scarce and maybe even threatened. These stories are not unfounded: Wira-wira has certainly been subject to testing as a potential AIDS drug (e.g., Abdel-Malek et al. 1996, Gugliucci and Menini 2002, Santos et al. 1999), and patents are being sought for various extraction processes for wira-wira. From a Bolivian herbalist's perspective, the testing and patenting of wira-wira represent an appropriation of Bolivian patrimony by outsiders, despite the potential benefit that a plant like wira-wira might provide as an immune booster to ailing people beyond Bolivia.

These stories about wira-wira, from different sources, illustrate the controversy over conflicting claims in the search for new drugs as this effort affects countries like Bolivia that are rich in both biodiversity and local/indigenous knowledge about the use of medicinal plants. These countries often serve as the sources for pharmaceutical raw materials but hold few rights over how these plants might be used and whether they can be patented.

Under U.S. patent law, "products of nature" such as the wira-wira plant itself cannot be patented, but compounds isolated from plant material can be if they meet certain requirements, such as being obtained by a new process (Roht-Arriaza, 1996; Yano, 1993). Nonetheless, there is a widespread perception in Bolivia that outsiders are expropriating and patenting the plants themselves. This belief undoubtedly persists because foreign companies do realize—and have in the past reaped—so much profit from the resources and knowledge of natural-resource-rich southern countries, which are the sources for many of their products.

For instance, in 1989 the maca root (*Lepidium peruvianum*) was labeled one of "the lost crops of the Incas" by the U.S.-based National Research Council, leading to a renewed interest in it and other crops deemed ancient and endangered. Public interest in this "rediscovery" of an "Inca" tuber translated into a maca boom when the plant was christened a "natural Viagra" because of its properties as a fertility enhancer for humans and animals, and as a stamina-builder (ETC Genotype, 2002). The maca tuber is a high-altitude crop that can grow at elevations beyond even the normal potato production zone. It is highly nutritious and has been grown for centuries as a food crop in the Andes. Farmers there dispute its classification as a "lost crop." Alejandro Argumedo, a member of the Cuzco-based Association for Sustainable Livelihoods (ANDES), explains:

> Maca may be a forgotten crop in the minds of foreign agronomists, but it
> has never been lost to indigenous peoples of the Andes .... indigenous
> communities have been using maca for food and medicinal purposes
> since before the Conquest. Ironically now we are in danger of losing
> maca—not to extinction, but to predatory U.S. patents. When it comes
> to maca, it's obvious that indigenous farmers are the true innovators,
> not chemists from New Jersey (ETC Genotype, 2002).

Unable to patent the maca plant as a whole organism, pharmaceutical companies have relied on the use of new and "innovative" extraction processes in their claims for patents. On June 28, 2002, a coalition of indigenous peoples' and farmers' organizations demonstrated in Lima, denouncing U.S. pharmaceutical companies for unfairly patenting maca extracts and protesting that "patenting indigenous knowledge is morally wrong and unacceptable" (ETC Genotype, 2002).

The patenting of extraction processes has effectively laid open a pathway to commercial use of many plants, wira-wira included. In the search for new drugs and patents, the leads provided by indigenous use of particular plants are very profitable: Bioprospectors who consult local or indigenous people increase their success ratio in trials for useful substances from 1 in 10,000 samples (random

Photo by Sarah Linn Gallardo

FIGURE 9.1   Vendors market their maca as "Andean Viagra," conscious of prevailing health trends.

biological testing) to 1 in 2 samples (Roht-Arriaza, 1996:928). Also, because it is so uncommon for the original users to receive any type of compensation for this information and guidance, the effects are similar to the plant itself being patented out from under the original holders.[2] From a global perspective, patents on crop plants, animals, and even human genetic material have pushed the parameters and thrown into question the justice of patent laws. As medicinal resources, plants and

2. In a related vein, Bolivians have disputed the claims made by mega-multinational corporation Bechtel over the company's claim of "profit loss" when it was forced out of its bid to bring privatized water to the Cochabamba valley. Bolivians protested the high water prices and the general privatization initiative that characterizes the Bolivian government's approach to public utilities, and argued against an outsider's "right" to sell them the water to which they had customary claim. Despite the IMF's "structural readjustments," which include the privatization of various public utilities, after seventeen years Bolivia remains the poorest country in Latin America (Finnegan 2003:45). Bolivia is involved in other natural resource "wars" such as the use of its natural gas reserves and the potential industrialization of coca. The use, benefits, and profits from medicinal plants fall under this broad rubric.

their patentability stand at the crux of the problem of indigenous knowledge versus intellectual property rights.

WIRA-WIRA AND TRADITIONAL MEDICINES AS COMMON RESOURCES

Wira-wira illustrates a case of how an herbal remedy can be exploited for the raw material itself (in this case, the plant wira-wira has been extensively tested) as well as for the knowledge and uses surrounding its ethnobotanical uses. A basic premise of ethnobotany is that the longer a particular group of people has used local plants, the greater the knowledge of those plants will be (Plotkin 1993). There is much variation in ethnobotanical knowledge, however, and ethnobotanist Mark Plotkin claims that "the most sophisticated 'native botanists' known to scientists today are found among South American Indians" (1993:56).

In the case of more isolated groups,[3] some researchers have posited that their unfamiliarity with crowd diseases and other infections that come with outside contact means that their medicinal plant repertoire is smaller, because it focuses on a small number of noncontagious conditions such as skin infections and fungal problems, along with herbal treatments for conditions such as childbirth and postpartum recovery. Ethnobotanists Wade Davis and James Yost (1983) have described how the Waorani, until recently a relatively isolated Amazonian group who inhabited the upland forests in Ecuador, had quite a small inventory of medicinal plants because they had dealt with smaller number of ailments. Reporting on a group on the other side of the Amazon, the ethnobotanist William Balée (1994) details the ethnobotanical knowledge of an indigenous group who migrated from the interior to a position closer to the coast. This group, the Ka'apor, uses a variety of plants to treat thirty-seven recognized diseases (p. 108). Baleé claims that the Ka'apor's traditional knowledge of medicinal plants is greater than that of the Waorani of Ecuador because the Ka'apor have had more contact with the non-Indians and the diseases they brought, but he also believes that the Waorani suffered a "regression of knowledge" due to conquest and its aftershocks (p. 113). In other words, groups of people will attempt to meet the challenges of contact by adapting in many ways, including their use of medicinal plants, but these groups may also suffer a loss of ethnobotanical knowledge if their numbers drop too quickly, and especially if their losses include individuals such as shamans who are the repositories of much ethnobotanical knowledge.

This discussion of the scope of knowledge surrounding medicinal plants and their uses among indigenous groups raises the issue of who controls and disseminates this knowledge within the group itself. Unlike the health care practiced under a biomedical system, within ethnomedical systems knowledge is more widely dispersed throughout the group. For many ailments, people simply treat themselves

---

3. It is more appropriate to talk about degrees of insulation from the neighboring groups and urban peoples given that all groups have now had at least some contact with "outsiders." Amazonian groups such as the Waorani and the Yanomami remained fairly isolated, however, until several decades back.

and their family members. Specialists do exist, however. In many Amazonian societies, the shaman is the healing specialist who has the most sophisticated ethnobotanical knowledge, which was passed on to him (and occasionally her) by an older shaman. Over time, information is passed not only vertically from generation to generation, but also horizontally from group to group. As a result, knowledge about a specific plant may become quite widespread geographically and even across ethnic groups. This generalized picture of ethnobotanical knowledge indicates the difficulty in addressing the related questions of where the knowledge comes from, how this knowledge is developed, and to whom it belongs.

In many parts of Bolivia, the health care that people have available to them can be described as medical pluralism, in that it combines elements from the biomedical system (present in clinics throughout rural areas) and from the system of traditional medicine commonly used for self-treatment, but also as practiced by Andean healers. The inventories of traditional medicine from various vendors surveyed in this book are examples of the material aspects of this medical pluralism.

Throughout South America, many of the plants used in this hybrid system of traditional medicine are the same ones. Some of them are derived from native plants (such as wira-wira, pupusa, and lamphaya) that have been used for as long as people remember. Others come from Hispanic tradition, having been introduced by the Spaniards and modeled after the uses in that system, but later adapted to Andean beliefs and uses. Such is the case with plants like chamomile, rosemary, rue, certain mints, and lavender. Introduced and native plants alike were part of the plant repertoire of the Andean healers who traveled to treat people (such as the Kallawaya healers) or the exchange networks of traders who bartered and later sold medicinal plants from the highlands, Amazon basin, and mid-altitude valleys. Through this means, plants have criss-crossed the Bolivian landscape, even serving as cultural links between groups unfamiliar with one another. In many areas, the marketplace now serves as the meeting place for these different medicines and traditions, bringing them together in a varied and complex pharmacopoeia that represents a mix from different traditions and eras.

Medicinal plants represent goods and services that have already been discovered, tested, and used by human subjects for years, and they provide fertile ground for pharmaceutical companies in their search for new drugs. Unfortunately for the Bolivian holders of this medicinal knowledge, the entire healthcare system is considered in the "public domain" by patent seekers and businesses. Thus traditional medicine practices can be exploited without consideration of any kind of permission from, or compensation paid to, the actual users of these plant products and traditions.

Looking again at the example of wira-wira in Bolivia, we find a plant commonly encountered across the Andean highlands that is recognized as coming in two variants, "highland wira-wira" and "valley wira-wira." The trajectories and uses of wira-wira also vary. Wira-wira is collected by individuals in rural villages in the highlands and used to treat coughs. Specialized medicine vendors in rural and urban marketplaces also sell it. This plant is an important component of the inventories of the vendors discussed in Chapters 4 through 6. Wira-wira is employed by curanderos in treatments they prescribe to customers to combat respiratory infections. Given this complex picture of the plant's usage, it is difficult to say where the knowledge of this plant originates or who should control its use. As in other cases of communal use, the very question of ownership may be inappropriate, as it is obvious that wira-wira is firmly part of *medicina popular* ("medicine of the people"), whose original innovators have been lost over the span of time because the plant has been used by so many people.

When a pharmaceutical company benefits from the use of wira-wira, the question of who should be compensated is difficult to answer. Clearly the company has benefited from the initial information that wira-wira has widespread medicinal use, and from the accumulated knowledge this use represents, but the entire Andean population is a very large group to be compensated, and it would prove impossible to attempt such a feat. The case of wira-wira illustrates how knowledge of medicinal plants is often community knowledge—a perspective that conflicts with the proprietary view taken by pharmaceutical companies that search for new drugs and patent the ensuing products. Writing on biopiracy, Vandana Shiva calls this effect the "enclosure of the intellectual commons" in that Western intellectual property rights, vested in individuals and their "innovations," are given priority over what she calls "common property knowledge and resource systems" (1997:17, 67). She argues that "the metaphor of bioprospecting thus hides the prior use, knowledge, and rights associated with biodiversity" (p. 73).

Many of the medicinal plants used by Bolivians face problems of scarcity and overexploitation. These serious problems need to be addressed both by national governments and by the companies interested in using them as medicinal resources. The ancient Greek case of the plant called *silphion* is a good example. Used for everything from hemorrhoids to uterine contractions, this wild plant was gathered in ancient Jordan with such commercial zeal that it was literally rooted out and became extinct (Tyler 1996). A few medicinal plants in Bolivia are already being subjected to intense commercial pressures and are becoming very hard to find (though they are not yet extinct). These plants include certain varieties of mint, a plant called *carqueja*, a tree named *quewiña*, and *Echinaceae* (now harvested around the world) (Carlos Prado, personal communication, 2000).

The renewed interest in traditional medicines and the competition surrounding them arise from the marketplace vendors; natural medicine companies add to these pressures; and the presence of *rescatadores* (gatherers, literally "rescuers") who collect traditional medicines for resale, compound them. In one Cochabamba business, these collectors bring in several hundred pounds of wild medicinal plants each week for sale (Maribel, personal communication, 2001). Adding further to the challenges, the destruction of habitat that accompanies the expansion of cities wipes out natural resources even before they can be exploited. This process of exploitation and deforestation has been going on for centuries in the Cochabamba Valley (see Gade 1999), but has accelerated in recent years as Cochabamba has expanded to a city of a half million inhabitants. The area around Cochabamba has become so polluted as a consequence of this rapid growth that conscientious naturopaths do not collect medicinal plants in its environs. It may be necessary to collect plants from at least thirty kilometers away to avoid this contamination (Grover Crespo, personal communication, June 12, 2001).

BIOTECHNOLOGY FIRMS VERSUS THE RIGHTS
OF PRIOR USE: PATENTS AND PROBLEMS

Biotechnology firms are able to make such a lucrative business out of the appropriation of Latin American plant medicines because they have patent law on their side. As members of powerful countries, they stand in a particular relationship to indigenous or ethnic groups that gives them a decided advantage over these smaller groups. Anthropologist John Bodley (1990) identifies the key issue as a question of scale: "Small-scale" cultures are characterized not only by small size but also by a communal ethic and a system of egalitarianism that unwittingly provides an opening for their exploitation by large-scale groups or countries.

The examples of land appropriation are legion, both historically and as part of the formation and transformation of modern states (Maybury-Lewis 1997). The myriad cases share a common thread: Indigenous people have faced difficulties in maintaining control over land for which they hold no legal titles or individual rights. The injustice of the many instances of land appropriation is well recognized, but the appropriation of resources and knowledge has not gained the public attention it deserves. In a volume called *Valuing Local Knowledge* (1996), Stephen Brush and Doreen Stabinsky cite the positive contributions found in local knowledge and resource systems. Some of these contributions take the form of the existing plant uses that are of potential benefit to the rest of the world. Another contribution is the maintenance of biodiversity, from which new uses come (Brush and Stabinsky 1996). Protecting local knowledge is thus not simply a human rights issue but a conservation issue as well (Riley and Moran 2001).

Patent law is as inadequate to provide protection to the original users of plant medicines as colonialism is to protect the land rights and sovereignty of a region's prior occupants. The fact that there is a long-standing prohibition against patenting "products of nature" puts herbal remedies at a disadvantage (in terms of indigenous peoples' proprietary claims over them) from the outset, even though no exact definition of a "product of nature" exists (Yano 1993). In particular, patent law places at a disadvantage those indigenous people who use the whole plant without intending to reduce it to its active components (p. 460). Patent law also requires that inventions be "new" or "novel" to warrant patent protection, which precludes patenting those plant uses that have been in existence since time immemorial. In addition, to be deemed patent-worthy, a product must meet a "utility" requirement, meaning that it must serve a potential industrial use, which is not a criterion considered by the original indigenous inventors. Because current patent law unfairly disadvantages indigenous inventors and users of local knowledge, Yano claims that the "current location of the line dividing patentability from nonpatentability" is inappropriate (p. 462). Although patent law ostensibly rewards innovations and their inventors, a closer look reveals that this relationship holds true only under certain systems and within specific cultural contexts (i.e., the business culture of the United States). Recognizing the ability of corporations to use patent law to take ownership of biomaterials, "since the second half of the 1980s, activists have condemned practices of what they call *patent piracy*" (Arts 1998:182).

Traditionally, plants have been enormously important sources for pharmaceuticals. Even today, when many compounds for drugs are synthesized in the laboratory, 25 percent of all prescriptions contain ingredients from whole plants (Farnsworth 1998). Of course, no one knows how many more plants have served as models for synthetic drugs (Tyler 1996:5). Consequently, it is important to protect plants not only from the perspective of indigenous peoples but also because they are sources of important and potentially life-saving drugs. In this way, "compensation should be defined as payment not for past services but for future options" (Brush and Stabinsky 1996:12).

The potential income from the plant derivatives is huge. For example, the two anticancer drugs derived from the rosy periwinkle—vincristine and vinblastine—earned $100 million for Eli Lilly and nothing for the people of Madagascar (Reid et al., 1996:149). A South American plant (the cinchona tree) became the source for the antimalarial drug quinine beginning in the 1700s, and this drug is still in use today—and quina-quina is a plant remedy found everywhere for sale in Andean marketplaces. The bark of the cinchona tree became so valuable in the 1700s that it was worth its weight in silver, spurring the "first conservation crisis" for a medicinal plant in the New World (King 1996:65). Its eventual transplantation to the Old World (India, Sri Lanka, and Southeast Asia) saved it from extinction, but also provided huge profits for the new suppliers of the bark (Honigsbaum 2001) rather than for the countries in South America. Currently, the world market for medicinal plants supplied by indigenous or local groups is estimated to amount to at least $43 billion (Shiva 1997:76). However, less than 0.001 percent of the profits from drugs originating in traditional medicine have gone to the indigenous people who led researchers to them (Yano 1993:446).

POTENTIAL SOLUTIONS

To set up a just system of compensation, a number of potential solutions must be considered. One idea is to expand and redefine the notion of intellectual property rights. Originally intended to protect the inventions of individuals by granting those persons patents to their innovations, intellectual property rights were not designed to protect the rights of indigenous groups who collectively hold knowledge about medicinal plants and their uses (Greaves 1996). To counter this shortcoming, the concept of indigenous intellectual property rights is being explored by many anthropologists and advocates of indigenous peoples (see, for example, *Cultural Survival Quarterly*, 2001). The Western legal definition of intellectual property rights, under which knowledge belonging to the public domain cannot be granted special status, complicates the notion of extending these rights to people whose knowledge is by definition already (though unfairly) considered part of the public domain (Riley 2001). If the definition of intellectual property rights can be adequately expanded or reworked, however, farmers could, for instance, gain control over their crop innovations (Brush and Stabinsky 1996).

In a slightly different vein, Vandana Shiva claims that intellectual property systems, which are restrictive because "they are recognized only when knowledge and innovation generate profits, not when they meet social needs" (1997:10), are an inadequate and unjust framework for recognizing the knowledge and innovations of all the world's citizens. Instead, she argues, we should develop a notion of "common property rights" that is not linked to commercially oriented patent laws in the same way that the concept of intellectual property rights is. Indigenous groups can take steps in this direction, too. Shiva has helped launch two grassroots networks that exemplify this new direction and emphasis: Navdanya is a national network in India to set up local seed banks to help protect biodiversity, and the Third World Network is a movement that supports the formalization of common property systems (pp. 39–40). The Center for International Environmental Law (CIEL) has also actively promoted a different legal definition of indigenous rights which it calls "community-based property rights" as a way to "advocate for communities and their rights to manage and control natural resources" (CIEL Brief 2002).

An interesting idea proposed by attorney Lester Yano (1993) links the issues of inadequate protection of indigenous ethnobiological knowledge to repatriation. Yano claims that just as there was a growing concern in the early 1900s about the Native Americans' loss of their cultural artifacts, so there is now an atmosphere for protecting ethnobiological knowledge. "Both ethnobiological knowledge and cultural artifacts personify something central to the cultural lore of the indigenous people, and in both cases it is inappropriate to allow one person or group to transfer that artifact or knowledge to another party outside of the cultural group" (p. 480). Perhaps just as the public can understand the need to support the repatriation of artifacts to Native American groups, so they can understand the need to protect the rights of indigenous people in terms of their knowledge and use of medicinal plants. In such an atmosphere, the idea of compensation becomes clear and acceptable.

As there is currently inadequate legal protection for indigenous groups and their knowledge, solutions to the patent-related problems must come through legal reforms, initiatives from indigenous groups, or arrangements made by the companies themselves. Fundamental to all of these initiatives will be the effort to provide a just legal foundation for protection of knowledge and rights. CIEL exemplifies this approach. Members of this organization are currently engaged in an effort to "develop and promote applied legal concepts that are more pro-community and more equitable" (CIEL Brief 2002). Claiming that property rights need not necessarily be based on state or formal recognition, CIEL seeks to help communities protect themselves from outside encroachment on "agricultural fields and fallows, gardens, planted or tended trees … wildlife, water, forest products, and marine products" (2002). Although these ideas are parameters for a broader solution and do not specifically name the protection of traditional medicines, CIEL's efforts to reform international law so as to offer more protection to communities would obviously provide an umbrella for a community's use of medicinal resources.

In the realm of business arrangements, Shaman Pharmaceuticals provided a good example of what a company could do to compensate for the services and knowledge it received from indigenous groups as it looked for new drugs. The company took this approach not only out of a commitment to equity, but also as part of an effort to alleviate human misery and promote conservation, as "one of the primary causes of tropical forest loss is poverty" (King 1996:63). To do so, the company helped create the Healing Forest Conservancy, whose goals were (1) to maintain medicinal plant biological diversity and (2) to provide a structure whereby a portion of the profits generated by commercialization were returned to the countries that participated in plant collection and collaborative activities with the company (p. 66). Shaman Pharmaceuticals also compensated the local groups of people from whose communities plants came that were tested at the company for their active principles—that is, not just those people from whose communities came the plants that actually made it into pharmaceuticals (Conte 1996). Although Shaman has since exited the pharmaceutical business, its model serves as a good example for future partnerships between companies and indigenous peoples (see the discussion of "dragon's blood" in Chapter 8 for more on Shaman Pharmaceuticals and its recent activities).

Another positive example of a commercial contract is the specific agreement reached between Costa Rican organizations and Merck & Company, a large pharmaceutical company. In Costa Rica, where its employees collect plants for use in the process of drug development, Merck entered into a contract with the Costa Rican National Biodiversity Institution (INBio); INBio, which is a private, non-profit organization, now works with Merck collecting plants and ethnobotanical data for the company. In turn, INBio has passed on 10 percent of its budget and 50 percent of its royalties to the National Park Fund, as a way to support the conservation of biodiversity in the country (Reid et al., 1996). Although these agreements are intended to stop the free (as in "uncompensated") flow of resources and knowledge from south to north, it has been argued that such commercial agreements do little for the local people, who actually had no say in the way this contract was set up (Shiva 1997:75). The Costa Rican agreement, though it represents an important step, was made neither with particular groups of disadvantaged people nor with the Costa Rican government. The solutions to protecting medicinal resources must, therefore, be sought through international arrangements, in-country regulation, and good coordination between the two.

What can be done in a country like Bolivia to gain protection for its medicinal resources and to counter the inequity of U.S. and other Western patent laws? A combination of broad institutional arrangements and more local agreements would likely provide benefits to the greatest number of people. Certainly, the government of Bolivia has made a beginning in framing this process. In 1992, the *Ley Del Medio Ambiente* ("Environmental Law," or Law 1333) was formulated, partly in response to that year's Earth Summit. One chapter stipulates protection for "wild flora and fauna." Article 55 states that it is "the duty of the state to preserve the biodiversity and the genetic patrimony" of these resources. Unfortunately, *medicinal* resources are not specifically named in Law 1333, nor is policy laid out explicitly for such protection. Article 57 adds the provision that the appropriate bodies will regulate and grant permission to those persons wishing to hunt or collect the wild resources, and will oversee the use and commercialization of the products, but once again a specific agency is not named.

In 1996, a special Forestry Law (Law 1700) was passed, focusing on the conservation of Bolivian forests. Taken together, Law 1333 and Law 1700 provide the broad framework for protection of Bolivia's natural resources, but have had little or no effect on the problem of protecting traditional medicines. As in most cases of national law reform, what is lacking is further specificity in the law and corresponding implementation.

There is a current move afoot in Bolivia, driven by a Commission for Defense of Traditional Medicines (a grassroots organization based in Cochabamba), to legally codify protection for medicinal resources and to bring national and international attention to this issue. The Commission is composed of healers, medicine vendors, lawyers, engineers, and representatives of nongovernmental organizations. Beginning in 2001, this committee initiated workshops in Cochabamba, soliciting the collaboration of various individuals and institutions in writing a manifesto that would allow for the protection of traditional medicines. In 2002, the group continued to meet as a way to provide information to the public and to involve people in a dialogue about the uses and importance of traditional medicines. For instance, the group sponsored an exhibit of traditional medicines and healing practices in Bolivia that was featured at the university's museum in downtown Cochabamba. During this time, several informal and informative "roundtables" were held, during which a variety of people were present and had the opportunity to speak. The topic of protection and defense of traditional medicines emerged as a key concern from these meetings. In collaboration with the group, one Bolivian M.A. student undertook a thesis project in which she called for "the construction of a law for the protection of biodiversity and intellectual property, in reference to the use of traditional medicine in Bolivia." The group as a whole urged an understanding that traditional knowledge forms part of a "collective patrimony" (known in other instances as "cultural patrimony"), and noted that to understand it one must begin with a survey of traditional knowledge of what the group's members call "original communities."

The process of forming a committee that acts collectively generated conflicts among various participants, such that since 2002 the group has been split into two factions with different outlooks. Here, the discussion follows the views of the Cochabamba-based group that continues to focus on securing rights from the more ample "common law" perspective than what they perceive is available under the current Bolivian constitutional law. Bolivia's legal system is based on so-called Roman Law, which evolved through the centuries into a common law used throughout many European countries and Latin America. When Bolivia achieved independence in 1825, it maintained this system of inherited law, which had been brought over by the Spaniards, though Bolivia's particular system is actually more closely modeled on the French code. According to Ciprian (one member of the group of people attempting to work toward protection of traditional medicine), the rights guaranteed under Bolivian law have always led to contradictions with the legal systems practiced by the country's indigenous peoples. The rights of indigenous people living in original Quechua, Aymara, and Guaraní communities are based on "traditional and customary uses with prehistoric origins that are currently categorized as common rights law." As an example, Ciprian cites the clash between

Photo by Sarah Linn Gallardo

F I G U R E 9.2   A number of people are active in the Commission for the Defense of Traditional Medicines, including Carlos Prado, a prominent *curandero* (here with the author).

criminal cases as judged by a community's traditional authority and as judged by the "official" Bolivian judicial authorities. The possibility of two different judgments or sentences leads to the problem of "two Bolivias" from the perspective of members of this group.

The Cochabamba committee emphasizes the need to work with indigenous people, who recognize a "different" legal system and whose rights could be defined as "customary" or "use rights" (*derechos consuetudinarios*). The group renamed itself in honor of these common law considerations as the Consultative Council in Defense and Protection of Earth Mother (in Spanish, *Consejo consultivo de defensa y protección de Pachamama*), which from the perspective of the new committee include the protection of natural resources, biodiversity, and traditional knowledge. In 2004, this committee composed and disseminated a manifesto with sixteen points, aimed at informing and working with institutions from the municipal level to the international level.

The points in this manifesto are broad ranging, encompassing everything from the knowledge and rights of local and indigenous groups to the efforts of groups such as Greenpeace and Rural Advancement Foundation International (RAFI; now Erosion, Technology, and Concentration [ETC]) to protect biological resources. To explore the stance of this concerned citizens' group, which sheds light on the broader debate over bioprospecting in Bolivia (and to some degree, in Latin America in general), this section highlights five points from this manifesto:

- The call for a moratorium
- A holistic emphasis
- Network building
- Intellectual property as collective
- Current emblematic issues in the traffic in biological products

In the manifesto, one of the main points made by the group is that the flora and fauna of their region is under siege—there has been a rapid and uncontrolled use of natural products such that no governing body can come to grips with it. Group members therefore ask for a moratorium of ten years—a "Primera Pausa ecológica Andino amazónica"—during which the region would be declared an "emergency zone" and the government would come up with a legal document "capable of protecting our tangible and intangible patrimony." The manifesto created by this group is a response to the deficits of Bolivian law that would require an adequate system to be put in place that account for the legal requirements of distinct indigenous groups.

The Cochabamba group further specifies that the approach should be "holistic," meaning members of the group will not approach the topic from solely a "legalistic" standpoint (which is the point of contention over the fissioning of the original group), nor solely "economic," "religious," or even "anthropological." They call these other approaches "partial" and insist that their activities be aimed at providing self-determination for indigenous "claimants." This position is of interest to anthropologists who work within a holistic methodological framework, but it also exposes the perceived pitfalls of protecting cultural patrimony from a local level. Many organizations have worked on these issues, but their efforts have apparently been deficient. As one member told me, "This is not just an environmental issue … it is easy to emphasize plants instead of people."

The composition of the Cochabamba group is itself an example of networking, in that many individuals have come together from different professions and backgrounds to work toward an equitable solution to the use of plant-based medicines. Throughout their discussions and documents, participants stress the importance of having many people collaborate in this process. Deemed even more important is the notion that the group's materials should reach a wide audience, thereby helping to build a national and international network that will provide further comments on their manifesto and help disseminate it as widely as possible. Within this framework, group members also call for an "educational component" to

their work, in which it would be everyone's "moral responsibility to give uncondi-
tional support and intellectual advising of a solitary and unpaid type."

Woven throughout the discussions and manifesto is the issue of what the
Cochabamba activists refer to as "collective intellectual property," so as to dis-
tinguish it from the intellectual property rights prevalent in Western societies on
which patent law rests. They speak out against monopoly and royalties, because in
their estimation royalties are not collective compensation, all too often benefiting
a few at the expense of the rest. Turning brief attention to the commercialization
of traditional medicines, they decry this practice as something that must also
benefit the collective good, mentioning that commercialization must have a
"democratic" bent.

Although this group got its start as a committee in defense of traditional
medicines, during the course of their discussions its members realized that broader
biological issues were at hand, which is why the committee was eventually renamed as a defense of "nature" and "Pachamama." Hence in their manifesto, the
Cochabamba activists make reference to other bioprospecting issues, such as denouncing the collection of blood from indigenous people, declaring Bolivia a
"GMO-free country" (GMO = genetically modified organism), and also making
reference to Greenpeace's initiative to boycott GMO products (genetically
modified foods and medicines).

Venezuela, which has rewritten its constitution to explicitly protect cultural
patrimony, including traditional medicines, may serve as a more concrete model for
grassroots organizations and the Bolivian government in their continuing efforts at
protection and conservation (for a discussion of the new Venezuelan constitution,
see Giordani and Villalón 2002). The Cochabamba committee discussed here needs
the help and financing of nongovernmental agencies. It is also necessary that international attention be brought to bear on individual cases and the ongoing controversy and dilemma of plant-based patents (such as that brought by farmers and
indigenous groups in the maca protest in Peru) and that pressure be exerted on the
United States to rethink its policy toward patents based in international products
and to reform its legal system in this regard. The United States could, by applying
more intense scrutiny, influence the activities of pharmaceutical companies.

Furthermore, contractual agreements entered into by companies such as Merck &
Company and Shaman Pharmaceuticals could provide some income and infrastructure to Bolivians as a whole. Given that the tropical regions of Bolivia (i.e., the
Amazon) may be of greater interest to bioprospectors, programs should benefit
Amazonian groups, but particularly in regard to ensuring conservation and halting
rampant deforestation, which would benefit all Bolivians. Initiatives that not only set
aside tracts of land, but also provide alternatives to logging and large-scale ranching
would improve the conditions under which forest management can thrive.

An organization like the Costa Rican INBio would be worthy of support, if
such an ecologically minded group had a presence in Bolivia (Gade 1999). Insisting
that bioprospectors obtain permits and pay user fees might help to build an organization such as the Traditional Medicine Research Center in Laos (Riley 2001),
which is dedicated to collecting information, helping to disseminate it, and
preserving this local knowledge in general. Latin American examples include the

Belize Association of Traditional Healers (BATH; see Kloppenburg and Balick 1996) and the Mexican Institute for the Study of Medicinal Plants (IMEPLAM; see Loayza 1996), both of which have been able to negotiate contractual agreements related to bioprospecting. Although a Bolivian Society for Traditional Medicine (SOBOMETRA, discussed in Chapter 8) does exist, this organization is more focused on the highlands of Bolivia, especially medicinal traditions around La Paz, and does not currently meet the goals of the conservation initiatives outlined here.

In general, guidelines to regulate bioprospecting need to be put in place for all companies and individuals engaged in these pursuits. These recommendations should include company–collector contracts, national policies, and a reexamination of property rights (Reid et al., 1996). Although it is very important for Bolivia to create national policies to protect its natural resources, an understanding by the U.S. public and the international community, accompanied by increased public awareness, must lead to new policies in regard to the cultural patrimony of our Latin American neighbors and Westerners' role in helping to protect it.

SUMMARY

Conflicts about who uses which resources and how they benefit from those resources will continue to surround the commercialization of traditional medicines, as well as other products originating from around the world. Only recently have intellectual property rights, which have long been a part of business dealings in the form of patents (protecting "inventors"), begun to be applied to the original uses and applications of products such as traditional medicines. Of course, such medicines also came into use through innovation on the part of local groups of people. Andean peoples themselves are pursuing the potential benefits of intellectual property rights, recognizing that their claims to products have been overlooked by Westerners. What might have been the effects of compensation for the use of traditional items in long-available commercial products—for instance, the use of coca leaf as an ingredient in Coca-Cola? Bolivian producers and consumers of traditional medicines, such as coca leaf, are asking questions like these, which might ultimately change the ways in which products are developed and commercialized in the future. Who should benefit?

Epilogue: The Future of Traditional Medicines in Bolivia

N ew medical directions, based in traditional practices, have come to Bolivia since I first began to gather information on the commercialization of traditional medicines several years ago. Not only is there intensified interest in the use of traditional medicines in new preparations—as described in this text— but recently the Bolivian government has begun to formalize the way in which traditional medicines will be used, marketed, and sold. After taking office in January 2006, Evo Morales, the new president of Bolivia, began to focus national and international attention on Bolivia's natural resources, their own- ership, and their unique uses. In his inaugural address, Morales stated, "We cannot privatize public needs like water. We are fighting for our water rights, for our right to plant coca, for control over national resources" (Burbach 2006). It would appear that in addition to natural gas—which is embroiled in a heated public debate as to how it should be used and who will control it—Morales considers resources such as coca and other traditional medicines to have roles to play in the national or cultural patrimony to which all Bolivian citizens share an interest and a stake.

Evo Morales is from an indigenous background. He grew up herding llamas on the altiplano and later worked as a coca grower in the Chapare region of Bolivia. His background as a native Aymara and rural dweller (termed *originario* these days) is a source of pride to Bolivians of indigenous background. Three years after his coming to office, they continue to say about their president, "He is one of us." Morales's years growing coca in the lowlands and working with labor unions there provided him with experience in organizing and mobilizing a very powerful political sector, and in so doing gave him the visibility that launched his political career.

A demonstration of the current president's concern for these facets of Bolivian culture and economy is the institution of two new Vice Ministries in the government: The Vice Ministry of Coca and Comprehensive Development is a brand-new section of the Ministry of Rural Development; the Vice Ministry of Traditional Medicines and Interculturality[1] is a new unit within the Ministry of Health. While I was conducting interviews in August 2007, in the second year after the government created these new ministries, it became clear to me that these two ministries had very different missions along with distinct issues to tackle, despite the fact that the administration considers them to be related in terms of managing natural resources.

The new Vice Minister of Traditional Medicines, a contemporary botanist and herbalist named Jaime Zalles, has a background in literature, philosophy, and theology, along with extensive experience working on various health campaigns in Bolivia over several decades. For instance, he was active in the creation of the Society for Traditional Medicines (SOBOMETRA; described in Chapter 8). The day that the Vice Minister received me in his office, I was as honored by his courteous reception as I was impressed by the simple existence of an office for traditional medicines in the middle of the big Ministry of Health and Sports. Zalles explained to me that Bolivia was the first Latin American country to recognize the validity of indigenous medicines through the creation of SOBOMETRA and to provide some form of regulation for their use. Since that time, however, it has fallen behind in the promotion and regulation of these products. The goals of his Vice Ministry are to revisit those issues.

So far, the Vice Ministry has concentrated its efforts on conducting a census of traditional healers, providing training programs in traditional medicine, and working on legislation that will both protect and regulate traditional healers. As part of the regulation campaign, the Vice Minister has recognized the need to regulate the very products that are manufactured and sold on a small scale throughout Bolivia, such as the traditional medicine cottage industries described in this book. According to Zalles, a dilemma because even though he and many people recognize the value and efficacy of the traditional medicines, their commercialization is unregulated, which can cause problems. He says, "This is my challenge: I have to structure a system that will show which product is good, and which is not ... but there is a war against the products, coming from the fact that the products aren't always organic. They can get contaminated with insecticides or other agricultural toxins. In one case some chamomile in Santa Cruz was contaminated with rat poison" (Jaime Zalles, interview, August 14, 2007).

To overcome these problems (and for other reasons), he has worked to set up licensing arrangements with natural medicine companies; those companies that have completed the process and been cleared by the Vice Ministry are allowed to publicize this fact on the labels of their products. One company that uses coca in

1. "Interculturality" is a term with a lot of currency in Bolivia's new administration. Perhaps because he is from an indigenous background himself, Morales has sought to portray the work of the new government as being based in the interaction of various ethnic groups—a cultural aspect of Bolivian life that the term "intercultural" seeks to convey.

its medicinal products, Ingacoca, had recently received its license from the Vice Ministry and proudly displayed it in the offices I visited in August 2007.

The Vice Ministry has also been charged with building an "intercultural" health model, in which traditional medicine and biomedicine will coexist. Zalles explains that this will avoid the "mutual exclusion" of the systems that existed before, and allow them to not "inter-mix" so much as to coexist so that patients can use them for different purposes. In his mind, it is the ability to choose any particular option that is a hallmark of the intercultural health system.

The Vice Ministry of Coca presents a different face. Embattled because of the demands of coca eradication programs on the one hand (largely sponsored by the U.S. government), and the politically mobilized coca growers and retailers on the other hand, this ministry has already had a stormy history, despite the enthusiasm with which it was inaugurated. The first Vice Minister was ousted, apparently due to misstatements about the extent of legal coca holdings; also, some critics suggested that he wasn't able to drive the new voluntary coca eradication programs adequately.[2] When his tenure came to an end just over a year after the inception of the ministry, he was replaced by the current Vice Minister, who had been in office for two months when I was in Bolivia in August 2007.

Jerónimo Meneses, the new Vice Minister, has been active in coca unions since the 1970s, and more recently was part of Morales's presidential campaign. Meneses is seen as more able to work with all the various coca constituencies, though so far his task has been far from easy. During my August 2007 stay, it was impossible to get an appointment with him. His days were occupied with a series of crises, requiring him to meet all day with coca producers and retailers, who are trying to change the regulations regarding how much coca they can sell at market.

Vice Minister Meneses, and the Morales administration in general, must deal with a long history of inconsistent and controversial coca regulation, imposed because of the way in which legal coca can be siphoned off into the illegal drug trade. In contrast to the manufacture of other herbal remedies, coca's industrialization faces different conditions. Coca is an agricultural crop, and not in danger of overexploitation (as the wild plant resources might be). Nonetheless, coca faces trade barriers because it is on the list of banned substances.[3] In January 2006, before Morales assumed the presidency, I interviewed Bolivian proponents of coca industrialization and U.S. officials alike, who cited a common figure of 12,000 hectares as the extent of land allowed for the production of coca for traditional uses, which includes coca-leaf for chewing, and the processing of coca leaf into tea, medicines, and other legal products. However, this amount of land has been arbitrarily determined. There are no precise studies about how much coca is used in the production of legal products, partly because many of these products

---

2. Programs to reduce the size and extent of coca holdings were formerly known by *erradicación* ("eradication") but have since adopted the less politically charged label of *racionalización*. Similar to the usage in English ("rationalization"), this term connotes the idea of having a reasonable amount, or organizing in a rational (and legal) manner. Therefore, in not pushing "rationalization" forward, the former Vice Minister of Coca was perceived as not cooperating with the U.S. government and was perhaps seen as a liability by the Bolivian government.

3. Coca is described as being on the "yellow list" and, therefore, cannot be exported.

are made in small cottage industries, sold on the street, and exported to only a limited extent.

Many people with whom I spoke in 2006 and 2007 alluded to a pending "demand study" being conducted by the European Union (EU), and one attaché from the U.S. Embassy in La Paz said that she had heard the EU was funding it with a half million dollars. Though in 2006 one U.S. Embassy official said that "The embassy doesn't have a position on legal coca industrialization" (Doman, personal communication, January 5, 2006), in 2007 another official told me that the U.S. government is opposed to industrialization of this plant (Urs, personal communication, August 14, 2007). What has happened since Morales took office is that coca production appears to have increased, despite continued eradication efforts on the part of the government. While eradication programs are still in place and drug interdiction efforts have continued, the flow of coca-for-cocaine has not been staunched. As one person told me, the dilemma is that there is now increasing illegal cocaine production, with labs being discovered in new places such as the Department of Oruro (previously not on the drug map) and in the booming altiplano city of El Alto, perched just minutes above La Paz's administrative center (Molina, personal communication, August 8, 2007; *La Prensa*, August 11, 2007). Because of this increased production, officials at the U.S. Embassy say that the U.S. government cannot support the project of legal coca industrialization, because from its position coca still provides the raw material for cocaine. In commenting on the U.S. position on legal coca production, then Ambassador Goldberg[4] told the Associated Press, "The narco-traffickers will always pay more than the toothpaste factory" (Keane 2006).

The wholesale coca-leaf marketplace in the La Paz barrio of Villa Fatima serves as a good example of the regulation and control of legal coca leaf in Bolivia. Villa Fátima itself is populated by migrants who have connections to the yungas,[5] so it is a logical location for a market dedicated solely to this regional product. The marketplace is run by coca farmers, and is overseen only to a certain extent by the Bolivian governmental agency DIGECO,[6] which controls the commercialization and transport of coca. The marketplace and its offices in Villa Fatima are part cooperative, part business, and part customs control. Collectively, they are referred to by the acronym ADEPCOCA (Association of Coca Producers), and the marketplace is modeled to some extent on the kind of rotating authority structure of traditional agricultural communities. The organization itself is composed of at least 14,000 members, who are all coca leaf producers from the yungas.

The marketplace organization of ADEPCOCA, and even its physical layout, allows it to maintain some degree of autonomy from DIGECO. On the day that a U.S. Agency for International Development (USAID) official visited in 2006, he

---

4. Bush-apointee Goldberg was expelled in September 2008 by Morales, who is waiting to take the next step when Obama takes office.

5. Many of the migrants go back and forth and maintain a kind of "double domicile" pattern, notable in many regions of Bolivia.

6. DIGECO is the government's coca control agency, which is financed entirely by U.S. government funds, and has gone by several different names. It works in conjunction with the U.S.-funded Bolivian force of anti-narcotics agents.

told me that it "wasn't a good time"—the visitors hadn't been welcomed there—so he decided not to go into the building on an unannounced visit with his official coterie (Francisco, personal communication, January 4, 2006). Once coca is bought at the central wholesale marketplace by the intermediaries or coca merchants, it is taken to interior markets throughout Bolivia, where it is sold in small quantities to chewers. A businessperson who wants to industrialize coca—for instance, in the production of coca tea or medicinal products—must get the same kind of permission from DIGECO that is obtained by a merchant who sells coca to middlemen or individuals. Additionally, a company specializing in the processing of coca to use in coca products must be inspected by DIGECO. Very few companies have been able to complete the entire legal sequence of paperwork to become legal coca manufacturers. Only nine companies (out of many more) were legally registered at DIGECO in 2006—these companies are allowed to buy a maximum of 500 pounds of coca per month for use in the manufacture of their products.[7] Given that the ability to export these products is in doubt, many companies remain at the level of cottage industries.[8]

By August 2007, there had been some loosening of the market restrictions for traditional medicine companies, including those incorporating coca. The new company Ingacoca not only received a special license for commercializing its products, but was also featured at an "Eco-fair" across from the presidential palace, in which products prepared from quinoa, honey, llama meat, and organic chocolate were showcased. While Jaime Zalles calls coca a "medical vegetable" (Becker 2007), Evo Morales claims that creating a legal market for coca would divert coca away from drug traffickers. Venezuelan President Hugo Chávez also announced that his government would promise to buy all legal products made from coca leaves as a way to stimulate and subsidize the market (Council on Hemispheric Affairs, July 2, 2007).

Coca producers have been one of the most vociferous and radical political voices in Bolivia; their decision to throw their political weight behind Morales was a large part of the president's successful bid for office. Even under the sympathetic administration of Morales they continue to mobilize. In fact, my difficulty in getting an interview with the new Vice Minister of Coca was related to the presence of ADEPCOCA producers, who were demanding that their legal right to commercialize the coca they bring up from the yungas be increased from the three *taques*[9] they can currently legally sell each month. The coca producers who

---

7. The Coca-Cola Company is the exception to this rule, as it has negotiated a special deal for large quantities of Andean coca leaf. The last time the company bought in Bolivia was 2002; in that year, it bought 50,000 pounds, or 100 times the amount that is legal for Bolivian-based companies. This is one of the reasons that Evo Morales said in his United Nations address, "It is not possible that the coca leaf is legal for Coca-Cola and that the coca leaf is illegal for other medicinal purposes in our country, and the whole world" (Morales 2006).

8. Some coca tea companies have been able to skirt the export obstacle to some extent. One businessman told me that although you cannot ship large quantities of coca leaf tea to the United States, you can export boxes of 100 tea bags to individual buyers. Tea cannot, however, be brought in through U.S. Customs, where it will be confiscated. The situation is a little more "open" in Europe, where individuals can bring in 100 tea bags each, and the product can be sent to buyers in larger quantities.

9. A *taque* is a traditional bundle of coca, which weighs 50 pounds.

bring their product to the legal wholesale market in Villa Fátima want to be allowed to sell eight to fifteen taques per month, which would put them on more equal footing with the coca middlemen (*rescatadores* or *intermediarios*), who are able to buy up and retail ten taques per month. During my August 2007 stay in Bolivia, a contingent of the ADEPCOCA producers marched into the La Paz streets and blocked one of the main thoroughfares to bring attention to their demands. This action led to their reception at the Vice Ministry, where negotiations began. Because they were not appeased immediately, some of these producers began to call for the new Vice Minister's resignation.

From these recent events, it is clear that the politics of coca will remain volatile, at least over the short term, even while coca products are promoted as an important way to start industrializing and possibly exporting Bolivia's traditional medicines. The use of coca leaf in traditional medicines stands out as an illustration of the processes of traditional medicine commercialization. Not only is coca leaf an important ingredient in Andean culture and traditional medicine—with a unique history of commoditization, both legal and illegal—but it is also the symbol of contemporary political struggle in Bolivia today. Its rocky road to commercialization provides a window into the dilemma faced by other traditional products as they seek to carve out a share of the market. How can a natural product like coca leaf be allowed the space to continue in its role in Andean culture and to gain a new status as a legal ingredient in new preparations of traditional medicine, in the face of its ongoing use in cocaine production and the international drug war? These are questions that the current Bolivian administration is addressing, and is doing so successfully in terms of forging new ministries to develop strategies for dealing with these volatile issues.

The traditional medicines of Bolivia today are not the property of one particular region and corresponding group of people in Bolivia, but rather amalgams of cures from different regions—highlands and lowlands alike—offered up in the setting of the marketplace. Simultaneously, medicinal ingredients and practices from "outside" sources such as other Latin American countries, China, and other indigenous traditions have become incorporated into the mix. Traditional medicine in Bolivia today is alive and well, albeit in an altered and richer form. From the vendors of fresh plants to natural medicine doctors and cottage industries based on traditional medicine, we see a pattern of flourishing traditional medicine, even as the biomedical system spreads, sometimes alongside the use of traditional remedies.

References

Abdel-Malek, Joseph Bastien, William Mahler, Qi Jia, Manfred Reinecke, W. Robinson, Yong-hua Shu, and Jaime Zalles-Asin. 1996. "Drug Leads from the Kallawaya Herbalists of Bolivia." *Journal of Ethnopharmacology* 50:157–166.

Alba, Juan José. 1988. *El Jampi Qhatu de Cochabamba.* Unpublished manuscript.

Alba, Juan José. 1989. *El Ocaso de una Feria Colonial: Vigencias y Transfiguraciones Sociales.* Unpublished manuscript.

Alba, Juan José, and Lila Tarifa. 1993. *Los Jampiris de Raqaypampa.* Cochabamba, Bolivia: CENDA.

Alberti, Amalia. 1988. From Recommendation Domains to Inter-Household Dynamics and Back: Attempts to Bridge the Gender Gap. In *Gender Issues in Farming Systems Research and Extension,* edited by S. Poats, M. Schmink, and A. Spring, pp. 61–72. Boulder, CO: Westview Press.

Alberti, G., and E. Mayer (eds.) 1974. *Reciprocidad y Intercambio en los Andes.* Lima: Instituto de Estudios Peruanos.

Albó, Xavier. 1991. El Retorno del Indio. *Revista Andina* 9(2):299–366.

Albro, Robert. 2000. The Populist Chola: Cultural Mediation and the Political Imagination in Quillacollo, Bolivia. *Journal of Latin American Anthropology* 5(2):30–88.

Allen, Catherine. 1988. *The Hold Life Has: Coca and Cultural Identity in an Andean Community.* Washington, DC: Smithsonian Institution Press.

Allen, Jim, and John Blashford Snell. 1999. *Atlantis: The Andes Solution.* Orion.

Arnold, Denise, and Juan de Dios Yapita. 2002. *Las Wawas del Inka: Hacia la Salud Materna Intercultural en Algunas Comunidades Andinas.* La Paz, Bolivia: Instituto de Lengua y Cultura Aymara.

Arts, Bas. 1998. *The Political Influence of Global NGOs: Case Studies on the Climate and Biodiversity Conventions.* Utrecht, Netherlands: International Books.

Ayala Loayza, Juan Luis. 1988. *Diccionario Español-Aymara.* Lima, Peru: Editorial Jaun Mejía Baca.

Babb, Florence. 1986. Producers and Reproducers: Andean Marketwomen in the Economy. In *Women and Change in Latin America,* edited by J. Nash and H. Safa, pp. 53–64. Massachusetts: Bergin and Garvey.

Babb, Florence. 1989. *Between Field and Cooking Pot: The Political Economy of*

Marketwomen in Peru. Austin, TX: University of Texas Press.

Baer, Hans. 2003. Contributions to a Critical Analysis of Medical Pluralism: An Examination of the Work of Libbet Crandon-Malamud. In *Medical Pluralism in the Andes*, edited by J. Koss-Chioino, T. Leatherman, and C. Greenway, pp. 42–60. London/ New York: Routledge Press.

Balée, William. 1994. *Footprints of the Forest: Ka'apor Ethnobotany: The Historical Ecology of Plant Utilization by the Amazonian People.* New York: Columbia University Press.

Balick, Michael, and Paul Alan Cox. 1997. *Plants, People, and Culture.* New York: Scientific American Library.

Barragán, Rossana. 1992. Entre Polleras, Lliqllas, y Ñañacas: Los Mestizos y la Emergencia de la Tercera República. In *Etnicidad, Economía y Simbolismo en los Andes*, edited by S. Arze, R. Barragán, L. Escobari, and X. Medinacelli, pp. 85–127. La Paz, Bolivia: Instituto de Historia Social Boliviana.

Basso, Keith. 1996. *Wisdom Sits in Places: Landscape, and Language among the Western Apache.* Albuquerque, NM: University of New Mexico Press.

Bastien, Joseph. 1978. *Mountain of the Condor.* Prospect Heights, IL: Waveland Press.

Bastien, Joseph. 1985. Qollahuaya-Andean Body Concepts: A Topographical–Hydraulic Model of Physiology. *American Anthropologist* 87(2): 595–611.

Bastien, Joseph. 1992. *Drum and Stethoscope.* Salt Lake City, UT: University of Utah Press.

Bastien, Joseph, and John Donahue. 1981. *Health in the Andes.* American Anthropological Association Special Publication No. 12.

Bender, Barbara. 1993. Introduction: Landscape—Meaning and Action. In *Landscape: Politics and Perspectives*, edited by B. Bender, pp. 1–17. Providence/Oxford, UK: Berg Press.

Bodley, John. 1990. *Victims of Progress.* Lanham, MD: AltaMira Press.

Brush, Stephen. 1977. *Mountain, Field, and Family: The Economy and Human Ecology of an Andean Village.* Philadelphia: University of Pennsylvania Press.

Brush, Stephen, and D. Stabinsky (eds.). 1996. *Valuing Local Knowledge: Indigenous People and Intellectual Property Rights.* Washington, DC: Island Press.

Buechler, Hans, and Judith-Maria. 1996. *The World of Sofia Velasquez: The Autobiography of a Bolivian Market Vendor.* New York: Columbia University Press.

Buechler, Judith Marie. 1997. The Visible and Vocal Politics of Female Traders and Small Scale Producers in La Paz. In *Women and Economic Change: Andean Perspectives,* edited by A. Miles and H. Buechler, pp. 75–88. Washington DC: Society for Latin American Anthropology Publication Series, American Anthropological Association.

Burchard, Roderick 1976. *Myths of the Sacred Leaf: Ecological Perspectives on Coca and Peasant Biocultural Adaptation in Peru* [Ph.D. dissertation]. Ann Arbor, MI: University Microfilms International.

Burchard, Roderick. 1978. Una Nueva Perspectiva Sobre la Masticación de la Coca. *América Indígena* 38(4): 809–835.

Cáceres Ch., Efrain. 1988. *Si Crees, Los Apus Te Curan: Medicina Andina e Indentidad Cultural.* Cuzco, Peru: Centro de Investigaciones de la Cultura y Tecnología Andina.

Calancha, Antonio de la. 1638/1972. *Crónicas Agustinianas del Perú.* Madrid: Consejo Superior de Investigaciones Científicas.

Calderón, Fernando, and Alberto Rivera. 1983. *La Cancha*. Cochabamba, Bolivia: CERES.

Center for International Environmental Law (CIEL) Brief. 2002. *Community Based Property Rights: A Concept Note.* 26 August–4 September.

Chiñas, Beverly. 1992. *The Isthmus Zapotecs: A Matrifocal Culture of Mexico.* Fort Worth, TX: Harcourt Brace.

Clapp, Roger, and Carolyn Crook. 2002. Drowning in the Magic Well: Shaman Pharmaceuticals and the Elusive Role of Traditional Knowledge. *Journal of Environment and Development* 11(1):79–102.

Clark, Gracia. 1994. *Onions Are My Husband: Survival and Accumulation by West African Market Women.* Chicago: University of Chicago Press.

Classen, Constance. 1993. *Inca Cosmology and the Human Body.* Salt Lake City, UT: University of Utah Press.

Cobo, Bernabé. 1653/1979. *History of the Inca Empire.* Trans. Roland Hamilton. Austin, TX: University of Texas Press.

Collins, Jane. 1986. The Household and Relations of Production in Southern Peru. *Comparative Studies in Society and History* 28(4):651–671.

Conte, Lisa. 1996. Shaman Pharmaceuticals' Approach to Drug Development. In *Medicinal Resources of the Tropical Forest: Biodiversity and Its Importance to Human Health,* edited by M. J. Balick, E. Elisabetsky, and S. Laird, pp. 94–100. New York: Columbia University Press.

Cosgrove, Denis. 1993. Landscapes and Myths, Gods and Humans. In *Landscape: Politics and Perspectives,* edited by B. Bender, pp. 281–305. Providence/ Oxford: Berg Press.

Crandon-Malamud, Libbet. 1991. *From the Fat of Our Souls: Social Change, Political Process, and Medical Pluralism in Bolivia.* Berkeley, CA: University of California Press.

Curtin, L. S. M., and Michael Moore. 1947/1997. *Healing Herbs of the Upper Rio Grande: Traditional Medicine of the Southwest.* Santa Fe, NM: Western Edge Press.

Dandler, Jorge. 1987. Diversificación, Procesos de Trabajo y Movilidad Espacial en los Valles y Serranías de Cochabamba. In *Participación Indígena en los Mercados Surandinos,* edited by O. Harris, B. Larson, and E. Tandeter, pp. 639–682. La Paz, Bolivia: CERES.

Davis, E. Wade, and James A. Yost. 1993. The Ethnomedicine of the Waorani of Amazonian Ecuador. *Journal of Ethnopharmacology* 273:282–283.

Deere, Carmen. 1990. *Household and Class Relations: Peasants and Landlords in Northern Peru.* Berkeley, CA: University of California Press.

de la Cadena, Marisol. 1995. "Women Are More Indian": Ethnicity and Gender in a Community Near Cuzco. In *Ethnicity, Markets, and Migration in the Andes,* edited by Brooke Larson and Olivia Harris, pp. 328–348. Durham, NC: Duke University Press.

Delgado, Guillermo. 1985. Industrial Stagnation and Women's Strategies for Survival at the Siglo XX and Uncía Mines. In *Miners and Mining in the Americas,* edited by W. Culver and I. Greaves, pp. 162–170. Manchester, UK: Manchester University Press.

De Lucca, Manuel, and Jaime Zalles. 1992. *Flora Medicinal Boliviana.* Cochabamba, Bolivia: Editorial Amigos del Libro.

De Soto, Hernando. 1989. *The Other Path.* New York: Harper and Row.

Dubberly, David. 1995. Commentary on the Ley Del Regimen de la Coca y Sustancias Controlodas. *American Bar Association: Inter-American Legal Materials* 6(3–4):278–294.

Espinoza Soriano, Waldemar. 1981. El Reino Aymara de Quillaca-Asanaques,

Siglos XV y XVI. *Revista del Museo Nacional* (Lima) 45:175–274.

ETC Genotype. July 3, 2002. Peruvian Farmers and Indigenous People Denounce Maca Patents. http://www.rafi.org/documents/macafinal1, accessed August 28, 2002.

Farnsworth, N. R. 1988. Screening Plants for New Medicines. In *Biodiversity*, edited by E. O. Wilson, pp. 83–97. Washington, DC: National Academy Press.

Farthing, Linda. 1991. After the Crash. *Report on the Americas (NACLA)* 25(1):24–29.

Farthing, Linda. 1997. Social Impacts Associated with Antidrug Law 1008. In *Coca, Cocaine, and the Bolivian Reality*, edited by M.B. Léons and H. Sanabria, pp. 253–269. Albany, NY: State University of New York Press.

Feld, Steven, and Keith Basso. 1996. Introduction. In *Senses of Place*, edited by S. Feld and K. Basso, pp. 3–11. Santa Fe, NM: School of American Research Press.

Fernández Juárez, Gerardo. 1999. *Médicos y Yatiris: Salud e Interculturalidad en el Altiplano Aymara*. La Paz, Bolivia CIPCA, OPS/CMS.

Finnegan, William. 2003. The Economics of Empire. *Harper's*, 306(1836): 41–54.

Ford, Richard. 1994. *The Nature and Status of Ethnobotany*. Ann Arbor, MI: University of Michigan Museum.

Forero, Juan. June 10, 2004. New Peruvian Soft Drink Packs a Punch. *Wall Street Journal*.

Foster, George. 1967. *Tzintzuntzan: Mexican Peasants in a Changing World*. Boston: Little, Brown.

Foster, George. 1988. The Validating Role of Humoral Theory in Traditional Spanish-American Therapeutics. *American Ethnologist* 15(1):120–135.

Foster, George. 1994. *Hippocrates' Latin American Legacy: Humoral Medicine in the New World*. Amsterdam: Gordon and Breach Science.

Gade, Daniel. 1999. *Nature and Culture in the Andes*. Madison, WI: University of Wisconsin.

Geertz, Clifford. 1996. Afterword. In *Senses of Place*, edited by S. Feld and K. Basso, pp. 259–262. Santa Fe, NM: School of American Research Press.

Ghersi, Enrique. 1997. The Informal Economy in Latin America. *Cato Journal* 17(1):99–108.

Gill, Lesley. 2000. *Teetering on the Rim: Global Restructuring, Daily Life, and the Armed Retreat of the Bolivian State*. New York: Columbia University Press.

Girault, Louis. 1987. *Kallawaya: Curanderos Itinerantes de los Andes*. La Paz, Bolivia: UNICEF, OPS, OMS.

Giordani, Lourdes, and María Eugenia Villalón. 2002. An Expansion of Citizenship in Venezuela. *NACLA Report on the Americas*, XXXV(6).

Gironda Cabrera, Eusebio. 2000. *Coca Inmortal*. La Paz, Bolivia: Plural Editores.

Goldstein, Daniel. 2004. *The Spectacular City: Violence and Performance in Urban Bolivia*. Durham, NC: Duke University Press.

Gose, Peter. 1994. *Deathly Waters and Hungry Mountains: Agrarian Ritual and Class Formation in an Andean Town*. Toronto: University of Toronto Press.

Gotkowitz, Laura. 2000. Commemorating the Heroínas: Gender and Civic Ritual in Early Twentieth-Century Bolivia. In *Hidden Histories of Gender and the State in Latin America*, edited by E. Dore and M. Molyneux, pp. 215–237. Durham, NC: Duke University Press.

Greaves, Thomas. 1996. Tribal Rights. In *Valuing Local Knowledge: Indigenous People and Intellectual Property Rights*, edited by S. Brush and D. Stabinsky, pp. 25–40. Washington, DC: Island Press.

Greene, Shane. 1998. The Shaman's Needle: Development, Shamanic Agency, and Intermedicality in Aguaruna Lands, Peru. *American Ethnologist* 25(4):634–658.

Griffiths, Nicholas. 1996. *The Cross and the Serpent: Religious Repression and Resurgence in Colonial Peru*. Norman, OK/ London: University of Oklahoma Press.

Grillo Fernández, Eduardo. 1994. *Género y Desarollo en los Andes*. Lima, Peru: PRATEC.

Gudeman, Stephen. 1976. *Relationships, Residence, and the Individual: A Rural Panamanian Community*. London: Routledge & Kegan Paul.

Gudeman, Stephen, and Alberto Rivera. 1990. *Conversations in Colombia: The Domestic Economy in Life and Text*. Cambridge, UK: Cambridge University Press.

Gugliucci, A., and T. Menini. 2002. Three Different Pathways for Human LDL Oxidation Are Inhibited by Water Extracts of the Medicinal Herb *Achyrocline satureioides*. *Life Sciences* 71:693–705.

Guillet, David. 1992. *Covering Ground: Communal Water Management and the State in the Peruvian Highlands*. Ann Arbor, MI: University of Michigan Press.

Hamilton, Sarah. 1998. *The Two-Headed Household: Gender and Rural Development in the Ecuadorean Andes*. Pittsburgh, PA: University of Pittsburgh Press.

Hardman, M. J. 1985. Aymara and Quechua: Languages in Contact. In *South American Languages: Retrospect and Prospect*, edited by H. E. Manelis Klein and L.R. Stark, pp. 617–643. Austin, TX: University of Texas Press.

Harris, Olivia. 1982. Labour and Produce in an Ethnic Economy, Northern Potosí, Bolivia. In *Ecology and Exchange in the Andes*, edited by David Lehmann, pp. 70–96. Cambridge, UK: Cambridge University Press.

Harris, Olivia. 1995. Ethnic Identity and Market Relations. In *Ethnicity, Markets, and Migration in the Andes: At the Crossroads of History and Anthropology*, edited by B. Larson and O. Harris, pp. 297–328. Durham, NC: Duke University Press.

Harris, Olivia. 2000. *To Make the Earth Bear Fruit: Ethnographic Essays on Fertility, Work, and Gender in Highland Bolivia*. London: Institute of Latin American Studies.

Himpele, Jeff. 2003. The Gran Poder and the Social Movement of the Aymara Middle Class: A Video Essay. *Visual Anthropology* 16(2–3).

Hirsch, Eric, and Michael O'Hanlon (eds.). 1995. *The Anthropology of Landscape: Perspectives on Place and Space*. Oxford, UK: Clarendon Press.

Huidobro Bellido, José. 1986. *Medicina del Hombre Andino*. La Paz, Bolivia: Alcegraf Editora.

Humphrey, Caroline. 1995. Chiefly Landscapes and Shamanist Landscapes in Mongolia. In *The Anthropology of Landscape*, edited by E. Hirsch and M. O'Hanlon, pp. 135–162. Oxford, UK: Clarendon Press.

Hurtado, Jorge. 1995. *Coca: The Legend*. La Paz, Bolivia: HISBOL.

Ingham, John. 1970. On American Folk Medicine. *American Anthropologist* 72(1):76–87.

Isbell, Billie Jean. 1978/1985. *To Defend Ourselves: Ecology and Ritual in an Andean Village*. Prospect Heights, IL: Waveland Press.

Jackson, John. 1994. *A Sense of Place, a Sense of Time*. New Haven/London: Yale University Press.

Jackson, Robert. 1994. *Regional Markets, and Agrarian Transformation in Bolivia: Cochabamba 1539–1960*. Albuquerque, NM: University of New Mexico Press.

Jordan, Brigitte, and Robbie Davies-Floyd. 1992. *Birth in Four Cultures*. Prospect Heights, IL: Waveland Press.

Kay, Margarita Artschwager. 1996. *Healing with Plants in the American and Mexican West*. Tucson, AZ: University of Arizona Press.

Keane, Dan. December 8, 2006. Bolivian President Takes Middle Path on Cocaine Policy. *Associated Press*.

King, Steven. 1996. Conservation and Tropical Medicinal Plant Research. In *Medicinal Resources of the Tropical Forest: Biodiversity and its Importance to Human Health*, edited by M. J. Balick, E. Elisabetsky, and S. Laird, pp. 63–74. New York: Columbia University Press.

Klein, Herbert. 1982. *Bolivia: The Evolution of a Multi-ethnic Society*. Oxford, UK: Oxford University Press.

Klinman, Edward. 1999. Evaluating Health Service Equity at a Primary Care Clinic in Chilimarca, Bolivia. *Social Science and Medicine* 49:663–678.

Koss-Chioino, Joan, Thomas Leatherman, and Christine Greenway (eds.). 2003. *Medical Pluralism in the Andes*. London/New York: Routledge.

Lakoff, George, and M. Johnson. 1980. *Metaphors We Live By*. Chicago: Chicago University Press.

Larson, Brooke. 1988. *Colonialism and Agrarian Transformation in Bolivia: Cochabamba, 1550–1900*. Princeton, NJ: Princeton University Press.

Léons, Madeline Barbara, and Harry Sanabria. 1997. Coca and Cocaine in Bolivia: Reality and Policy Illusion. In *Coca, Cocaine, and the Bolivian Reality*, edited by M. B. Léons and H. Sanabria, pp. 1–46. Albany, NY: State University of New York Press.

Lira, Jorge. 1985. *Medicina Andina: Farmacopea y Ritual*. Cuzco, Peru: Centro Bartolomé de las Casas.

Lloyd, G. E. R. 1964. The Hot and the Cold, the Dry and the Wet in Greek Philosophy. *Journal of Hellenic Studies* 84:92–106.

Loayza, Xavier. 1996. Medicinal Plants of Mexico: A Program for Their Scientific Validation. In *Medicinal Resources of the Tropical Forest: Biodiversity and Its Importance to Human Health*, edited by M. J. Balick, E. Elisabetsky and S. Laird, pp. 311–316. New York: Columbia University Press.

Long, Norman, and B. Roberts. 1984. *Miners, Peasants, and Entrepreneurs: Regional Development in the Central Highlands of Peru*. Cambridge, UK: Cambridge University Press.

Loza-Balsa, Gregorio. 1995. *Enciclopedia de la Medicina Aymara*. La Paz, Bolivia: Panamerican Health Organization and World Health Organization.

Luykx, Aurolyn. 2000. Gender Equity and Interculturalidad: The Dilemma in Bolivian Education. *Journal of Latin American Anthropology* 5(2):150–178.

MacLean, Daniel. July 23, 2000. Piratas de la Vida. *Los Tiempos, Cochabamba*, pp. 13–16.

Mariani, Angelo. 1892. *Coca and Its Therapeutic Applications*. New York: J. N. Jaros.

Mariani, Angelo. 1902. *Eminent Physicians* (compiled from the *Album Mariani*). New York: J. N. Jaros.

Mariani & Company. 1896. *Erythroxylon Coca: Its Uses in the Treatment of Disease*. New York: J. N. Jaros.

Maybury-Lewis. 1997. *Indigenous Peoples, Ethnic Groups, and the State*. Boston: Allyn and Bacon.

Mayer, Enrique. 2002. *The Articulated Peasant: Household Economies in the Andes.* Boulder, CO: Westview Press.

McElroy, A., and P. Townsend. 1996. *Medical Anthropology in Ecological Perspective.* Boulder, CO: Westview Press.

McKee, Lauris. 1997. Women's Work in Rural Ecuador: Multiple Resource Strategies and the Gendered Division of Labor. In *Women and Economic Change: Andean Perspectives,* edited by A. Miles and H. Buechler, pp. 13–30. American Anthropological Association and Society for Latin America.

Metzger, Thomas. 1998. Who Put the Coke in Coca-Cola? http://209.238.229.175/Articles/WhoPut.htm, accessed August 2, 2002.

Miller, M. October 28, 1994. Quality Stuff: Firm Is Peddling Cocaine, and Deals Are Legit. *Wall Street Journal,* p. A1.

Molina Rivera, Ramiro. 1986. Estratégias Socio Económicos y Reproductivas en la Comunidad de Pampa-Aullagas Oruru. In *Tiempo de Vida y Muerte,* edited by J. Izko, R. Molina, and R. Pereira, pp. 169–276. La Paz, Bolivia: CONAPO and CIID.

Molina Rivera, Ramiro. 1987. La Tradicionalidad como Medio de Articulación al Mercado: Una Comunidad Pastoril en Oruro. In *Participación Indígena en los Mercados Surandinos,* edited by O. Harris, B. Larson, and E. Tandeter, pp. 603–636. La Paz, Bolivia: CERES.

Morales, Edumundo. 1989. *Cocaine: White Gold Rush in Peru.* Tucson, AZ: University of Arizona Press.

Mortimer, W. Golden. 1901/1974. *History of Coca: "The Divine Plant" of the Incas.* San Francisco: And/Or Press.

Moseley, Michael. 1992. *The Incas and Their Ancestors: The Archaeology of Peru.* London: Thames and Hudson.

Murra, John. 1987. ¿Existieron el Tributo y los Mercados antes de la Invasión Eruopeo? In *La Participación Indígena en los Mercados Surandinos,* edited by O. Harris, B. Larson, and E. Tandeter, pp. 51–61. La Paz, Bolivia: CERES.

Nash, June. 1979. *We Eat the Mines and the Mines Eat Us: Dependency and Exploitation in Bolivia Tin Mines.* New York: Columbia University Press.

Oblitas Poblete, Enrique. 1963. *Cultura Callawaya.* La Paz, Bolivia: Talleres Gráficos Bolvianos.

Ortner, Sherry. 1984. Theory in Anthropology since the Sixties. *Society for Comparative Study of Society and History* 26(1):126–166.

Ortner, Sherry. 1999. *Life and Death on Mt. Everest.* Princeton, NJ: Princeton University Press.

Parry, Jonathan, and Maurice Bloch (eds.). 1989. *Money and the Morality of Exchange.* Cambridge, UK: Cambridge University Press.

Paulson, Susan, and Pamela Calla. 2000. Gender and Ethnicity in Bolivian Politics: Transformation or Paternalism. *Journal of Latin American Anthropology* 5(2):112–149.

P"axsi Limachi, Rufino. 1983. *Medicina Natural.* La Paz, Bolivia: Mundo Aymara.

Pendergrast, Mark. 1993. *For God, Country, and Coca-Cola: The Unauthorized History of the Great American Soft Drink and the Company That Makes It.* New York: Scribner's.

Platt, Tristan. 1982. *Estado Boliviano y Ayllu Andino: Tierra y Tributo en el Norte de Potosí.* Lima, Peru: IEP.

Plotkin, Mark. 1993. *Tales of a Shaman's Apprentice: An Ethnobotanist Searches for New Medicines in the Amazon Rain Forest.* New York: Penguin Books.

Plowman, Timothy. 1984. The Ethnobotany of Coca. *Advances in Economic Botany* 1:62–111.

Quieser Morales, Waltraud. 1992. *Bolivia: Land of Struggle.* Boulder, CO: Westview Press.

Raintree Nutrition Database. 2003. Tropical Plant Database: *Achyrocline satureoides*. www.rain-tree.com/macela. htm, accessed April 25, 2003.

Rasnake, Roger. 1988. *Domination and Cultural Resistance: Authority and Power among an Andean People*. Durham, NC: Duke University Press.

Reid, Walter, Sarah Laird, Carrie Meyer, Rodrigo Gómez, Ana Sittenfeld, Daniel Janzen, Michael Gollin, and Calestous Juma. 1996. Biodiversity Prospecting. In *Medicinal Resources of the Tropical Forest: Biodiversity and Its Importance to Human Health*, edited by M. J. Balick, E. Elisabetsky and S. Laird, pp. 142–173. New York: Columbia University Press.

Riley, Mary. 2001. The Traditional Medicine Research Center (TMRC): A Potential Tool for Protecting Traditional and Tribal Medicinal Knowledge in Laos. *Cultural Survival Quarterly* 24(2):21–24.

Riley, Mary, and Katy Moran. 2001. Protecting Indigenous Intellectual Property Rights: Tools That Work. *Cultural Survival Quarterly* 24(4):6–9.

Roht-Arriaza, Naomi. Summer 1996. Of Seeds and Shamans: The Appropriation of the Scientific and Technical Knowledge of Indigenous and Local Communities. *Michigan Journal of International Law* 17:919–965.

Romanucci-Ross, Lola. 1989. The Hierarchy of Resort in Curative Practices: The Admiralty Islands. In *Culture, Disease, and Healing: Studies in Medical Anthropology*, edited by D. Landy, pp. 481–487. Macmillan.

Rösing, Ina. 1996. *Rituals Para Llamar la Lluvia*. La Paz, Bolivia: Amigos Del Libro.

Rubel, Arthur. 1998. The Epidemiology of a Folk Illness: Susto in Hispanic America. *Ethnology* 3(3):268–283.

Santos, A., D. Ripoll, V. Nardi, and V. Bassani. 1999. Immunomodulatory Effect of *Achyrocline satureioides* (LAM.) D.C. Aqueous Extracts. *Phytotherapy Research* 13(1):65–66.

Seligmann, Linda. 1989. To Be in Between: The Cholas as Market Women. *Comparative Studies in Society and History* 31(4):694–721.

Seligmann, Linda. 1993. Between Worlds of Exchange: Ethnicity Among Peruvian Market Women. *Cultural Anthropology* 8(2):187–213.

Seligmann, Linda. 2001. Introduction. In *Women Traders in Cross-Cultural Perspective: Mediating Identities, Marketing Wares*, edited by L. Seligmann, pp. 1–24. Stanford, CA: Stanford University Press.

Shiva, Vandana. 1997. *Biopiracy: The Plunder of Nature and Knowledge*. Boston: South End Press.

Sikkink, Lynn. 1994. *House, Community, and Marketplace: Women as Managers of Exchange Relations and Resources on the Southern Altiplano of Bolivia*. Unpublished Ph.D. dissertation, Department of Anthropology, University of Minnesota, Minneapolis, MN.

Sikkink, Lynn. 1997. Water and Exchange: The Ritual of *Yaku Cambio* as Communal and Competitive Encounter. *American Ethnologist* 24(1):170–189.

Sikkink, Lynn. 2001a. Traditional Medicines in the Marketplace: Identity and Ethnicity among Female Vendors. In *Women Traders in Cross-Cultural Perspective: Mediating Identities, Marketing Wares*, edited by L. Seligmann, pp. 209–225. Stanford, CA: Stanford University Press.

Sikkink, Lynn. 2001b. Home Sweet Market Stand: Work, Gender, and Getting Ahead among Bolivian Traditional Medicine Vendors.

Anthropology of Work Review
22(3):1–6.

Sikkink, Lynn, and Braulio Choque. 1999. Landscape, Gender, and Community: Andean Mountain Stories. *Anthropological Quarterly* 72(4):167–182.

Silverblatt, Irene. 1978. Andean Women in the Inca Empire. *Feminist Studies* 4(3):37–61.

Silverblatt, Irene. 1987. *Moon, Sun, and Witches: Gender Ideologies and Class in Inca and Colonial Peru.* Princeton, NJ: Princeton University Press.

Soux, María. 1993. *La Coca Liberal.* La Paz, Bolivia: CID.

Spedding, Alison. 2005. *Kawsachun Coca.* La Paz, Bolivia: EDOBOL.

Stark, Louisa. 1985. The Quechua Language in Bolivia. In *South American Languages: Retrospect and Prospect*, edited by H. Manelis Klein and L. Stark, pp. 516–545. Austin, TX: University of Texas Press.

Starn, Orin 1991. Missing the Revolution: Anthropologists and the War in Peru. *Cultural Anthropology* 6(1):63–91.

Stephenson, Marcia. 1999. *Gender and Modernity in Andean Bolivia.* Austin, TX: University of Texas Press.

Stewart, Kathleen. 1996. An Occupied Place. In *Senses of Place*, edited by S. Feld and K. Basso, pp. 137–165. Santa Fe, NM: School of American Research Press.

Taylor, Leslie. 1998. *Herbal Secrets of the Rainforest.* Rocklin, CA: Prima.

Troll, Carl. 1968. The Cordilleras of the Tropical Americas. In *Geo-ecology of the Mountainous Regions of the Tropical Americas*, edited by C. Troll. Bonn, Germany: Ferd. Dummlers.

Tyler, Varro. 1996. Natural Products and Medicine: An Overview. In *Medicinal Resources of the Tropical Forest: Biodiversity and Its Importance to Human Health*, edited by M. J. Balick, E. Elisabetsky and S. Laird, pp. 3–10. New York: Columbia University Press.

van den Berg, Hans. 1990. *La Tierra no Da Así Nomás.* La Paz, Bolivia: HISBOL—UCB/ISET.

Wayland, Carol, and Jerome Crowder. 2002. Disparate Views of Community in Primary Health Care: Understanding How Perceptions Influence Success. *Medical Anthropology Quarterly* 16(2):230–247.

Weismantel, Mary. 1988. *Food, Gender and Poverty in the Ecuadorian Andes.* Philadelphia: University of Pennsylvania Press.

Weismantel, Mary. 2001. *Cholas and Pishtacos: Stories of Race and Sex in the Andes.* Chicago: University of Chicago Press.

West, Terry. 1981. *Sufriendo Nos Vamos: From a Subsistence to a Market Economy in an Aymara Community of Bolivia* [Ph.D. dissertation]. New School for Social Research, Ann Arbor, MI: University Microfilms International.

Wilson, David. 1992. *Indigenous South Americans of the Past and Present.* Boulder, CO: Westview Press.

Yano, Lester I. 1993. Protection of the Ethnobiological Knowledge of Indigenous Peoples. *UCLA Law Review* 41(2):443–486.

Zorn, Elayne. 1997. Coca, Cash, and Cloth in Highland Bolivia. In *Coca, Cocaine, and the Bolivian Reality*, edited by M. B. Léons and H. Sanabria, pp. 71–98. Albany, NY: State University of New York Press.

Index